The Socioeconomic Impact of COVID-19 on Eastern European Countries

The year 2020 went down in economic history due to the dramatic and drastic changes in economic and social conditions that resulted from the outbreak of the global pandemic of COVID-19. This book offers a multi-level narrative about the pandemic, written from national and international perspectives, enabling the authors to construct several macro- and mega-scenarios.

The book consists of six chapters. Four of them discuss the process of the COVID-19 pandemic caused by the SARS-CoV-2 virus in Europe in 2020, i.e. the directions and dynamics of the spread and its socioeconomic consequences, and provide a comparative analysis of fiscal and monetary packages employed by Europe, with an emphasis on Eastern European countries. The remaining two chapters contain forecasts and scenarios. The fifth chapter, dedicated to forecasts, provides readers with a comprehensive description of possible consequences of any epidemic leading to severe social losses such as high percentages of infected and dead, limited interpersonal contacts as a result of lockdown, a lowered level of general individual and social well-being, as well as economic losses, for example a decline in production as a result of the collapse of aggregate demand and a reduction in the supply capacity of the economy, consequently slowing down the pace of capital accumulation. The sixth, final chapter describes possible scenarios of the spread of the pandemic in Poland and Ukraine, depending on measures taken by the governments of those countries.

The Socioeconomic Impact of COVID-19 on Eastern European Countries is designed as a practical reference for scholars, researchers and policymakers.

Paweł Dykas is Assistant Professor at the Department of Mathematical Economics of the Jagiellonian University, Krakow, Poland.

Rafał Wisła is Professor of Economics at the Department of Economics and Innovation of the Jagiellonian University, Krakow, Poland.

Routledge Studies in the European Economy

57 The European Monetary Union After the Crisis
From a Fiscal Union to a Fiscal Capacity
Nazaré da Costa Cabral

58 Empirical Macroeconomics and Statistical Uncertainty
Spatial and Temporal Disaggregation of Regional Economic Indicators
Mateusz Pipień and Sylwia Roszkowska

59 Economic Transformation in Poland and Ukraine
National and Regional Perspectives
Edited by Rafał Wisła and Andrzej Nowosad

60 Competitiveness and Economic Development in Europe
Prospects and Challenges
Edited by Sławomir I. Bukowski, Alina Hyz and Marzanna B. Lament

61 Brexit and the Political Economy of Ireland
Creating a New Economic Settlement
Paul Teague

62 The Economic and Legal Impact of Covid-19
The Case of Poland
Edited by Jerzy Menkes and Magdalena Suska

63 Brexit and the Future of the European Union
Firm-Level Perspectives
Edited by Marian Gorynia, Barbara Jankowska and Katarzyna Mroczek-Dąbrowska

64 The Socioeconomic Impact of COVID-19 on Eastern European Countries
Edited by Paweł Dykas and Rafał Wisła

For more information about this series, please visit www.routledge.com/series/SE0431

The Socioeconomic Impact of COVID-19 on Eastern European Countries

Edited by Paweł Dykas and Rafał Wisła

LONDON AND NEW YORK

First published 2022
by Routledge
2 Park Square, Milton Park, Abingdon, Oxon OX14 4RN

and by Routledge
605 Third Avenue, New York, NY 10158

Routledge is an imprint of the Taylor & Francis Group, an informa business

© 2022 selection and editorial matter, Paweł Dykas and Rafał Wisła; individual chapters, the contributors

The right of Paweł Dykas and Rafał Wisła to be identified as the authors of the editorial material, and of the authors for their individual chapters, has been asserted in accordance with sections 77 and 78 of the Copyright, Designs and Patents Act 1988.

The Open Access version of this book, available at www.taylorfrancis.com, has been made available under a Creative Commons Attribution-Non Commercial-No Derivatives 4.0 license.

Trademark notice: Product or corporate names may be trademarks or registered trademarks, and are used only for identification and explanation without intent to infringe.

British Library Cataloguing-in-Publication Data
A catalogue record for this book is available from the British Library

Library of Congress Cataloging-in-Publication Data
Names: Dykas, Paweł, editor. | Wisła, Rafał, editor.
Title: The socioeconomic impact of COVID-19 on Eastern European countries/edited by Paweł Dykas and Rafał Wisła.
Description: Abingdon, Oxon; New York, NY: Routledge, 2022. | Series: Routledge studies in the European economy |
Includes bibliographical references and index.
Identifiers: LCCN 2021032959 (print) | LCCN 2021032960 (ebook) | ISBN 9781032078717 (hardback) | ISBN 9781032078731 (paperback) | ISBN 9781003211891 (ebook)
Subjects: LCSH: COVID-19 (Disease)–Social aspects. | COVID-19 (Disease)–Economic aspects. | COVID-19 Pandemic, 2020—Social aspects–Europe, Eastern. | COVID-19 Pandemic, 2020—Economic aspects–Europe, Eastern.
Classification: LCC RA644.C67 S624 2022 (print) |
LCC RA644.C67 (ebook) | DDC 362.1962/41400947–dc23
LC record available at https://lccn.loc.gov/2021032959
LC ebook record available at https://lccn.loc.gov/2021032960

ISBN: 978-1-032-07871-7 (hbk)
ISBN: 978-1-032-07873-1 (pbk)
ISBN: 978-1-003-21189-1 (ebk)

DOI: 10.4324/9781003211891

Typeset in Sabon
by Deanta Global Publishing Services, Chennai, India

Contents

List of figures vii
List of tables xii
List of maps xiv
List of contributors xvi
Introductory remarks xix
RAFAŁ WISŁA AND PAWEŁ DYKAS
Acknowledgements xxi

1 The coronavirus SARS-CoV-2 and its impact on the world 1
   ANDRZEJ NOWOSAD, ÜMIT TURANLI, AND KATARZYNA LORENC

2 Impact of the COVID-19 pandemic on the differentiation of selected macroeconomic variables characterizing the EU economies over a short period 20
   MONIKA BOLIŃSKA, RAFAŁ WISŁA, AND MICHAŁ WŁODARCZYK

3 Fiscal interventions in 2020: A comparative analysis of EU states' policies 46
   MICHAŁ WŁODARCZYK, RAFAŁ WISŁA, AND MONIKA BOLIŃSKA

4 Effect of the COVID-19 pandemic on selected economies in Eastern Europe 68
   OLESIA CHORNENKA, OLEKSIJ KELEBAJ, MONIKA BOLIŃSKA, PAWEŁ DYKAS, AND RAFAŁ WISŁA

5 Modelling the social and economic impact of an epidemic 89
   MONIKA BOLIŃSKA, PAWEŁ DYKAS, TOMASZ TOKARSKI, AND RAFAŁ WISŁA

6 Simulations of the pandemic propagation patterns on the example of Poland and Ukraine 116
PAWEŁ DYKAS, KATARZYNA FILIPOWICZ, OLESIA CHORNENKA, OLEKSIJ KELEBAJ, AND TOMASZ TOKARSKI

Key findings 147
RAFAŁ WISŁA AND PAWEŁ DYKAS

Index 149

Figures

2.1 A dendrogram of GDP per capita in the member states of the EU (2006–2020, Euclidean distance). Source: own calculation based on https://ec.europa.eu/eurostat/data/database   22

2.2 Changes in the unemployment rate in the EU economy (in %, 2006–2020, quarterly data). Source: own calculation based on https://ec.europa.eu/eurostat/data/database   26

2.3 A dendrogram of unemployment rates in the EU (2006–2020, Euclidean distance). Source: own calculation based on https://ec.europa.eu/eurostat/data/database   27

2.4 Gross fixed capital formation per capita in the EU (2006–2020, % of GDP, quarterly data). Source: own calculation based on https://ec.europa.eu/eurostat/data/database   32

2.5 A dendrogram of gross fixed capital formation in the EU (2006–2020, Euclidean distance). Source: own calculation based on https://ec.europa.eu/eurostat/data/database   33

2.6 Dynamics of changes in exports of goods and services in the EU (2006–2020, % of GDP, quarterly data). Source: own calculation based on https://ec.europa.eu/eurostat/data/database   36

2.7 A dendrogram of similarities in exports (2006–2020, Euclidean distance). Source: own calculation based on https://ec.europa.eu/eurostat/data/database   37

2.8 Dynamics of changes in imports in the EU (the years 2006–2020, % of GDP, quarterly data). Source: own calculation based on https://ec.europa.eu/eurostat/data/database   41

2.9 A dendrogram of similarities in imports (the years 2006–2020, Euclidean distance). Source: own calculation based on https://ec.europa.eu/eurostat/data/database   42

4.1a Changes in Gross Domestic Product per capita, at PPP, quarter-over-quarter (2006–2020, 2020 = 100) in (a) Ukraine. Source: own calculation based on http://www.ukrstat.gov.ua/ (accessed: 2021-01-30)   71

viii *Figures*

4.1b Changes in Gross Domestic Product per capita, at PPP, quarter-over-quarter (2006–2020, 2020 = 100) in (b) Russia. Source: own calculation based on https://eng.rosstat.gov.ru (accessed: 2021-01-30) 71

4.1c Changes in Gross Domestic Product per capita, at PPP, quarter-over-quarter (2006–2020, 2020 = 100) in (c) the European Union. Source: own calculation based on https://ec.europa.eu/eurostat/data/database (accessed: 2021-01-30) 72

4.2a Changes in Gross Domestic Product per capita, at PPP, quarter-over-quarter (2019–2020) in (a) Ukraine. Source: own calculation based on http://www.ukrstat.gov.ua/; https://eng.rosstat.gov.ru; https://ec.europa.eu/eurostat/data/database (accessed: 2021-01-30) 74

4.2b Changes in Gross Domestic Product per capita, at PPP, quarter-over-quarter (2019–2020) in (b) Russia. Source: own calculation based on http://www.ukrstat.gov.ua/; https://eng.rosstat.gov.ru; https://ec.europa.eu/eurostat/data/database (accessed: 2021-01-30) 75

4.2c Changes in Gross Domestic Product per capita, at PPP, quarter-over-quarter (2019–2020) in (c) the European Union. Source: own calculation based on http://www.ukrstat.gov.ua/; https://eng.rosstat.gov.ru; https://ec.europa.eu/eurostat/data/database (accessed: 2021-01-30) 76

5.1a Curves of S, I, H and P in scenarios I, V and IX (at $\kappa_t = 1 - \sqrt{I_{t-1}}$) Scenario I. Source: own calculations 100

5.1b Curves of S, I, H and P in scenarios I, V and IX (at $\kappa_t = 1 - \sqrt{I_{t-1}}$) Scenario V. Source: own calculations 101

5.1c Curves of S, I, H and P in scenarios I, V and IX (at $\kappa_t = 1 - \sqrt{I_{t-1}}$) Scenario IX. Source: own calculations 101

5.2a Curves of S, I, H and P in scenarios II, VI and X (at $\kappa_t = 1 - I_{t-1}$) Scenario II. Source: own calculations 101

5.2b Curves of S, I, H and P in scenarios II, VI and X (at $\kappa_t = 1 - I_{t-1}$) Scenario VI. Source: own calculations 102

5.2c Curves of S, I, H and P in scenarios II, VI and X (at $\kappa_t = 1 - I_{t-1}$) Scenario X. Source: own calculations 102

5.3a Curves of S, I, H and P in scenarios III, VII and XI, at $\kappa_t = \begin{cases} 1 \, dla \, \bar{I}_{Gt} < 0.0005 \\ 0.85 \, dla \, \bar{I}_{Gt} \geq 0.0005 \end{cases}$ Scenario III. Source: own calculations 103

5.3b Curves of S, I, H and P in scenarios III, VII and XI, at $\kappa_t = \begin{cases} 1 \, dla \, \bar{I}_{Gt} < 0.0005 \\ 0.85 \, dla \, \bar{I}_{Gt} \geq 0.0005 \end{cases}$ Scenario VII. Source: own calculations 103

5.3c	Curves of *S, I, H* and *P* in scenarios III, VII and XI, at $\kappa_t = \begin{cases} 1\, dla\, \bar{I}_{Gt} < 0.0005 \\ 0.85\, dla\, \bar{I}_{Gt} \geq 0.0005 \end{cases}$ Scenario XI. Source: own calculations	104
5.4a	Curves of *S, I, H* and *P* in scenarios IV, VIII and XII, at $\kappa_t = \begin{cases} 1\, dla\, \bar{I}_{Gt} < 0.001 \\ 0.95\, dla\, \bar{I}_{Gt} \geq 0.001 \end{cases}$ Scenario IV. Source: own calculations	104
5.4b	Curves of *S, I, H* and *P* in scenarios IV, VIII and XII, at $\kappa_t = \begin{cases} 1\, dla\, \bar{I}_{Gt} < 0.001 \\ 0.95\, dla\, \bar{I}_{Gt} \geq 0.001 \end{cases}$ Scenario VIII. Source: own calculations	105
5.4c	Curves of *S, I, H* and *P* in scenarios IV, VIII and XII, at $\kappa_t = \begin{cases} 1\, dla\, \bar{I}_{Gt} < 0.001 \\ 0.95\, dla\, \bar{I}_{Gt} \geq 0.001 \end{cases}$ Scenario XII. Source: own calculations	105
5.5a	Curves representing social utility in scenarios I–IV. A poorly developed economy. Source: own calculations	109
5.5b	Curves representing social utility in scenarios I–IV. A strongly developed economy. Source: own calculations	109
5.6a	Curves representing social utility in scenarios V–VIII. A poorly developed economy. Source: own calculations	110
5.6b	Curves representing social utility in scenarios V–VIII. A strongly developed economy. Source: own calculations	110
5.7a	Curves representing social utility in scenarios IX–XII. A poorly developed economy. Source: own calculations	111
5.7b	Curves representing social utility in scenarios IX–XII. A strongly developed economy. Source: own calculations	111
6.1	Trajectories of proportions *S, I* and *H* for the baseline scenario. Source: the author's own study	122
6.2	Trajectories of proportions *S, I* and *H* for scenario A_1 (without a vaccine). Source: the author's own study	122
6.3	Trajectories of proportions *S, I, H* and *P* for scenario A_2 (50% of the population vaccinated). Source: the author's own study	123
6.4	Trajectories of proportions *S, I, H* and *P* for scenario A_3 (75% of the population vaccinated). Source: the author's own study	124
6.5	Trajectories of proportions *S, I, H* and *P* for scenario A_4 (25% of the population vaccinated). Source: the author's own study	124
6.6	Trajectories of death rates for Scenario A. Source: the author's own study	125
6.7	Trajectories of proportions *S, I* and *H* for scenario B_1 (without a vaccine). Source: the author's own study	126

6.8	Trajectories of proportions S, I, H and P for scenario B_2 (50% of the population vaccinated). Source: the author's own work	127
6.9	Trajectories of proportions S, I, H and P for scenario B_3 (75% of the population vaccinated). Source: the author's own study	128
6.10	Trajectories of proportions S, I, H and P for scenario B_4 (25% of the population vaccinated). Source: the author's own study	129
6.11	Trajectories of death rates for Scenario B. Source: the author's own study	129
6.12	Trajectories of proportions S, I and H for scenario C_1 (without a vaccine). Source: the author's own study	130
6.13	Trajectories of proportions S, I, H and P for scenario C_2 (50% of the population vaccinated). Source: the author's own study	130
6.14	Trajectories of proportions S, I, H and P for scenario C_3 (75% of the population vaccinated). Source: the author's own work	131
6.15	Trajectories of proportions S, I, H and P for Scenario C_4 (25% of the population vaccinated). Source: the author's own study	131
6.16	Trajectories of death rates for Scenario C. Source: the author's own study	132
6.17	Trajectories of proportions S, I and H for the baseline scenario. Source: the author's own study	133
6.18	Trajectories of proportions S, I and H for scenario A_1 (without a vaccine). Source: the author's own study	134
6.19	Trajectories of proportions S, I, H and P for scenario A_2 (60% of the population vaccinated). Source: the author's own study	135
6.20	Trajectories of proportions S, I, H and P for scenario A_3 (90% of the population vaccinated). Source: the author's own study	135
6.21	Trajectories of proportions S, I, H and P for scenario A_4 (30% of the population vaccinated). Source: the author's own study	136
6.22	Trajectories of death rates for Scenario A. Source: the author's own study	136
6.23	Trajectories of proportions S, I and H for scenario B_1 (without a vaccine). Source: the author's own study	137

6.24	Trajectories of proportions S, I, H and P for scenario B_2 (60% of the population vaccinated). Source: the author's own study	138
6.25	Trajectories of proportions S, I, H and P for scenario B_3 (90% of the population vaccinated). Source: the author's own study	139
6.26	Trajectories of proportions S, I, H and P for scenario B_4 (30% of the population vaccinated). Source: the author's own study	139
6.27	Trajectories of death rates for Scenario B. Source: the author's own study	140
6.28	Trajectories of proportions S, I and H for scenario C_1 (without a vaccine). Source: the author's own study	140
6.29	Trajectories of proportions S, I, H and P for scenario C_2 (60% of the population vaccinated). Source: the author's own study	141
6.30	Trajectories of proportions S, I, H and P for scenario C_3 (90% of the population vaccinated). Source: the author's own study	141
6.31	Trajectories of proportions S, I, H and P for scenario C_4 (30% of the population vaccinated). Source: the author's own study	142
6.32	Trajectories of death rates for Scenario C. Source: the author's own study	142

Tables

3.1 Objectives of the Multiannual Financial Framework 2021–2027 and Next Generation EU and their financing — 48

3.2 Fiscal measures implemented in the European Union member states and in the United Kingdom in 2020 — 65

4.1 Estimates of the parameters of equation (4.4) for the European Union, Russian Federation and Ukraine — 81

4.2 Estimates of the parameters of equation (4.8) for the European Union, Russian Federation and Ukraine — 82

5.1 Scenarios of epidemic development — 99

5.2 Epidemiological indicators in consecutive scenarios — 100

5.3 Economic indicators in consecutive scenarios at $K_1/K^*=0.4$ (a poorly developed economy) — 107

5.4 Economic indicators in consecutive scenarios at $K_1/K^*=0.9$ (a strongly developed economy) — 108

6.1 Minimum proportion of uninfected persons (S_m), maximum proportion of infected persons (I_M), maximum proportion of vaccinated persons (P_M), maximum proportion of convalescents (H_M) and the deceased (D_M), day of the epidemic with the highest number of infections (T) for scenario A with different variants — 123

6.2 Minimum proportion of uninfected persons (S_m), maximum proportion of infected persons (I_M), maximum proportion of vaccinated persons (P_M), maximum proportion of convalescents (H_M) and the deceased (D_M), day of the epidemic with the highest number of infections (T) for scenario B with different variants — 126

6.3 Minimum proportion of uninfected persons (S_m), maximum proportion of infected persons (I_M), maximum proportion of vaccinated persons (P_M), maximum proportion of convalescents (H_M) and the deceased (D_M), day of the epidemic with the highest number of infections (T) for scenario C with different variants — 129

6.4	Minimum proportion of uninfected persons (S_m), maximum proportion of infected persons (I_M), maximum proportion of vaccinated persons (P_M), maximum proportion of convalescents (H_M) and the deceased (D_M), day of the epidemic with the highest number of infections (T) for scenario A with different variants	134
6.5	Minimum proportion of uninfected persons (S_m), maximum proportion of infected persons (I_M), maximum proportion of vaccinated persons (P_M), maximum proportion of convalescents (H_M) and the deceased (D_M), day of the epidemic with the highest number of infections (T) for scenario B with different variants	137
6.6	Minimum proportion of uninfected persons (S_m), maximum proportion of infected persons (I_M), maximum proportion of vaccinated persons (P_M), maximum proportion of convalescents (H_M) and the deceased (D_M), day of the epidemic with the highest number of infections (T) for scenario B with different variants	140

Maps

2.1a Spatial differentiation of GDP per capita in the second quarters of 2019 in the member states of the European Union (in EUR, constant prices from Q2 of 2020). Source: own calculation based on https://ec.europa.eu/eurostat/data/database 24

2.1b Spatial differentiation of GDP per capita in the second quarters of 2020 in the member states of the European Union (in EUR, constant prices from Q2 of 2020). Source: own calculation based on https://ec.europa.eu/eurostat/data/database 25

2.2a Unemployment in the second quarter of 2019 in the EU countries (in %). Source: own calculation based on https://ec.europa.eu/eurostat/data/database 29

2.2b Unemployment in the second quarter of 2020 in the EU countries (in %). Source: own calculation based on https://ec.europa.eu/eurostat/data/database 30

2.3a Gross fixed capital formation in the second quarters of 2019 in the member states of the European Union (in EUR, constant prices from Q2 of 2020). Source: own calculation based on https://ec.europa.eu/eurostat/data/database 34

2.3b Gross fixed capital formation in the second quarters of 2020 in the member states of the European Union (in EUR, constant prices from Q2 of 2020). Source: own calculation based on https://ec.europa.eu/eurostat/data/database 35

2.4a Exports per capita in the second quarters of 2019 in the member states of the European Union (in EUR, constant prices from Q2 of 2020). Source: own calculation based on https://ec.europa.eu/eurostat/data/database 38

2.4b Exports per capita in the second quarters of 2020 in the member states of the European Union (in EUR, constant prices from Q2 of 2020). Source: own calculation based on https://ec.europa.eu/eurostat/data/database 39

2.5a	Imports per capita in the second quarters of 2019 in the member states of the European Union (in EUR, constant prices from Q2 of 2020). Source: own calculation based on https://ec.europa.eu/eurostat/data/database	43
2.5b	Imports per capita in the second quarters of 2020 in the member states of the European Union (in EUR, constant prices from Q2 of 2020) Source: own calculation based on https://ec.europa.eu/eurostat/data/database	44
4.1a	Spatial differentiation of GDP per capita in Q2 of 2019 in the member states of the European Union, the Russian Federation and Ukraine (in USD, fixed prices from Q2 of 2020) Source: own calculations. based on https://ec.europa.eu/eurostat/data/database, http://www.ukrstat.gov.ua and https://rosstat.gov.ru	77
4.1b	Spatial differentiation of GDP per capita in Q2 of 2020 in the member states of the European Union, the Russian Federation and Ukraine (in USD, fixed prices from Q2 of 2020) Source: own calculations. based on https://ec.europa.eu/eurostat/data/database, http://www.ukrstat.gov.ua and https://rosstat.gov.ru	78

Contributors

Monika Bolińska is a doctoral student at the Jagiellonian University (Krakow, Poland) in the faculty of Management and Social Communication. She is the author and co-author of 14 academic publications, such as *Spatial diversity of unemployment in Ukraine* (2019), *Demographic forecasts and volatility of investment rates vs. labour productivity trajectories* (2019) and *An impact of the variable technological progress rate on the trajectory of labour productivity* (2020). Her research is mainly based on regional development and labor market analysis. In her research, she studies economic development in Eastern Poland and Western Ukraine.

Olesia Chornenka has an MSc in economics from the Jagiellonian University (Krakow, Poland). She is the author and co-author of over 15 academic publications, such as *Selecting the optimal method to assess the level of financial safety of enterprise* (2018), *Spatial diversification of Ukraine's GDP* (2019) and *Spatial diversity of unemployment in Ukraine* (2019). Her main interests include the impact of socio-political factors on regional development in Ukraine.

Paweł Dykas is Assistant Professor at the Faculty of Management and Social Communication in the Jagiellonian University (Krakow, Poland). He is the author of over 50 academic publications, such as *The neoclassical model of economic growth and its ability to account for demographic forecasts* (2018), *Demographic forecasts and volatility of investment rates vs. labour productivity trajectories* (2019) and *An impact of the variable technological progress rate on the trajectory of labour productivity* (2020). His main interests include the mathematical theory of economic growth, an analysis of the spatial diversity of economic development and an analysis of regional differences in the labour market.

Katarzyna Filipowicz is Assistant Professor at the Department of Mathematical Economics of the Jagiellonian University (Krakow, Poland). She is the author and co-author of over 50 academic publications devoted to this issue, *The impact of domestic and foreign gravity effects on the diversity of economic development of Poland* (2017),

Diversification of economic development of EU countries on the basis of the gravity growth model (2018) and *The influence of spatial interactions on the differentiation of economic development of Poland* (2019). Her research interests are mathematical models of economic growth and the spatial differentiation of economic development.

Oleksij Kelebaj is a doctoral student of economy and finance of the Doctoral School in Social Sciences at the Jagiellonian University (Krakow, Poland). His main interests include the regional and local differentiation of economic development and mathematical models of economic growth.

Katarzyna Lorenc is a Ph.D. candidate at the Faculty of Management and Social Communication of the Jagiellonian University (Krakow, Poland). She is the author of the book *Dynamika wolności mediów na świecie* (The Dynamics of Media Freedom in the World, 2017) and several research articles, including *Wolność mediów a bezpieczeństwo państwa* (Freedom of expression and security of state, 2016), *Dobór i konstrukcja twierdzeń kwestionariusza w nawigatorach wyborczych (Voting Advice Applications): od problemów metodologicznych po ideologię* (Statement choice and structure in Voting Advice Applications (VAAs): from methodological issues to ideological framework, 2018), *Voting Advice Applications as tools for researching and influencing voters: agenda setting and framing in European VAA* (2019), and *Women in South African politics: gender equality in the Republic of South Africa* (2019). Her research interests focus mainly on online astroturfing and social bots, new media in political campaigns, and media freedom in the world.

Andrzej Nowosad is Associate Professor at the Institute of Journalism, Media and Social Communication of the Jagiellonian University (Krakow, Poland). He is the author and co-author of over 100 academic publications such as *Media i władza w Bułgarii* (The media and the state in Bulgaria, 2008), *Zróżnicowanie rozwoju wspołczesnej Europy* (The differentiation of development in contemporary Europe, co-authored with Rafal Wisla 2016), *Klastery medialnie jako kapitał społeczny na Bałkanach* (Media clusters as social capital in the Balkans, 2019), *Nieformalne komunikowanie o pracy w krajach bałkańskich* (Informal communication about work in the Balkan countries, 2019), and *Economic transformation in Poland and Ukraine: national and regional perspectives* (co-authored with Rafal Wisla, 2020). His main interests include the diversity of paths of regional development and economic, socio-political and media transformation in the world.

Tomasz Tokarski is Professor at the Department of Mathematical Economics of the Jagiellonian University (Krakow, Poland). He is the author and co-author of over 200 academic publications, such as *Wybrane modele podażowych czynników wzrostu gospodarczego* (Selected supply models of economic growth, 2005), *Ekonomia matematyczna modele mikroekonomiczne* (Microeconomic models of mathematical economics, 2011), *Ekonomia matematyczna modele makroekonomiczne* (Macroeconomic models of mathematical economics, 2011) as well as extensive research and publications dealing with economic growth models and problems related with regional and local development. He is the Director of the Department of Mathematical Economics in the Institute of Economics, Finance and Management at the Jagiellonian University. His main interests include gravitational growth models and the differentiation of spatial economic development in Europe.

Ümit Turanlı is doing an undergraduate degree in international management, a master's degree in intercultural relations at the Institute of Intercultural Studies and a master's degree in oriental languages and literature, all at the Jagiellonian University (Krakow, Poland). He is the author and co-author of several academic publications such as *Institutional conditions for the functioning of the Polish and Ukrainian economies* (co-authored with Rafal Wisla and Andrzej Nowosad, 2020) and *Rynek prasy drukowanej w Turcji w latach 2012–2020* (Press market in Turkey in 2012–2020, co-authored with Andrzej Nowosad and Margreta Grigorova, 2020). His main interests include the economic, political, social, and intercultural relations between Asia and Europe.

Rafał Wisła is Professor of Economics at the Department of Economics and Innovation of the Jagiellonian University (Krakow, Poland). He is the author of over 80 academic publications, such as *Innovation in the pharmaceutical and medical technology industries of Poland* (2018), *Developmental diversification of contemporary Europe* (2016) and *Regional patterns of technology accumulation in Central and Eastern Europe countries* (2014). Recently, he has co-edited and contributed to *Economic transformation in Poland and Ukraine* (2020). He is the Doctoral Program Coordinator in Economics and Finance at Jagiellonian University (2019–2023) and the Deputy Director of the Institute of Economics, Finance and Management of the Jagiellonian University (2016–2020). The issues which he deals with are technological changes and innovation activity from a regional perspective.

Michał Włodarczyk is a doctoral student at the Faculty of Management and Social Communication at the Jagiellonian University (Krakow, Poland). He is the author and co-author of academic publications in the field of financial innovations, new technologies and the fintech sector, such as *Between social responsibility and potential profit. The technological giants' dilemma* (2018) and *Financial clusters and fintech agglomerations – location factors* (2020). He is also a co-founder of *Stać Mnie*, a scientific YouTube channel focused on financial education and popularizing economics among young people.

Introductory remarks

Rafał Wisła and Paweł Dykas

The problem of distortion in the social and economic sphere, caused by a dramatic increase in incidence or other health issues, was not systematically studied in economics over recent decades. However, it must be emphasized that in the 1980s and 1990s, economic consequences of tuberculosis, malaria and HIV/AIDS in Africa, Asia, and selected European and American countries were analyzed.

The scale and dynamics of the spread of the COVID-19 pandemic, caused by a coronavirus, in 2020 and 2021 entailed serious disturbances in social and economic life. The 2020+ pandemic was not only the most serious global health crisis since the Spanish flu of 1918 but also one of the most economically expensive pandemics on a global scale. The events observed give rise to several questions. Those questions relate to the balance of costs and benefits of a lockdown policy, the substitution between public health and economic growth under pandemic conditions.

The 2020+ pandemic is a health phenomenon that strongly affects society (limited spatial mobility, losses in social capital, increased mortality of people at various ages) and the economy (decelerated or inhibited business activity in dozens of industries, dramatic growth in public debt, the deepest recession since World War II in 2020).

The outbreak of the coronavirus pandemic could not be foreseen in 2019. Closed border checkpoints, severe limitations to the freedom of movement and an almost complete ban on service activities (especially in the hospitality industry) were beyond the imagination in early 2020.

In view of this type of unpredictable major external shock, all attempts to propose a forecast entail a substantial risk of losing touch with reality. It is difficult to construct reliable scenarios of the future spread or halt of the pandemic, the effect of vaccination on lifting restrictions imposed on social and economic life or the future pace of economic growth in European countries, but the authors of this book take on this challenge.

The book consists of six chapters. Four of them discuss the process of COVID-19 pandemic caused by the SARS CoV-2 virus in Europe in 2020 (the directions and dynamics of pandemic spread, its socio-economic consequences and measures of fiscal and monetary intervention implemented in European countries with an accent on Eastern European countries). The remaining two sections contain forecasts and scenarios. The fifth chapter dedicated to forecasts aims to provide readers with a comprehensive description of possible consequences of (any) epidemic leading to severe social losses (high percentages of infected and dead, limited interpersonal contacts as a result of lockdown, a lowered level of general individual and social well-being) and economic losses (a decline in production as a result of the collapse of aggregate demand and a reduction in the supply capacity of the economy, consequently slowing down the pace of capital accumulation). The sixth, final chapter, describes possible scenarios of the spread of the pandemic in Poland and Ukraine, depending on measures taken by the governments of those countries.

It must be clearly emphasized that nobody could imagine the future in early 2020. The potential consequences of the pandemic were unknown. First, the scale of hazard to public health and lives of people had to be identified before considering economic consequences. The COVID-19 pandemic caused by the SARS-CoV-2 virus will come to an end. But its economic and social consequences will be suffered for a long time. This book principally constructs a picture of the global pandemic of 2020, a major demand and supply shock in the global economy, unprecedented in the economic history of recent decades.

Acknowledgements

We gratefully acknowledge constructive and insightful comments provided by Prof. Adam Krawiec (Jagiellonian University in Kraków), Prof. Eugeniusz Kwiatkowski, Prof. Michał Majsterek, Prof. Iwona Świeczewska (University of Lódź), Prof. Krzysztof Malaga (Poznań University of Economics) and Prof. Tomasz Misiak (Rzeszow University of Technology).

The open access license of the publication was funded by the Priority Research Area Society of the Future under the programme "Excellence Initiative – Research University" at the Jagiellonian University in Krakow.

1 The coronavirus SARS-CoV-2 and its impact on the world

Andrzej Nowosad, Ümit Turanli, and Katarzyna Lorenc

1.1 Introduction

Severe acute respiratory syndrome coronavirus (SARS-CoV-2)[1] (Gorbalenya et al. 2020: 536) is the virus that causes the coronavirus disease 2019 (COVID-19), the respiratory illness responsible for the COVID-19 pandemic (BBC: February 11, 2020).[2] The World Health Organization (WHO) declared the disease a Public Health Emergency of International Concern on January 30, 2020 and a pandemic on March 11, 2020 (WHO: January 30, 2020; WHO: March 11, 2020). The last time WHO announced a pandemic was during the 2009 H1N1 outbreak[3] (the 2009 swine flu pandemic), which infected nearly a quarter of the world's population.[4]

The so-called Wuhan virus (COVID-19) spreads among people primarily through close contact and via respiratory droplets produced by coughs or sneezes, and epidemiological studies estimate each infection results in 5.7 new ones (Sanche et al. 2020). Each case of infection has an individual

---

1 SARS-CoV-2 is a positive-sense single-stranded RNA virus (Machhi et al. 2020: 359–386) and hence Baltimore class IV (Baltimore 1971) that is contagious in humans (Chan et al. 2020). As described by the US National Institutes of Health, it is the successor to SARS-CoV-1, the virus that caused the 2002–2004 SARS outbreak (NIH: March 17, 2020).
2 Colloquially known simply as 'the coronavirus', it was previously referred to by its provisional name, 2019 novel coronavirus (2019-nCoV) (WHO January 2020 Report; CDC February 11, 2020) and has also been called human coronavirus 2019 (HCoV-19 or hCoV-19) (Andersen et al. 2020: 450–452).
3 In virology, influenza A virus subtype H1N1 (A/H1N1) is a subtype of Influenza A virus. Well-known outbreaks of H1N1 strains in humans include the 2009 swine flu pandemic as well as the 1918 flu pandemic. It is an orthomyxovirus that contains the glycoproteins haemagglutinin and neuraminidase. For this reason, they are described as H1N1, H1N2 etc. depending on the type of H or N antigens they express with metabolic synergy (Lim, Mahmood 2011).
4 The 2009 swine flu pandemic was an influenza pandemic that lasted about 19 months, from January 2009 to August 2010. The number of lab-confirmed deaths reported to the World Health Organization (WHO) is 18,449, though the 2009 H1N1 flu pandemic is estimated to have actually caused about 284,000 (range from 150,000 to 575,000) deaths.

DOI: 10.4324/9781003211891-1

course of the disease. Usually, the virus causes a severe inflammation of the airways but it also affects other organs and organ systems.

As of September 8, 2021, there have been 222,903,649 total confirmed cases of SARS-CoV-2 infection during the ongoing pandemic and the number of virus infections is increasing quickly, particularly in the United Kingdom and in the United States. The total number of deaths attributed to the virus is 4,603,035 (CSSE: September 8, 2021). And although it should be noted that many recoveries from both confirmed and untested infections go unreported since some countries do not collect this data, at least 199,461,542 people have recovered from confirmed infections (CSSE: September 08, 2021). The number of confirmed cases is lower than the number of actual cases; the main reason for that is limited testing.

The large scale of the COVID-19 pandemic is causing unprecedented human and economic costs throughout the world. Trying to reduce the spread of the virus and thus the number of people infected and deceased, most state governments in the world introduced limitations for many industries and activities, which contributed to the ongoing economic decline. In this chapter, we analyze the origins, development, and current state of the COVID-19 epidemic, the ways in which the governments are trying to fight the deadly virus and the economic crisis caused by the pandemic, and the differences in perception of the threat caused by COVID-19. We also mention new challenges the world faces in 2021 as well as introduce the reader to the broad spectrum of costs of the pandemic, including the possible costs for people's mental health.

1.2 Origin and spread of SARS-CoV-2

The origin of SARS-CoV-2 coronavirus has not yet been explained. *Journal of Medical Virology* (three special issues on the Novel Coronavirus (COVID-19), 2019, 2020) indicated snakes (*serpentes*), then bats (*chiroptera*), and currently Asiatic pangolins, sometimes known as scaly anteaters (*manidae*),[5] as the source of the coronavirus disease. There are also a lot of theories on how the virus transferred to humans. However, none of them is coherent and reliable enough and publications on this subject are increasingly moving away from the norms of scientific literature.

Coronavirus SARS-CoV-2 (originally called 2019-nCoV) was officially identified for the first time in the Chinese city of Wuhan (武漢市) in the province Hubei (湖北) in central China in December 2019. However, it can be assumed that it had already affected humans earlier as Spanish virologists found traces of the novel coronavirus in a sample of Barcelona wastewater collected in March 2019, nine months before the COVID-19 disease was

---

5 Shou-Jiang (ed.) 'Three special issues on the Novel Coronavirus (COVID-19)', *Journal of Medical Virology*, monthly editions for years 2019–2020.

identified in China (Reuters: June 26, 2020). But there is no reliable data on the source of the SARS-CoV-2 and the geography of its spread before it was identified in Wuhan, and this very fact caused speculations that China spread the virus around the world.

Currently, there are many hypotheses about how this dangerous virus was released – from global warming and melting glaciers to being artificially created in a military laboratory as a new kind of biological weapon. Disagreements on this topic among scientists and members of the public are accompanied by conspiracy theories pouring globally into the media, thanks to which they gain the popularity and trustworthiness of scientific theories.

The claims of virologists and "experts" are also not consistent. Some claim that they have sufficient evidence that SARS-CoV-2 coronavirus was produced naturally, in wildlife not in a laboratory, and that SARS-CoV-2 coronavirus is not suitable for biological weapons. Others say the opposite and claim that the virus has "escaped" from a Chinese laboratory (see the statement by the US President Donald Trump from May 1, 2020 (The Guardian: May 1, 2020)).[6]

1.3 SARS, MERS and COVID-19

The human coronavirus was first identified in 1962 in a child with cold symptoms and was called B814. Since then, six species of this type of virus have appeared in the world. The most severe diseases were caused by SARS in 2003, with 812 deaths, and MERS-CoV which between 2012 and 2017 resulted in the deaths of 712 people. SARS-CoV-2 is the seventh known coronavirus that is dangerous for humans. COVID-19 does not cause high mortality compared to acute respiratory failure MERS-CoV or SARS. However, it spreads rapidly and has already caused more deaths worldwide than SARS and MERS combined.

According to Worldometer Data (WMD) (https://www.worldometers.info/coronavirus/, data collected as of December 31, 2020), there were 83,135,180 global cases of COVID-19 infection by the end of 2020, of which 1,813,389 cases resulted in humans' death, and 58,933,056 people recovered. The coronavirus COVID-19 is affecting 218 countries and

---

6 "Donald Trump claims to have seen evidence to substantiate the unproven theory that the coronavirus originated at the Wuhan Institute of Virology, despite US intelligence agencies' conclusion that the virus was 'not manmade or genetically modified'. 'We're going to see where it comes from,' Trump said at a White House event on Thursday. 'We have people looking at it very, very strongly. Scientific people, intelligence people, and others. We're going to put it all together. I think we will have a very good answer eventually. And China might even tell us.' Pressed to explain what evidence he had seen that the virus originated in a Chinese lab, Trump responded, 'I can't tell you that. I'm not allowed to tell you that'" (The Guardian: May 1, 2020).

territories around the world and two international conveyances. The fatality rate is still being assessed (WMD: December 31, 2020).

When it comes to the pandemic's development over time, as of September 08, 2021, we are expecting the fourth wave, we are experiencing the third wave of an increased number of people infected. After originally erupting in China in November and December 2019, the first worldwide wave of the COVID-19 pandemic started at the end of March 2020 and peaked in April 2020. Governmental responses across countries differed greatly at that time, from severe lockdown introduced in Italy – the country most affected among those in Europe – to the United Kingdom and Sweden who were convinced that the economic and social costs of a lockdown would be too big and decided against introducing severe restrictions, at least at the beginning. The summer of 2020 brought hope, encouraging many governments to lower restrictions and people to protest against the restrictions as the numbers of new COVID-19 cases dropped in many countries. However, in October and November 2020 it became clear that the second wave of the pandemic was inevitable. This time, similar but often less severe restrictions were introduced around the world. Spirits were kept up by the news about vaccines against the deadly virus which were already invented and during the last phases of testing. After reaching peaks in the winter of 2020, the beginnings of 2021 saw a decline in the worldwide number of new COVID-19 cases. From late December 2020, the vaccination process started as well, letting some experts believe that the COVID-19 pandemic was a thing of 2020. However, as new virus mutations appeared in the United Kingdom and South Africa and the European Union governments avoided early implementation of a new lockdown, in March 2021 the third wave of the pandemic began, leaving experts to wonder about the future (Johns Hopkins University: March 25, 2021).

Geographically, the highest number of cases of infection and death have been reported in the United States (41,206,672 total cases and 669,022 total deaths), India (33,096,718 total cases and 441,443 total deaths), Brazil (20,913,578 total cases and 584,208 total deaths), Russia (7,065,904 total cases and 189,582 total deaths), the United Kingdom (7,056,106 total cases and 133,483 deaths), France (6,854,028 total cases and 115,159 total deaths), Turkey (6,542,654 total cases and 58,651 total deaths), Argentina (5,211,801 total cases and 112,851 total deaths), Iran (5,210,978 total cases and 112,430 total deaths), Colombia (4,921,410 total cases and 125,378 total deaths), Spain (4,892,640 total cases and 85,066 total deaths), Italy (4,579,502 total cases and 129,638 total deaths), Indonesia (4,147,365 total cases and 137,782 total deaths) and Germany (4,029,849 total cases and 92,949 total deaths), Mexico (3,449,295 total cases and 264,541 total deaths), Poland (2,891,602 total cases and 75,403 total deaths), (September 08, 2021).

Moreover, it should be noted that many cases and deaths have not been statistically recorded as they have been asymptomatic, and not every country has provided reliable data on cases and deaths.

1.4 Virus denial and miscalculations

One of the biggest problems connected with the pandemic is that many countries around the world have denied the existence of the pandemic and the virus itself, or have neglected the threat. The well-known examples of such a denial include Russia, Belarus, Turkmenistan, and Azerbaijan, which even decided to organize mass sporting events during the pandemic. What is more, the US President Donald Trump, the British Prime Minister Boris Johnson, the Russian President Vladimir Putin, the Polish President Andrzej Duda, the Brazilian President Jair Bolsonaro, and the Mexican President Andres Manuel Lopez Obrador have repeatedly downplayed the coronavirus threat. This "cavalier" leadership approach as well as the lack of social safety nets and strong public health systems have worsened the crisis. The lack of an effective response to the virus's spread in the United States, the United Kingdom, Brazil, Poland or Russia has been one of the most surprising developments of the pandemic.

With some political leaders openly neglecting the threats of the COVID-19 pandemic, so do the people as well. Those affected strongly by governmental restrictions – denied the right to run their businesses, losing jobs, or just opposing the fact that a lot of human, political, and social rights have been suspended for a year now and probably also for the indefinite future – express their skepticism towards the measures taken by the governments and even raise concerns about the existence and extent of the pandemic itself. According to the YouGov-Cambridge Globalism Project that included a survey of about 26,000 people in 25 countries, significant groups of people believe that the death rate of the virus is deliberately exaggerated to a large extent. This statement is believed by 59% of Nigerians; 46% of Greeks; over 40% of Poles, South Africans, and Mexicans; about 38% of Americans; 36% of Hungarians; 30% of Italians; 28% of Germans; and 22% of Britons. In 10 out of 25 countries studied, 20–30% of respondents go even further, claiming that the pandemic is a hoax to deceive people (The Guardian: October 26, 2020).

Even if not doubting COVID-19 itself, many people around the world are tempted to believe in one or more of several leading conspiracy theories connected with the virus. More than 50% of Nigerians; more than 40% of South Africans, Poles, and Turks; more than 30% of Americans and Brazilians; and more than 20% of French, Britons, Italians, and Germans believe that the virus has been deliberately created and spread by China (The Guardian: October 26, 2020). There are also many others who think that COVID-19 is not more harmful than regular flu, that there is no need to wear a mask and that the vaccines are unsafe or include miniature devices that may be used to spy on people (Scientific American: October 12, 2020).

Those skeptical of the COVID-19 threat and the necessity of measures taken to fight it do not only express their concerns through social surveys but also engage in many communication activities, from Facebook groups dedicated to different COVID-19-related conspiracy theories to public gatherings organized to protest against the restrictions. For example, on August 29, 2020, over 10,000 unmasked people gathered in Trafalgar Square to protests about the so-called "new normal" order (The Guardian: September 4, 2020) while a protest against the government restrictions in Germany took place the same day in Berlin, including over 38,000 participants (RBB: August 29, 2020). Similar protests raised in many cities around the United States (BBC: April 19, 2020), together with the political implications of the presidential election campaign, kept the US federal government from introducing more severe restrictions similar to those implemented in Europe.

Another problem the world faced during the pandemic was that in many countries the statistics about the cases and deaths were forged. This problem has been emphasized by the European Centre for Disease Prevention and Control (ECDC) and WHO which repeatedly expressed a lack of reliability of the data provided. Many countries did not provide real statistics on the spread of the disease and deaths due to COVID-19 for political reasons. Moreover, more than a dozen countries in Africa, Asia, and Eurasia were not connected to the "global COVID-19 disease and death rate" because they did not have access to electronic instrumentation to record data – required to be a part of the global database (The Guardian: June 4, 2020).

It should be noted that only the number of deaths in 2019 and 2020 compared to other years can give reliable data on mortality due to COVID-19. For example, in the case of Poland, according to *Gazeta Wyborcza* article from December 28, 2020 that was based on a comparative big data analysis, in 51 weeks of 2020, 60,000 more people died than in the whole of 2019 – although official statistics show that in 2019 and 2020, a little over 27,000 people died in Poland because of COVID-19. *Gazeta Wyborcza*'s analysis was conducted on the data obtained from the Registers of Civil Status in Poland from 1945 to 2020 and concluded that the pandemic caused the highest mortality rate in Poland in the last 70 years. The mortality rate was similar only in 1951, just six years after the end of the Second World War, and at that time was caused by disability and chronic diseases such as malnutrition, yellow fever, tuberculosis, diphtheria, whooping cough, tetanus, or epidemic typhus (Gazeta Wyborcza: December 28, 2020). In Poland, vaccination against these diseases began only in the late 1950s. Similar research conducted on the data from other countries around the world may offer interesting results.

1.5 Coping with the pandemic

Data published by the *Bloomberg Covid Resilience Ranking* on December 21, 2020 ('The Best and Worst Places to Be in Covid: U.S. Sinks in Ranking' by Rachel Chang, Jinshan Hong and Kevin Varley, published: November 24, 2020, updated: December 21, 2020) shows that many countries around the world are not coping well enough with the pandemic, either in terms of healthcare security or economics. *Bloomberg*'s ranking took into account economies whose gross domestic product (GDP) was above $200 billion in 2019. The list included 53 countries, including Poland, and the assessment was based on 10 indicators:

- daily increase in infections,
- mortality rate of COVID-19,
- percentage of positive results among all virus tests,
- possibilities of the health care system,
- strengthening of the functioning of enterprises,
- blockade of the functioning of enterprises,
- restrictions on social and political freedoms,
- restrictions on movement,
- quality of pandemic strategy,
- quality of vaccination strategies.

(Bloomberg: December 21, 2020)

These key metrics cover the increase in virus cases to the overall mortality rate and testing capabilities. The capacity of the local healthcare system, the impact of virus-related restrictions like lockdowns on the economy, and freedom of movement are also taken into account.

It should be noted that only data officially provided by national governments were taken into account and that the last two factors included in the ranking reflect the number of doses of vaccine, the number of contracts signed for the supply of vaccine, and the percentage of the population that can be vaccinated with the doses ordered. The percentage of the population that does not want to be vaccinated due to a lack of trust in the vaccine or political power was not taken into account.

According to *Bloomberg*'s ranking, countries such as New Zealand (1st place in the ranking), Taiwan (2), Australia (3), Norway (4), Singapore (5), Finland (6), Japan (7), Korea (8), China (9), and Denmark (10) are best at dealing with the pandemic. The worst include Mexico (53rd; last place in the ranking), Argentina (52), Peru (51), Greece (50), and Italy (49) (Bloomberg: December 21, 2020).

When it comes to the regions of the world, Asia-Pacific countries have the best achievements in the fight against COVID-19, while the worst are noticed in Africa, both Americas and Europe. This is not surprising because the virus first attacked in Asia, while both Europe and the Americas were skeptical of Chinese "revelations" about the "deadly" virus.

In *Bloomberg*'s ranking, Poland, a member of the European Union, was ranked in the low 47th place, one place lower than Iran. What is more, other economies and countries significantly less developed than Poland, including India (39th place), Brazil (36), Nigeria (31), Pakistan (29), Egypt (24), Russia (18), and Vietnam (12), are dealing with COVID-19 much better than Poland. A similar situation is also visible in some other EU countries, including Romania (48), Greece (49), and Italy (49), which rank the lowest among European and EU countries (Bloomberg: December 21, 2020).

Difficulties in coping with COVID-19 result in economic decline and healthcare security. Most countries in Africa, Asia, and Latin America will be unable to return to pre-pandemic growth levels until 2023 and to the previous level of per capita income until 2025, later than anywhere else, according to *Bloomberg: Covid Resilience Ranking* published (Bloomberg: December 21, 2020). Many countries also faced the difficult choice between limiting mortality by announcing a lockdown and trying to maintain the economy by keeping it open.

Still, the countries that have responded most successfully were able to avoid choosing between the two: they avoided the trade-off between high mortality and a high socioeconomic impact of the pandemic. New Zealand and Israel has been able to bring infections down and open up their country internally. Other island nations were also able to almost entirely prevent an outbreak (like Taiwan, Australia, and Iceland). What is more, not only islands were able to bend the curve of infections and prevent large outbreaks – Norway, Uruguay, Thailand, Finland, and South Korea are examples of countries which dealt with the pandemic successfully. These countries not only suffered a smaller direct impact but they also limited the indirect impact because they were able to release lockdown measures earlier (see Our World in Data: January 11, 2021). Unfortunately, the fourth wave of the COVID-19 Pandemic, again shuts down societies and economies in late 2021.

1.6 Vaccination problems

Introducing lockdowns and COVID-19 restrictions was only a half-measure. The main goal of the year 2020 was to invent a cure or a vaccine that could successfully deal with the disease and help to end the pandemic. The end of 2020 brought such an invention – several companies worldwide managed to produce a vaccine against the deadly virus, including Pfizer and BioNTech, Moderna, AstraZeneca, Johnson & Johnson as well as Russian (Sputnik V), and Chinese (Sinovac, Sinopharm) vaccines (Pharmaceutical Processing World: February 5, 2021). In December 2020, the first countries started their vaccination programs. However, with the invention of vaccines, new problems also arose.

The first problem is the reluctance of people to get vaccinated. Many people in the world still downplay the virus. According to a survey conducted by several agencies, institutions, and newspaper editors, it is clear that nearly 50% of people do not want to get vaccinated. They claim: "99.7% recovery from COVID-19 – why do we need vaccine" (demonstrator holding an anti-vaccine placard in east London December 5, 2020).

According to a survey conducted by the Polish Institute for Market and Social Research (IBRiS, Instytut Badań Rynkowych i Społecznych) in

Poland, only 47% of the adult population wants to be vaccinated, while 44% does not want the vaccine and 9% are not sure. The largest group of those opposing vaccination (42%) believe that vaccines were not tested enough because they were created too quickly and thus are dangerous (IBRiS: December 28, 2020).

In the United Kingdom, one in five say they are unlikely to take the vaccine, according to YouGov research published in November 2020, citing a variety of different reasons. Around half of this group (47%, or 10% of all Britons) say they simply want to wait and see if the vaccine is safe first. An additional 15% of this group (equivalent to 3% of all Britons) currently say they would not get vaccinated because they see themselves as low risk and therefore, do not need the vaccine (YouGov: November 16, 2020).

When it comes to the United States, in December 2020, 42% of US adults say they would not get a vaccine. This shows a decrease since September 2020, when 50% did not want to get a vaccine, according to Gallup Panel 19, but it still poses significant challenges for public health and government officials in achieving mass public compliance with vaccine recommendations (Gallup 2020).

Another current problem is the insufficient number of vaccines connected with the low pace of vaccine production and the international quest for vaccines among the governments. Although AstraZeneca is planning to produce up to 3 billion doses of the vaccine, Pfizer and BioNTech 1.3 billion, and Johnson & Johnson, Sinovac, Sinopharm, and Moderna 1 billion doses each (Pharmaceutical Processing World: February 5, 2021), there are still important issues to arise, such as who will be vaccinated first. Since whole populations are to be vaccinated and there are not enough doses produced yet, governments began the vaccination process with different social groups that were considered the most vulnerable: doctors, teachers, critical workers, the elderly, or chronic patients. However, such a vaccination process design also encourages malpractice – the vaccines as well as fake vaccination certificates are already available on the darknet (BBC: March 23, 2021).

Differences in the pace of vaccination are also clearly visible between countries. Israel intends to be the first country to vaccine the whole population with 50% Israelis fully vaccinated and 60% having had the first dose as of March 15, 2021. At the same time in the United States, 12% of the population had been fully vaccinated and 21% had received the first dose (Health Affairs: March 18, 2021). But while some countries increase the pace of vaccination, other face unexpected delays in the supplies delivered. The European Union had to deal with this problem when Pfizer, AstraZeneca, and Moderna delayed or lowered the numbers of vaccines delivered to the member states at the beginning of 2021 (Reuters: February 17, 2021).

Finally, some experts raise doubts about the effectiveness of the vaccination process itself. With some new mutations in the virus causing the current fourth wave of the pandemic, there are concerns about whether the already existing vaccines can successfully prevent this new mutation as well (CNBC: March 5, 2021).

1.7 New challenges

Due to the COVID-19 pandemic, the global economy has slowed down significantly. All over the world, apart from New Zealand, people welcomed the New Year 2021 in total or partial lockdown: banned from leaving homes, traveling, with closed hotels and restaurants, and restrictions on the public gatherings for New Year's Eve (depending on the region of the world, up to 5–10 people). Although many people believed that the year 2021 would turn the situation around and allow the world to come back to the pre-pandemic state, new challenges connected with COVID-19 arose in the first quarter of 2021.

In December 2020, a new virus mutation (B.1.1.7) was detected in South Africa and the United Kingdom. Several countries in Europe and the Middle East banned air travel from the United Kingdom because of concerns over a mutant strain of the coronavirus that had been spreading rapidly in England in December 2020. The borders were kept closed also in January 2021; this was particularly difficult for the United Kingdom, which left the European Union on January 1, 2021. The B.1.1.7 mutation is believed to be more adept at human-to-human transmission, causing a much quicker spread of the virus within populations (Science: January 10, 2021). In January, in Japan, another new variant of COVID-19 was also detected – one that appears to have arrived with four passengers who came to Tokyo from Brazil. The newest variant of the virus appears to differ from the highly contagious strains in Britain and South Africa (CNBC: January 11, 2021). The new mutations of the virus shattered the hopes for a quick comeback to the pre-pandemic world and caused the current third wave of the pandemic.

2021 is to become a year of global vaccination. Vaccinations started to be introduced worldwide at the end of December 2020 – firstly, in the medical services and then, depending on the country, targeted at politicians, the elderly or different professional groups. As of December 31, 2020, the first dose of the vaccine had been taken by 2.1 million people worldwide. Most people were vaccinated with the vaccines produced by Pfizer/BioNTech and from January 2020, by Moderna (Our World in Data: January 1, 2021). On the one hand, the vaccines offer hope for a quick return to normality, but on the other hand, some problems with vaccine production and distribution as well as new virus mutations rapidly spreading infections leave people with the question "how will it all end?"

Since the pandemic has proven to be a long-lasting problem for humanity, not just a one-quarter-long anomaly in world development, one of the most pressing current problems is how to adjust to the new situation in the long term. Although we are already facing the fourth wave of the pandemic, many governmental solutions and the state of public healthcare have still not been developed enough in many countries to face the ongoing situation. What is more, citizens are not as understanding and mobilized as they were at the beginning of 2020, knowing now that their savings have disappeared, job opportunities have dropped, and hopes for normality are once again delayed. And even if humanity is to successfully combat the COVID-19 pandemic in the near future, there still will be a likely scenario of a big economic crisis for years to come.

1.8 The costs of the pandemic

The COVID-19 pandemic has caused a lot of implications for almost every aspect of people's lives. It certainly brought social distance and distrust of others as well as the erosion of public trust in researchers, politicians, and all sorts of "specialists in everything", and above all, the erosion of trust in governments and public institutions. It also has led to a dispersion of trust-based social capital, which money value no one has yet estimated.

What is more, the end of 2020 and the first quarter of 2021 brought numerous restrictions on civil and economic freedoms. In some regions, national governments closed country borders, some of them introducing a total lockdown. On January 5, 2021 a total lockdown was introduced by the United Kingdom, due to the discovery of a new virus mutation.

The first lockdown was introduced in China on November 17, 2019, and on March 1, 2020 the World Health Organization stated that the world was dealing with a pandemic of infectious disease with COVID-19 and suggested that countries "social distance". In the second half of February 2020, big outbreaks of infections with hundreds of patients started in South Korea, Italy, and Iran. Due to the pandemic, travel has been reduced worldwide, quarantine and curfew have been introduced, and a number of sporting, religious, and cultural events have been postponed or cancelled. Many countries have closed their borders or introduced severe restrictions on foreign travel, including restrictions on people crossing borders such as enforcing complete isolation for a period of 10 to 14 days – depending on the country – called "quarantine". Schools and universities went into remote online learning mode, which has affected nearly 1.27 billion students globally (72.4% of all students) (UNESCO: May 8, 2020). Soon after, enterprises stopped operations and started online work, especially after April 5, 2020, when the threshold of 2 million registered cases was crossed – most of them in the USA, Spain, Italy, and Brazil. Infections in South America have grown rapidly, causing a humanitarian crisis with significant socioeconomic implications. The fear of the virus has caused a decrease in consumer spending and thus, the collapse of traditional trade, transport, tourism and gastronomy around the world.

According to the World Bank, the costs of the pandemic can be divided into three main categories: about 12% of the total cost comes from increased mortality, 28% is due to high absenteeism, and as much as 60% comes from behavioral changes – that is because a person tries to avoid another people for fear of being infected. The estimated loss to the world economy as of October 24, 2020 is $30 billion, according to the World Bank.

As of February 24, 2020, there have been significant declines in stock markets around the world (Nikkei – 5.3%, Dow Jones – 13.3%, FTSE 100 – 19.3%). What is more, oil prices fell sharply, reaching their lowest price in 30 years on March 9, 2020. Many regions of the world faced a lack of food, and a few faced hunger. Even before COVID-19 reduced incomes and disrupted supply chains, chronic and acute hunger were on the rise due to various factors including conflicts, socioeconomic conditions, natural disasters, climate change, and pests. But 2020 marks the most severe increase in global food insecurity, impacting vulnerable households in almost every country. These phenomena may intensify in the following years because of the economic and agricultural losses, particularly in Latin America, Africa and Asia.

In the first year of the pandemic, transport and tourism industries suffered the most, while trade (especially online) and online games increased their profits. There was a high increase in house prices, caused by a stagnation in the construction industry, which, however, has later fallen due to massive asset sales and the bankruptcy of individuals and businesses (Williams 2020). Currently, the crisis is engulfing the insurance and banking spheres (46% decrease in profits). In most sectors of the economy, strategies have been put in place to survive and stock up during these uncertain times.

With many economic sectors closed, including tourism, entertainment, restaurants, and shopping malls, and companies unsure how to react in extremely unstable economic and legal conditions, many people lost their jobs and were unable to find a new one, had to do a job they are overqualified for or had their income cut. According to the International Monetary Fund, in 2020 compared with 2019, the unemployment rate rose from 2.4% to 3.3% in Japan, from 3.1% to 4.3% in Germany, from 3.8% to 5.4% in the United Kingdom, from 9.9% to 11% in Italy, from 11.9% to 13.4% in Brazil, from 3.7% to as much as 8.9% in the United States and from 5.7% to 9.7% in Canada (BBC: January 24, 2021). This generated significant costs for governments in a form of unemployment allowance and support for companies to prevent further redundancies. The coronavirus pandemic has affected all sectors of the economy, triggering one of the biggest economic crises in the last 100 years. According to the Organisation for Economic Co-Operation and Development (OECD), the COVID-19 pandemic has generated the worst health, economic, and social crisis in our lifetime. No country, no economy, no society has been spared. And no country, no economy, or no society can face it alone. Over 1.1 million people have lost their lives and more than 42 million infections have been recorded so far. In the 2022, we are expected to witness the worst recession since the Second World War, with a projected fall in global GDP of 4.5%. Many economies will not recover their 2019 output levels until 2022 at the earliest. The crisis has already wiped out all the jobs created since the global financial crisis of 2008 (OECD: October 10, 2020).

Although it is said that the coronavirus has plunged the world into a "crisis like no other", global growth is expected to rise to 5.8% in 2022 if the pandemic fades in the second half of 2021. This forecast is driven primarily by the predicted growth in countries such as India and China. Recovery in big, services-reliant economies that have been hit hard by the COVID-19 outbreak, such as the United Kingdom or Italy, is expected to be a much slower process.

1.9 Critical mental health services

Fear, worry and stress are normal responses to perceived or real threats and when people face uncertainty or the unknown. Therefore, it is normal and understandable that people are experiencing fear in the context of the COVID-19 pandemic. The fear of contracting the virus in a pandemic such as COVID-19 is accompanied by the significant changes to our daily lives caused by the restrictions introduced to slow down the spread of the virus. When facing the new realities of working from home, temporary unemployment, home-schooling, and a lack of physical contact with other family members, friends, and colleagues, we need to look after both our mental and physical health.

The COVID-19 pandemic has disrupted or halted critical mental health services in 93% of countries worldwide while the demand for mental health care is increasing, according to a new WHO survey. The survey of 130 countries provides the first global data showing the devastating impact of COVID-19 on access to mental health services. According to WHO, the pandemic is increasing demand for mental health services. Bereavement, isolation, loss of income, and fear are triggering mental health conditions or exacerbating existing ones. Many people may be facing increased levels of alcohol and drug use, insomnia, and anxiety.

What is more, COVID-19 itself can lead to neurological and mental complications, such as delirium, agitation, and stroke. People with pre-existing mental, neurological or substance use disorders are also more vulnerable to SARS-CoV-2 infection – they may stand a higher risk of severe outcomes and even death. While many countries (70%) have adopted telemedicine or teletherapy to overcome disruptions to in-person services, there are significant disparities in the uptake of these interventions. More than 80% of high-income countries reported deploying telemedicine and teletherapy to bridge gaps in mental health, compared with less than 50% of low-income countries.

According to the WHO survey, countries reported widespread disruption of many kinds of critical mental health services, including:

- over 60% reported disruptions to mental health services for vulnerable people, including children and adolescents (72%); older adults (70%); and women requiring antenatal or postnatal services (61%);

- disruptions to counseling and psychotherapy were reported by 67%; 65% reported disruptions to critical harm reduction services; and 45% to opioid agonist maintenance treatment for opioid dependence;
- more than a third (35%) reported disruptions to emergency interventions, including those for people experiencing prolonged seizures; severe substance use withdrawal syndromes; and delirium, often a sign of a serious underlying medical condition;
- disruptions to access to medications for mental, neurological and substance use disorders were reported by 30%;
- around three-quarters reported at least partial disruptions to school and workplace mental health services (78% and 75% respectively).

(WHO: October 5, 2020)

1.10 COVID-19 databases

Thanks to the Internet, it is possible to check the status of the pandemic daily. The most popular databases of active cases of COVID-19 include:

- Worldometers (https://www.worldometers.info/coronavirus/), based on Geoshemie UN public statistics (https://unstats.un.org/unsd/methodology/m49/),
- WHO Coronavirus Disease (COVID-19) Dashboard (https://covid19.who.int/),
- Our World in Data (https://ourworldindata.org/coronavirus-data),
- OCHA – Asia Pacific COVID-19: Humanitarian Data Portal (https://interactive.unocha.org/data/ap-covid19-portal/),
- The Coronavirus in Asia and ASEAN – Live Updates by Country (https://www.aseanbriefing.com/news/coronavirus-asia-asean-live-updates-by-country/),
- COVID-19 Research Response. The Global Health Network (https://coronavirus.tghn.org/regional-response/asia-ncov/),
- The Lancet – Regional Health (https://www.thelancet.com/journals/laninf/article/PIIS1473-3099(20)30708-8/fulltext),
- The South African Resource Portal (https://sacoronavirus.co.za/),
- CDC – Centers for Disease Control and Prevention, US Federal Government Agency, Part of the Department of Health and Human Services (https://www.cdc.gov/coronavirus/2019-ncov/covid-data/covidview/index.html),
- Europe: European Centre for Disease Prevention and Control, An Agency of the European Union (https://www.ecdc.europa.eu/en/covid-19/data),
- Eurostat – COVID-19: Statistics Serving Europe (https://ec.europa.eu/eurostat/web/covid-19/overview).

1.11 Conclusions

The COVID-19 pandemic has taken the world and world leaders by surprise, significantly changing all aspects of our lives. The virus and the disease spread so quickly and took so many lives around the world that it has become the most important topic of 2020 and 2021, influencing all aspects of the economy, society, politics, and culture. No part of humanity was spared – many people are dying, healthcare systems are collapsing, economies are suffering because of lockdown, governments are facing distrust and in some countries are even facing uprisings of people who are dissatisfied with the way the COVID-19 crisis has been handled.

In the face of the crisis, it is no wonder that COVID-19 has immediately become the main topic of research conducted around the world in a wide range of disciplines – from medicine and virology to social sciences trying to explain its impact on society and its members. Large amounts of funds targeted at all types of COVID-19 research projects led to a lot of important discoveries, including different types of tests, medical procedures to treat COVID-19 patients, statistics allowing for study of the development of the pandemic, and finally vaccines against the deadly virus. However, despite all these applied studies and recent discoveries, humanity still faces a lot of problems connected with the virus's impact.

One of the most important problems is denial of the virus's existence and miscalculated statistics on its spread. Not every government and politician took the disease seriously and many of them tried to use the situation for their own political gain. As a consequence, in some countries governments did not act upon the virus as quickly and forcefully as they could have done, causing severe implications not only for these countries but also for their neighbors.

What is more, the lack of knowledge about the origins or initial spread of the virus combined with miscalculated data on the scope of pandemic has led to many misunderstandings, mistakes, and even conspiracy theories, which unfortunately have been spread through the media and the Internet, affecting numerous people. Politicians and different kinds of 'experts' did not stop these revelations which only fueled them and led to social and political distrust to the extent that when the vaccine for the COVID-19 was finally introduced, huge parts of society did not want to take it for fear of the possible side effects or mistrust for the government.

There is also huge economic loss connected with the COVID-19 pandemic. The global economy, which became a highly interconnected network during the last 30 years, started to split and collapse. Many branches which were based on international exchange and social contacts, especially services, have suffered a lot since the very beginning of the pandemic. Others have been hit hard later, when initial lockdowns led to unemployment, withdrawal of assets, and general pessimism when it comes to investments.

All these factors combined allow experts to predict the occurrence of a big economic crisis connected with the pandemic in the near future.

Economic pressures are also closely connected with social loss. Although globalization in the last 30 years allowed for the quick development of ideas and improvement of life conditions, the virus caused a lot of personal and social damage. Problems such as the deaths of people who may otherwise have lived for much longer time, unemployment, healthcare, and mental health problems, home-schooling, lack of contact with others, and decrease of trust will probably be the long-lasting effects of the COVID-19 pandemic.

References

Andersen, K., Rambaut, A., Lipkin, W., Holmes, E., Garry, R. (2020) Correspondence: The proximal origin of SARS-CoV-2. *Nature Medicine*. No. 26 (4), 450–452.

Baltimore, D. (1971). Expression of animal virus genomes. *Bacteriological Reviews*. No. 35 (3), 235–241.

BBC (February 11, 2020). *Coronavirus disease named Covid-19*. Archived from the original on 15 February 2020. Retrieved January 15, 2021.

BBC (April 19, 2020). *Coronavirus: US protests against and for lockdown restrictions*. Retrieved March 25, 2021. https://www.bbc.com/news/av/world-us-canada-52344540.

BBC (January 24, 2021). *Coronavirus: How the pandemic has changed the world economy*. Retrieved March 30, 2021. https://www.bbc.com/news/business-51706225.

BBC (March 23, 2021). *Covid-19: Vaccines and vaccine passports being sold on darknet*. Retrieved March 25, 2021. https://www.bbc.com/news/technology-56489574.

Bloomberg (December 21, 2020). Rachel Chang, Jinshan Hong, Kevin Varley, *The Covid resilience ranking. The best and worst places to be in covid: U.S. sinks in ranking*. Bloomberg. November 24, 2020, Updated: December 21, 2020, Retrieved 15 January 2021. https://www.bloomberg.com/graphics/covid-resilience-ranking/.

CDC (February 11, 2020). *About novel coronavirus (2019-nCoV)*. Archived from the original on February 11, 2020. Retrieved February 25, 2020. https://www.who.int/docs/default-source/coronaviruse/situation-reports/20200130-sitrep-10-ncov.pdf?sfvrsn=d0b2e480_2.

CDC-Led Collaboration (2012). *First global estimates of 2009 H1N1 pandemic mortality released*. cdc.gov. June 25, 2012. Access: January 10, 2021. https://www.cdc.gov/flu/spotlights/pandemic-global-estimates.htm; https://www.thelancet.com/journals/laninf/article/PIIS1473-3099(12)70121-4/fulltext.

Chan, J., Yuan, S., Kok, K., To, K., Chu, H., Yang, J., et al. (2020). A familial cluster of pneumonia associated with the 2019 novel coronavirus indicating person-to-person transmission: A study of a family cluster. *The Lancet*. No. 395 (10223), 514–523.

CNBC (March 5, 2021). *How the different Covid vaccines will handle new variants of the virus.* Retrieved March 25, 2021. https://www.cnbc.com/2021/03/05/how-the-different-covid-vaccines-will-handle-variants.html.

CNBC TV (January 11, 2021). *Japan has found a new Covid variant. Here's how it compares to virus strains in the UK. South Africa.* Retrieved January 11, 2021. https://www.cnbc.com/2021/01/11/japan-covid-variant-how-it-compares-to-strains-in-uk-south-africa.html.

CSSE – Center for Systems Science and Engineering (January 11, 2021). *COVID-19 dashboard by the center for systems science and engineering (CSSE) at Johns Hopkins University (JHU).* ArcGIS, Johns Hopkins University, Coronavirus Resource Center. Retrieved January 10, 2021. https://coronavirus.jhu.edu/map.html.

Gallup (November 17, 2020). *More Americans now willing to get COVID-19 vaccine.* Archived from the Retrieved original on January 10, 2021. https://news.gallup.com/poll/325208/americans-willing-covid-vaccine.aspx.

Gazeta Wyborcza (December 28, 2020). *Zgony. Niestety, 2020 r. zapisze się w naszej powojennej historii jako rekordowy,* edited by Pawłowska, D. "Gazeta Wyborcza BiQ DATA.pl" BiG DATA.pl, Retrieved December 28, 2020. https://biqdata.wyborcza.pl/biqdata/7,159116,26642808,zgony-niestety-2020-r-zapisze-sie-w-naszej-powojennej-histori.html.

Gorbalenya, A. E., Baker, S. C., Baric, R. S., de Groot, R. J, Drosten, C., Gulyaeva, A. A., et al. (2020). The species Severe acute respiratory syndrome-related coronavirus: Classifying 2019-nCoV and naming it SARS-CoV-2. *Nature Microbiology.* No. 5 (4), 536–544.

Health Affairs (March 18, 2021). *Lessons In COVID-19 vaccination from Israel.* Retrieved March 25, 2021. https://www.healthaffairs.org/do/10.1377/hblog20210315.476220/full/.

IBRIS (December 28, 2020). *Polish institute for market and social research.* <u>Survey: Wciąż sporo osób nie chce się zaszczepić. Dominuje jeden argument przeciw.</u> 'Rzeczpospolita'. Retrieved December 28, 2020. https://wiadomosci.onet.pl/kraj/koronawirus-sondaz-ile-osob-w-polsce-chce-sie-zaszczepic/9m6pr2k.

Johns Hopkins University (March 25, 2021). *COVID-19 dashboard.* Retrieved March 25, 2021. https://coronavirus.jhu.edu/map.html.

Lim, B. H., Mahmood, T. A. (2011). Influenza A H1N1 2009 (Swine Flu) and pregnancy. *Journal of Obstetrics and Gynaecology.* No. 61 (4), 386–393.

Machhi, J., Herskovitz, J., Senan, A. M., Dutta, D., Nath, B., Oleynikov, M. D., et al. (2020). The natural history, pathobiology, and clinical manifestations of SARS-CoV-2 infections. *Journal of Neuroimmune Pharmacology. The Official Journal of the Society on Neuroimmune Pharmacology.* No. 15 (3), 359–386.

NIH – National Institutes of Health (March 17, 2020). *New coronavirus stable for hours on surfaces.* NIH.gov. Archived from the original on March 23, 2020. Retrieved May 4, 2020. https://www.nih.gov/news-events/news-releases/new-coronavirus-stable-hours-surfaces.

OECD (October 10, 2020). *Ministerial council meeting opening remarks by Angel Gurría.* OECD Secretary-General. Retrieved January 10, 2021. https://www.oecd.org/coronavirus/en/.

Our World in Data (January 1, 2021). *How many people have received a coronavirus vaccine?* Retrieved January 10, 2021. https://ourworldindata.org/covid-vaccinations.

Pharmaceutical Processing World (February 5, 2021). *Which companies will likely produce the most COVID-19 vaccine in 2021?* Retrieved March 25, 2021. https://www.pharmaceuticalprocessingworld.com/which-companies-will-likely-produce-the-most-covid-19-vaccine-in-2021/.

RBB (August 29, 2020). *Fast 40.000 Menschen bei Corona-Demos – Sperren am Reichstag durchbrochen.* Retrieved March 25, 2021. https://www.rbb24.de/politik/thema/2020/coronavirus/beitraege_neu/2020/08/demonstrationen-samstag-corona-querdenken-gegendemos.html.

Reuters (June 26, 2020). *Coronavirus traces found in March 2019 sewage sample, Spanish study shows.* Archived from the original on June 26, 2020 7:22 PM. Retrieved January 10, 2021. https://www.reuters.com/article/us-health-coronavirus-spain-science-idUSKBN23X2HQ.

Reuters (February 17, 2021). *Exclusive: Pfizer COVID-19 vaccine supply to the EU about 10 million doses short of plan -sources.* Retrieved March 25, 2021. https://www.reuters.com/article/us-health-coronavirus-eu-pfizer-exclusiv-idUSKBN2AH1E3.

Sanche, S., Lin, Y. T., Xu, C., Romero-Severson, E., Hengartner, N., Ke, R. (2020). High contagiousness and rapid spread of severe acute respiratory syndrome coronavirus 2. *Emerging Infectious Diseases.* No. 26 (7), 1470–1477.

Science (January 10, 2021). *Kupferschmidt Kai, Mutant coronavirus in the United Kingdom sets off alarms, but its importance remains unclear, Science's COVID-19 reporting.* Retrieved January 10, 2021. https://www.sciencemag.org/news/2020/12/mutant-coronavirus-united-kingdom-sets-alarms-its-importance-remains-unclear.

Scientific American (October 12, 2020). *Eight persistent COVID-19 myths and why people believe them.* Retrieved March 25, 2021. https://www.scientificamerican.com/article/eight-persistent-covid-19-myths-and-why-people-believe-them/.

Shou-Jiang, G. (ed.) *Journal of Medical Virology.* Three special issues on the Novel Coronavirus (COVID-19), monthly editions for years 2019–2020. Retrieved January 10, 2021. https://onlinelibrary.wiley.com/journal/10969071; https://papers.ssrn.com/sol3/papers.cfm?abstract_id=3557504.

The Guardian (May 1, 2020). Trump claims to have evidence coronavirus started in Chinese lab but offers no details. *Support the Guardian.* Retrieved January 10, 2020. https://www.theguardian.com/us-news/2020/apr/30/donald-trump-coronavirus-chinese-lab-claim.

The Guardian (June 4, 2020). *Covid-19 investigations unreliable data: How doubt snowballed over Covid-19 drug research that swept the world.* The Guardian. Retrieved January 10, 2021. https://www.theguardian.com/world/2020/jun/04/unreliable-data-doubt-snowballed-covid-19-drug-research-surgisphere-coronavirus-hydroxychloroquine; https://papers.ssrn.com/sol3/papers.cfm?abstract_id=3557504.

The Guardian (September 4, 2020). *How coronavirus has brought together conspiracy theorists and the far right.* Retrieved March 25, 2021. https://www.theguardian.com/commentisfree/2020/sep/04/coronavirus-conspiracy-theorists-far-right-protests.

The Guardian (October 26, 2020). *Survey uncovers widespread belief in 'dangerous' Covid conspiracy theories.* Retrieved March 25, 2021. https://www.theguardian.com/world/2020/oct/26/survey-uncovers-widespread-belief-dangerous-covid-conspiracy-theories.

UNESCO (May 8, 2020). *COVID-19 educational disruption and response*. Retrieved January 10, 2021. https://en.unesco.org/news/covid-19-educational-disruption-and-response; https://papers.ssrn.com/sol3/papers.cfm?abstract_id=3557504.

WHO – World Health Organization (January 2020). *Surveillance case definitions for human infection with novel coronavirus (nCoV): Interim guidance v1, January 2020 (report)*. Retrieved January 10, 2021. https://papers.ssrn.com/sol3/papers.cfm?abstract_id=3557504;hdl:10665/330376.WHO/2019-nCoV/Surveillance/v 2020.1.=

WHO – World Health Organization (January 30, 2020). *Statement on the second meeting of the International Health Regulations (2005) Emergency Committee regarding the outbreak of novel coronavirus (2019-nCoV)*. (Press release). Archived from the original on January 31, 2020. Retrieved January 10, 2021. https://www.who.int/news/item/30-01-2020-statement-on-the-second-meeting-of-the-international-health-regulations-(2005)-emergency-committee-regarding-the-outbreak-of-novel-coronavirus-(2019-ncov).

WHO – World Health Organization (March 11, 2020). *WHO Director-General's opening remarks at the media briefing on COVID-19 – 11 March 2020*. (Press release). Archived from the original on March 11, 2020. Retrieved March 12, 2020. https://www.who.int/director-general/speeches/detail/who-director-general-s-opening-remarks-at-the-media-briefing-on-covid-19---11-march-2020.

WHO – World Health Organization (October 5, 2020). *COVID-19 disrupting mental health services in most countries, WHO survey. World Mental Health Day on 10 October to highlight urgent need to increase investment in chronically underfunded sector, October 5, 2020*. https://www.who.int/news/item/05-10-2020-covid-19-disrupting-mental-health-services-in-most-countries-who-survey.

Williams, C. Ch. (2020). Impacts of the coronavirus pandemic on Europe's tourism industry: Addressing tourism enterprises and workers in the undeclared economy. *International Journal of Tourism Research*. No. 23 (1): 79–88. Retrieved July 27, 2020. https://doi.org/10.1002/jtr.2395.

WMD – Worldometer Data. Archived from the original on January 31, 2020. Retrieved September 9, 2021. https://www.worldometers.info/coronavirus/.

2 Impact of the COVID-19 pandemic on the differentiation of selected macroeconomic variables characterizing the EU economies over a short period

Monika Bolińska, Rafał Wisła, and Michał Włodarczyk

2.1 Introduction

The COVID-19 pandemic cast a long shadow over the world's economies in 2020 and the economic outlook in 2021 is very uncertain (OECD, 2020). The scale and dynamics of the spread of the COVID-19 pandemic, caused by a coronavirus, entailed serious disturbances in social and economic life. The 2020+ pandemic is not only the most serious global health crisis since the Spanish flu of 1918 but also one of the most economically expensive pandemics on a global scale. The World Bank stated that the COVID-19 pandemic has plunged the global economy into its deepest recession since World War II. Per capita incomes are expected to decline in about 90% of countries in 2020, the largest fraction since 1870 (Dieppe, 2020).

Looking at the four quarters of 2020, it is clear that the restrictions on social and economic life, imposed in line with various rules, had a stronger effect on the value of aggregate demand (and due to the Keynesian multiplier effect, on the volume of production) than on the supply aspect of the economy. Consumer expenditures in the household sector represent the most important component of domestic demand and account for about 55% of the situation of European economies (the dynamics of changes in the gross domestic product (GDP) and its structure, labor market condition, and indirectly the condition of public finance and international competitive advantage, etc.). Considering an additional decrease in the volume of exports and gross fixed capital formation (that is aimed to strengthen the economy's manufacturing potential), a grim picture of the European economies in 2020 emerges.

The International Monetary Fund (IMF) argues that most economies will suffer a durable loss in their manufacturing potential due to the 2020+ pandemic, and this will decelerate growth in the following years. It will take time for the labor market to recover to its pre-2020 condition, as investments will be postponed due to uncertainty, and unemployment and loss

DOI: 10.4324/9781003211891-2

of schooling will cause erosion in human and social capital (Dieppe, 2020). The crisis caused by the pandemic would be more severe if it were not for rapid counteraction by governments and central banks that supported enterprises in maintaining their financial liquidity and to a significant extent upheld employment and household income (IMF, 2020). The European Union has responded to the outbreak of COVID-19 and its consequences by adopting a wide range of measures in many areas: public health, society, economy, etc.[1]

The COVID-19 pandemic has generated a very large volume of research related to the basic biology of coronavirus infection, its detection, treatment and evolution,[2] but also related to its economic consequences.[3] In terms of economics, most of the research is focused on aggregate macroeconomic effects (Atkeson, 2020; Baumeister, Guérin, 2020; Ludvigson, Ma & Ng, 2020), labor markets (Forsythe, Kahn, Lange & Wiczer, 2020), costs of the pandemic and its containment (Brock, Xepapadeas, 2020; Lik Ng, 2020).

This chapter aims to assess the impact of the COVID-19 pandemic on the differentiation of selected macroeconomic variables in the European Union (EU) economies. The study examined 27 European countries that were members of the European Union at the time of the announcement of the pandemic by the World Health Organization (WHO) on March 11, 2020. The analysis did not include the United Kingdom, which left the European Union on January 31, 2020. The following macro-indicators were analyzed and assessed: gross domestic product per capita, the unemployment rate, gross fixed capital formation per capita, exports of goods and services per capita, and imports of goods and services per capita. The research project included both a long (2006–2020) and a short (Q2 of 2020 vs. Q2 of 2019)[4] period.

The macro-indicators are discussed in this analysis using a dynamic approach (in time) and a spatial approach (the level of countries). The economies of the EU member states are classified in quintile groups with the lowest (five countries), low (five), average (six), high (five) and the highest (five) values of the analyzed variables. The groups have different compositions in the analysis of unemployment because the changes in unemployment rates in those countries were insignificant between Q2 of 2019 and Q2 of 2020.

Short-term comparative analyses cover the second quarters of 2019 and 2020, the period of the sharpest decreases in the discussed macroeconomic

---

1 European Parliament's EU response (https://www.europarl.europa.eu/news/en/headlines/priorities/eu-response-to-coronavirus); European Commission (https://ec.europa.eu/info/live-work-travel-eu/coronavirus-response_en).
2 See, for example, the websites at https://www.nature.com/collections/hajgidghjb.
3 See: https://www.nber.org/wp_covid19.html or https://covid-19.iza.org/publications/.
4 Both the analyzed period and the selected macroeconomic variables were determined by the availability of statistics on the EUROSTAT website: https://ec.europa.eu/eurostat/data/database.

aggregates. Slovakia is classified in a separate group with a 0 value on the maps due to the absence of statistics for that country (except the unemployment map). This chapter contains a cluster analysis employing Ward's method with Euclidean distance, and a study into variations of selected macroeconomic characteristics in quarterly periods in the years 2006–2020.

2.2 Gross domestic product per capita

If we assume that GDP per capita gives a synthetic, general, albeit imperfect image of the level of wealth of an average citizen of a country and build a tree of clusters of similarities and differences in this macro-indicator in the group of 27 member states of the European Union (Figure 2.1), the general conclusions discussed below can be drawn. The highest similarities in this macroeconomic variable in the period 2006–2020 (considering quarterly values) were characteristic of the following country pairs: Belgium and Finland, Denmark and the Netherlands, Cyprus and Slovenia, Greece and Latvia, Latvia and Lithuania, Croatia and Poland, and Germany and France. An analysis of clusters of EU countries also led to the distinction

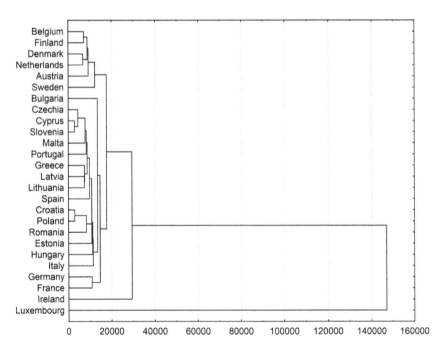

Figure 2.1 A dendrogram of GDP per capita in the member states of the EU (2006–2020, Euclidean distance). Source: own calculation based on https://ec.europa.eu/eurostat/data/database.

Impact on macroeconomic variables 23

of three main similarity clusters. The first cluster is formed by Belgium, Finland, Germany, the Netherlands, Austria and Sweden. The second cluster includes the Czech Republic, Cyprus, Slovenia, Malta, Portugal, Greece, Latvia, Lithuania and Spain. The last cluster is formed by Croatia, Poland, Romania, Estonia, Hungary and Italy. Luxembourg and Ireland with their high values of GDP per capita clearly stand out from the other countries.

Between the years 2006 and 2020, the lowest values of GDP per capita were recorded in Bulgaria (EUR 1,338.78), Croatia (EUR 3,995.16), Poland (EUR 4,131.15), Romania (EUR 4,398.21) and Lithuania (EUR 5,643.06). The highest values of the analyzed variable were recorded in Luxembourg (EUR 35,117.87), one of the largest global financial centers. The group of countries with the highest values of GDP per capita included: the Netherlands (EUR 15,571.39), Denmark (EUR 15,606.95), Sweden (EUR 16,052.14) and Austria (EUR 16,316.64).

The analysis of long-term similarities and differences is juxtaposed below with an analysis of a very short period of the sharpest decrease in the values of discussed macroeconomic aggregates since the end of World War II, i.e. in Q2 of 2020.

Maps 2.1(a) and 2.1(b) show the value of GDP per capita in Q2 of 2019 and Q2 of 2020. Over the analyzed period, the greatest falls in GDP per capita occurred in the economies of Luxembourg (a decrease by EUR 3,048.36 in Q2 of 2020 vs. Q2 of 2019), Austria (EUR 2,271.61), the Netherlands (EUR 2,027.30), Belgium (EUR 1,902.88), France (EUR 1,869.73), Spain (EUR 1,589.29), Sweden (EUR 1,556. 00) and Malta (EUR 1,504.74). These countries are classified in the groups with average, high and the highest values of the discussed variable.

The slightest falls of GDP per capita were recorded in Bulgaria (a decrease by EUR 367.08 in Q2 of 2020 vs. Q2 of 2019), Lithuania (EUR 627.21), Croatia (EUR 677.73), Portugal (EUR 700.33), Romania (EUR 710.99), Poland (EUR 711.31), Latvia (EUR 771.12), Greece (EUR 815.90) and Estonia (EUR 905.01). These states constituted the groups with the lowest, low and average values of GDP per capita.

Eight countries changed their positions in the ranking of average wealth between Q2 of 2019 and Q2 of 2020. Austria, Hungary, Spain, Cyprus, Estonia, Finland and Poland changed their positions by one within the quintile groups they belong to until the end of 2019. The Czech Republic dropped to the quintile group with lower values of GDP per capita. Estonia entered in the second quarter of 2020 the group with higher values of the analyzed variable, compared to the corresponding period in the preceding year.

The depth of decreases in GDP (and consequently GDP per capita) in the second quarter of 2020 was unprecedented in the post-war history of the member states of the former European Communities and the current European Union. The greatest falls in GDP were recorded in Spain (−21.5% in Q2 of 2020 vs. Q2 of 2019), France (−18.9%), Italy (−18.0%),

24 *Monika Bolińska et al.*

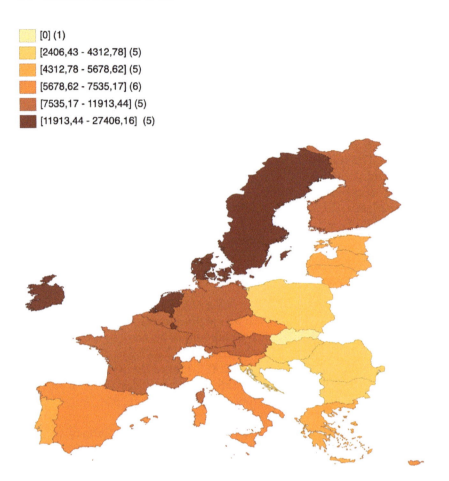

- [0] (1)
- [2406,43 – 4312,78] (5)
- [4312,78 – 5678,62] (5)
- [5678,62 – 7535,17] (6)
- [7535,17 – 11913,44] (5)
- [11913,44 – 27406,16] (5)

Map 2.1a Spatial differentiation of GDP per capita in the second quarters of 2019 in the member states of the European Union (in EUR, constant prices from Q2 of 2020). Source: own calculation based on https://ec.europa.eu/eurostat/data/database.

Malta, Portugal, Croatia, Greece, Austria, Belgium, Hungary (decreases by –16.7% to –13.5%); relatively slighter decreases were recorded in Lithuania (–4.6%) and Ireland (–3.5%). The third quarter of 2020 still saw a downward trend in GDP values, except Ireland (8.1% growth in Q3 of 2020 vs. Q3 of 2019). Despite a decrease in GDP by 1.8% in the third quarter, Poland increased its proportion of EU GDP from 3.82 to 3.94 percent, i.e. by 0.12 percentage points. Proportions of EU GDP increased by higher percentages only in the case of Ireland, the Netherlands and Sweden.

Impact on macroeconomic variables 25

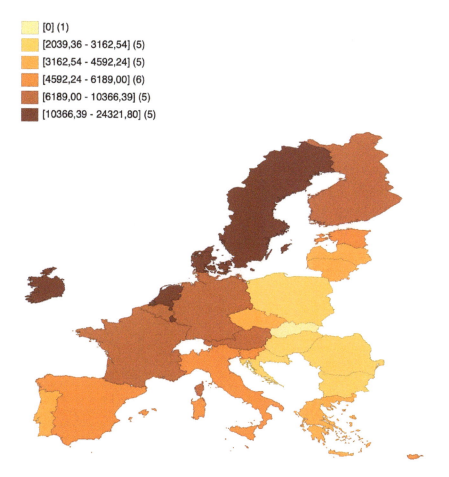

Map 2.1b Spatial differentiation of GDP per capita in the second quarters of 2020 in the member states of the European Union (in EUR, constant prices from Q2 of 2020). Source: own calculation based on https://ec.europa.eu/eurostat/data/database.

2.3 Unemployment

The unemployment rate is correlated with the curve of the economic situation, both at the level of member states and that of the entire EU economy.

Figure 2.2 shows the changes in the unemployment rate in the European Union countries, from this figure we can conclude the following statements. A decrease in the unemployment rate was observed between the first quarter of 2006 and the corresponding quarter of 2008 due to a favorable economic situation in the European Union. The decrease in the unemployment rate

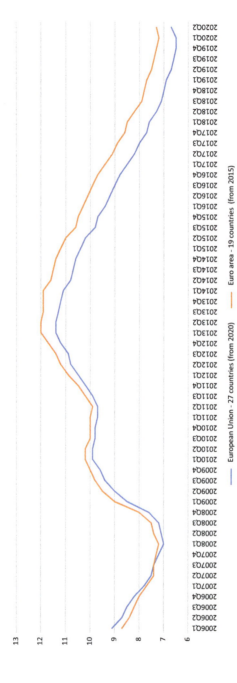

Figure 2.2 Changes in the unemployment rate in the EU economy (in %, 2006–2020, quarterly data). Source: own calculation based on https://ec.europa.eu/eurostat/data/database.

in that time interval amounted to more than 1%. The unemployment rate grew in the following quarters (from the second quarter of 2008 to the third quarter of 2013). This unfavorable trend was caused by a global shock (the crisis of 2008+), exogenous in its nature to the EU economy. The greatest increase in the unemployment rate was recorded between the last quarter of 2008 and the first quarter of 2009. The average increase in the rate of unemployment between Q2 of 2008 and Q3 of 2013 amounted to 2.4%. In the following periods, the unemployment rate dropped, by 0.1% on average period-over-period, until the second quarter of 2020, when unemployment grew by 0.1 percentage points compared to the first quarter of that year. The increase in the unemployment rate resulted from the economic restrictions imposed by European economies in response to the spread of the SARS-CoV-2 virus. Figure 2.3 represents a clustering tree of similarities and differences in unemployment rates in the member states of the EU in the years 2006–2020 (including the second quarter of 2020).

The dendrogram identifies the following pairs of similar countries: Belgium and Finland, Malta and Romania, Luxembourg and Austria, Hungary and Poland, Ireland and Lithuania, Croatia and Portugal, and Greece and Spain. An analysis of the clustering tree demonstrates the following similarity clusters. The first cluster is formed by Croatia, Slovakia and

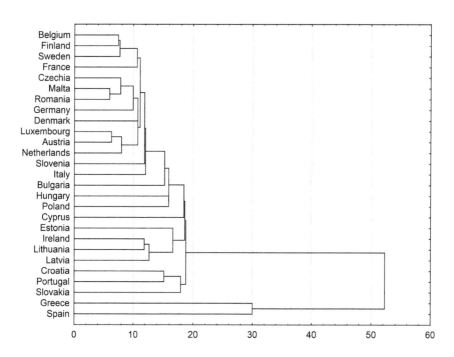

Figure 2.3 A dendrogram of unemployment rates in the EU (2006–2020, Euclidean distance). Source: own calculation based on https://ec.europa.eu/eurostat/data/database.

Portugal, where the average unemployment rate amounted to about 11% in the analyzed time interval. Another cluster is formed by three states located in the north-eastern part of Europe: Lithuania, Latvia and Estonia, plus Ireland. The third cluster includes Belgium, Finland, Sweden and France, where the average unemployment rate amounted to about 8%. The last and largest cluster is formed by the Czech Republic, Malta, Denmark, Romania, Germany, Luxembourg, Austria and the Netherlands.

The highest average unemployment rates in the years 2006–2020 occurred in Greece (17.85%), Spain (17.81%), Croatia (12.00%), Slovakia (11.06%) and Latvia (10.86%). The lowest average unemployment rates were recorded in Iceland (4.43%), Austria (5.12%), the Netherlands (5.13%), the Czech Republic (5.16%) and Luxembourg (5.38%).

The analysis of long-term similarities and differences is juxtaposed below with an analysis of short-term responses of unemployment rates to the circumstances between Q2 of 2019 and Q2 of 2020. Maps 2.2(a) and 2.2(b) represent spatially differentiated rates of registered unemployment in the 27 member states of the EU in the second quarters of 2019 and 2020.

The lowest unemployment rates both in 2019 and in 2020 were recorded in the central area of the European Union. Twenty-one states changed their positions in the ranking between Q2 of 2019 and Q2 of 2020: 11 states dropped in the ranking and 10 were ranked higher. The largest fall affected Lithuania; the country dropped by eight positions in the ranking of registered unemployment rates. Also, Estonia dropped by six positions; the countries that dropped by five positions in the ranking were Latvia, Bulgaria and Sweden. The group of states that went down also includes Romania (down four positions), Austria (down two positions), and Finland, Germany, Hungary and the Netherlands (down one position).

In contrast, Portugal advanced by seven positions, Belgium advanced by six positions, and Croatia, Ireland and Cyprus each advanced by five positions. The group of states that reached higher positions also included France (by four positions), Italy (by three positions), Poland (by two positions), and Malta and Denmark (by one position).

Both a decrease and an increase in the unemployment rate was observed between the discussed quarters. The unemployment rate fell only in seven countries. Between Q2 of 2019 and Q2 of 2020, the unemployment rate fell in Italy (2.1 percentage points), France (1.3 percentage points), Portugal (0.7 percentage points), Belgium (0.5 percentage points), Greece (0.3 percentage points) and Poland and Ireland (0.2 percentage points each). The unemployment rate grew in 20 states in the analyzed time interval. The largest increases (exceeding 1.5 percentage points) were recorded in Bulgaria (1.5 percentage points), Romania (1.6 percentage points), Latvia (1.7 percentage points), Estonia (1.9 percentage points), Sweden (1.9 percentage points) and Lithuania (2.4 percentage points).

This variety of responses of labor markets to the supply and demand shock in Q2 of 2020 can be interpreted from various perspectives. The causes of such diversity should be sought in the varying scenarios of the

Impact on macroeconomic variables 29

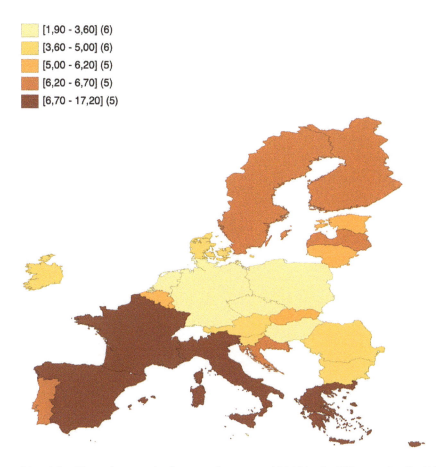

Map 2.2a Unemployment in the second quarter of 2019 in the EU countries (in %). Source: own calculation based on https://ec.europa.eu/eurostat/data/database.

implementation of lockdown measures. First, a rapid introduction of lockdown measures has a stronger effect on accumulated social and economic activity than continual increases and decreases in the severity of restrictions on that activity. Second, a scenario of strong rapid lockdown has the most serious adverse consequences for the economy, both in terms of the sharpness of decrease in production, the time of staying on the relatively lowest growth path, and the expected accumulated decrease in production. Similar conclusions concern the changes in social utility and labor market.

The unemployment rate in Poland amounted in October 2020 to 3.5%, as per the EU standard methods, while in the Czech Republic it reached 2.9% – the best result in this category in the European Union. The number of unemployed in the European Union by the end of October 2020 amounted to 13.8 million. This was 1.7 million (13.9%) more than in

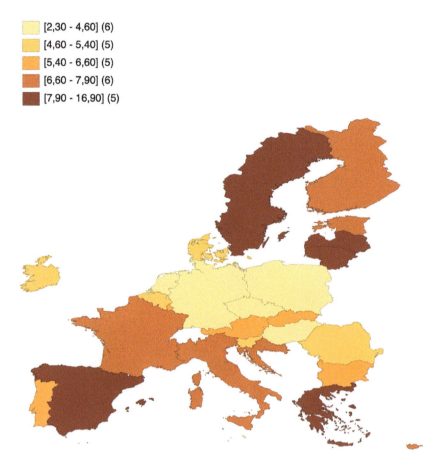

Map 2.2b Unemployment in the second quarter of 2020 in the EU countries (in %).
Source: own calculation based on https://ec.europa.eu/eurostat/data/database.

2019. The largest increases in the numbers of unemployed were recorded in Germany and Spain.

Employment rose in Q3 of 2020 in Poland (by 0.5%) and Malta (by 2.4%). In the remaining countries of the European Union (except Luxembourg), a continued decrease in the employment rate was observed. Employment in the EU economy dropped by 2% year-over-year, by 4.3 million people in total.

2.4 Gross fixed capital formation per capita

Investing activities of business entities have a direct effect on global demand, production volume, employment and capital accumulation.

On the basis of Figure 2.4 we can conclude that the gross fixed capital formation in the EU economy as a whole, considered in quarterly periods in the years 2006–2020, underwent three distinct processes. The gross fixed capital formation rose in the European Union until the first quarter of 2008 but began to dramatically drop in the advent of a financial crisis that in the following years evolved into an economic crisis. The EU member states reduced the value of gross fixed capital formation by 0.65% per annum in the years 2008–2015.

The highest gross fixed capital formation was recorded in the fourth quarter of 2007 (23.6%) and that value was not reached until the second quarter of 2020. The lowest value was recorded in the first quarter of 2015 (19.6%). The value of expenditures on gross fixed capital formation bought or produced in the EU economy has significantly fluctuated since 2015. The greatest fall (by 1.1 percentage points) of gross fixed capital formation was recorded both between the second and third quarters of 2019 and between the first and second quarters of 2020. The average decrease of the analyzed variable between the first quarter of 2006 and the last quarter of 2020 amounted to 0.09% per annum.

The above general picture of fluctuations in the gross fixed capital formation is supplemented by an analysis of clusters shown in Figure 2.5. In the clustering tree, six pairs of national economies similar in their gross fixed capital formation can be distinguished. The pairs of similar countries comprise Belgium and Finland, Germany and France, Croatia and Poland, Greece and Romania, the Czech Republic and Italy, and Hungary and Slovenia. Four clusters can be distinguished in the 26 analyzed economies (excluding Slovakia). The first includes Belgium, Finland, Austria, Denmark, the Netherlands and Sweden – the analyzed variable assumed on average the highest values in those states. Another cluster is formed by the states with the lowest average value of gross expenditures on gross fixed capital formation in the EU: Bulgaria, Croatia, Poland and Portugal. The third, smallest cluster is formed by Greece, Romania and Lithuania.

The last cluster is formed by the Czech Republic, Italy, Spain, Hungary, Slovenia and Cyprus; these economies (except Cyprus) displayed the same trend in the value of capital expenditures in the analyzed period. Luxembourg is characterized by significantly greater values of the discussed macroeconomic variable (like in the case of GDP). This country clearly stands out from the other member states. The highest average values of per-capita gross expenditures on property and plant equipment in the years 2006–2020 were observed in Luxembourg (EUR 6,486.09), Ireland (EUR 3,904.46), Sweden (EUR 3,793.09), Austria (EUR 3,738.34), Belgium (EUR 3,410.30) and Finland (EUR 3,298.32). The lowest average values of the discussed variable occurred in Bulgaria (EUR 544.91), Poland (EUR 825.60), Croatia (EUR 907.67), Greece (EUR 1,030.93) and Portugal (EUR 1,114.27).

Maps 2.3(a) and 2.3(b) depict the spatial differentiation of gross fixed capital formation in Q2 of 2019 and Q2 of 2020. Sixteen states changed

32 *Monika Bolińska et al.*

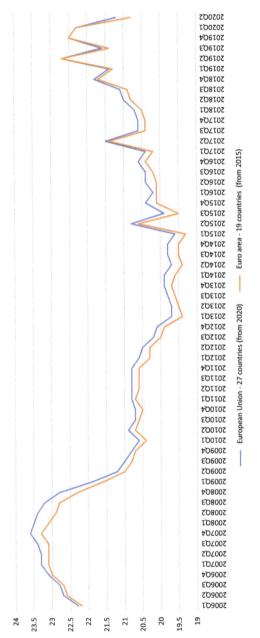

Figure 2.4 Gross fixed capital formation per capita in the EU (2006–2020, % of GDP, quarterly data). Source: own calculation based on https://ec.europa.eu/eurostat/data/database.

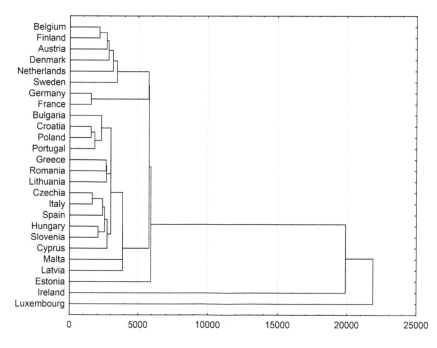

Figure 2.5 A dendrogram of gross fixed capital formation in the EU (2006–2020, Euclidean distance). Source: own calculation based on https://ec.europa.eu/eurostat/data/database.

their positions in the ranking of quintile groups in the analyzed period, due to their reductions in expenditures on gross fixed capital formation bought or produced. The group of countries that reduced their gross fixed capital formation between the analyzed periods included Austria, Belgium, Cyprus, Estonia, Poland and Sweden. The greatest fall, by six positions, affected Cyprus. Additionally, Cyprus and Austria fell to lower quintile groups. Croatia, the Czech Republic, Denmark, Finland, Germany, Hungary, Malta, Portugal, Slovenia and Spain rose in the ranking but remained in their quintile groups. A significant rise was experienced by Portugal (by 3 positions). In the group of ten countries that rose in the ranking, two (Finland and Slovenia) were reclassified in higher quintile groups.

All of the 26 analyzed economies (excluding Slovakia) recorded a general reduction in the per-capita expenditures on gross fixed capital formation. The greatest decreases took place in Ireland (a reduction by EUR 9,150.12 in Q2 of 2020 compared to Q2 of 2019), and Luxembourg (EUR 1,074.45). Significant declines were observed in Cyprus (EUR 663.18), Belgium (EUR 631.57) and France (EUR 566.94). The slightest falls (below EUR 100) were observed in Denmark (EUR 96.50), Romania (EUR 90.07), Portugal (EUR 79.65), Bulgaria (EUR 61.42) and Greece (EUR 40.04).

34 *Monika Bolińska et al.*

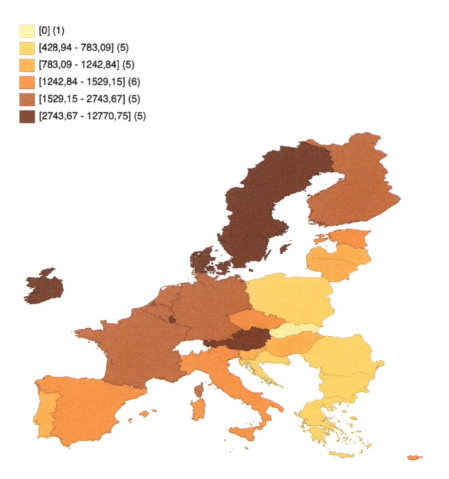

Map 2.3a Gross fixed capital formation in the second quarters of 2019 in the member states of the European Union (in EUR, constant prices from Q2 of 2020). Source: own calculation based on https://ec.europa.eu/eurostat/data/database.

2.5 Exports of goods and services

Figure 2.6 represents the dynamics of changes in the proportion of exports of goods and services in GDP. The proportion of exports in GDP rose by 0.9% p.a. on average in 2006–2008 (Q1). The value of exports suddenly collapsed in Q3 of 2008 for the subsequent three quarters (by more than 5 percentage points) due to a severe downturn in international trade caused by the loss of trust in the global financial system. The proportion of exports in GDP in the European Union fell to the lowest value of 35.6% in the second quarter of 2009. Thereafter, the proportion of exports began to rise and was free from significant fluctuations until the outbreak of the pandemic. The value of

Impact on macroeconomic variables 35

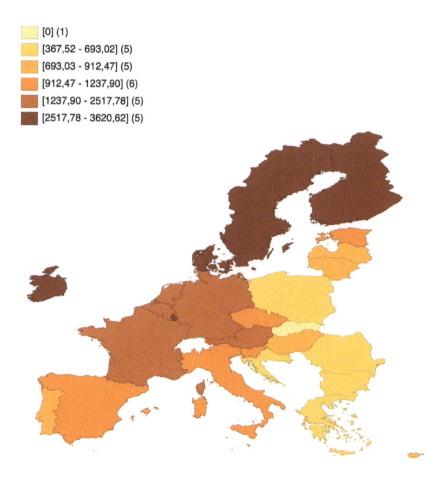

Map 2.3b Gross fixed capital formation in the second quarters of 2020 in the member states of the European Union (in EUR, constant prices from Q2 of 2020). Source: own calculation based on https://ec.europa.eu/eurostat/data/database.

exports of goods and services dramatically fell between the first and second quarter of 2020 – by more than 5 percentage points. The average annual rate of increase in the value of exports between the second quarter of 2009 (the lowest value of exports) and the first quarter of 2020 amounted to 0.72%.

An analysis of differences and similarities shown on the Figure 2.7 in the volumes of exports per capita in the EU member states leads to the following generalizations. The strongest similarities in the values of the discussed variable were characteristic of 8 pairs of states: Malta and the Netherlands, Greece and Croatia, Poland and Portugal, Spain and Italy, France and Lithuania, the Czech Republic and Slovenia, Estonia and Finland, and Denmark and Austria. Luxembourg is characterized by a value of exports

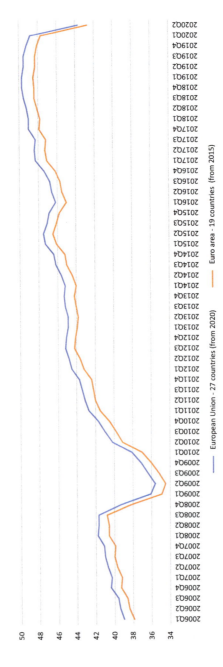

Figure 2.6 Dynamics of changes in exports of goods and services in the EU (2006–2020, % of GDP, quarterly data). Source: own calculation based on https://ec.europa.eu/eurostat/data/database.

Impact on macroeconomic variables 37

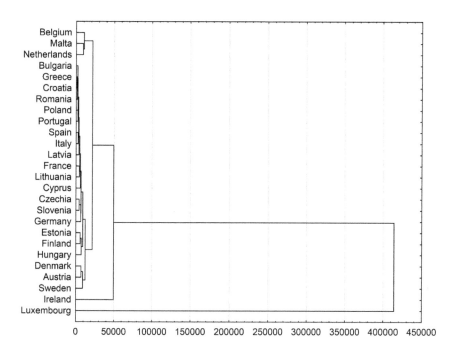

Figure 2.7 A dendrogram of similarities in exports (2006–2020, Euclidean distance).
Source: own calculation based on https://ec.europa.eu/eurostat/data/database.

per capita significantly exceeding those achieved by the other states, and as such clearly stands out. In the clustering tree, similarity clusters can also be distinguished. The first cluster includes Denmark, Austria and Sweden, countries that achieved an average value of exports per capita of about EUR 8,000. Another cluster is formed by Estonia, Finland and Hungary with an average value of exports of goods and services amounting in the analyzed period to about EUR 5,000. The third cluster includes the Czech Republic, Slovenia and Germany; the fourth Belgium, Malta and the Netherlands, which achieved high average values of per-capita exports (excluding the outstanding economies of Luxembourg and Ireland). The last and largest cluster includes Bulgaria, Greece, Croatia, Romania, Poland and Portugal.

The states classified in the largest cluster were characterized in the analyzed period by the lowest average values of exports per capita. The lowest values of the analyzed variable, not exceeding EUR 2,000 per capita, were recorded in Bulgaria (EUR 1,348.55), Romania (EUR 1,441.82), Greece (EUR 1,555.14), Croatia (EUR 1,639.16) and Poland (EUR 1,861.38); those countries also recorded, in the first two quarters of 2020, the slightest falls of exports resulting from the restrictions imposed by governments and aimed to control the spread of the SARS-CoV-2.

The highest values of exports per capita (exceeding EUR 10,000) were recorded in the Benelux countries: Belgium (EUR 11,644.97), the Netherlands (EUR 11,723.06) and Luxembourg (EUR 67,531.70); also in Malta (EUR 11,033.99) and Ireland (EUR 15,077.92).

Maps 2.4(a) and 2.4(b) represent the spatial differentiation of exports of goods and services in the 26 European economies in the second quarter of 2019 and in the second quarter of 2020. 15 states changed their positions in the general ranking of quintile groups; seven of them rose and eight fell in the ranking. The group of countries that achieved rises: Poland, by three positions; Bulgaria, by two positions; Cyprus, Estonia, Germany, Latvia and Malta by one position. Poland was the only country to change its quintile group from that with the lowest values into that characterized by low

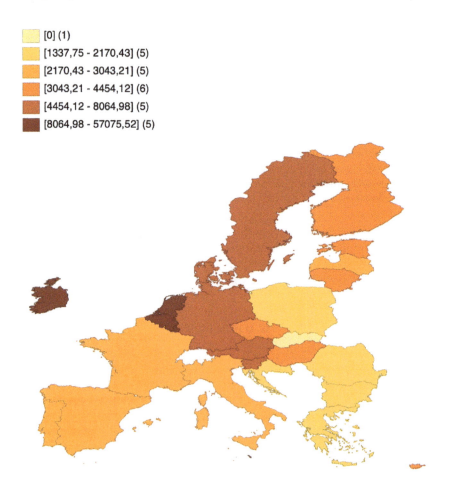

Map 2.4a Exports per capita in the second quarters of 2019 in the member states of the European Union (in EUR, constant prices from Q2 of 2020). Source: own calculation based on https://ec.europa.eu/eurostat/data/database.

Impact on macroeconomic variables 39

values. Croatia and the Czech Republic fell in the ranking by two positions while France, Italy, the Netherlands, Portugal, Slovenia and Spain fell by one position. Also, Portugal changed its quintile group.

All member states of the European Union recorded reductions in exports of goods and services in the second quarter of 2020 compared to the corresponding period in 2019 due to the imposed restrictions. The greatest decrease in exports was recorded in Luxembourg (by EUR 5,281.44 per capita between Q2 of 2019 and Q2 of 2020). A significant fall also affected the other Benelux countries: the Netherlands (by EUR 2,403.19) and Belgium (by EUR 1,803.15). The value of exports also significantly dropped (by EUR 1,942.67) in Malta, with foreign trade and financial services as its main economic sectors. Only a few among the EU economies recorded

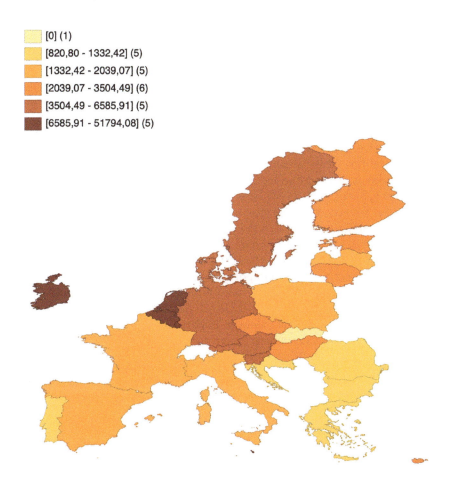

Map 2.4b Exports per capita in the second quarters of 2020 in the member states of the European Union (in EUR, constant prices from Q2 of 2020). Source: own calculation based on https://ec.europa.eu/eurostat/data/database.

40　*Monika Bolińska et al.*

slight decreases in exports: Latvia (by EUR 574.10), Poland (EUR 544.42), Romania (EUR 516.95) and Bulgaria (EUR 461.23).

2.6 Imports of goods and services

Figure 2.8 represents the dynamics of changes in the proportion of imports of goods and services in GDP. The proportion of imports in GDP rose by 0.8% per annum on average between 2006 and Q3 of 2008. The variable sharply dropped thereafter (by 6.4 percentage points over the three subsequent quarters). The value of imports and its proportion in GDP continually grew since H2 of 2009. The proportion amounted to 46.6% in the second quarter of 2019. The average annual rate of growth in the discussed period amounted to 0.8%. The second quarter of 2020 saw a severe reduction in the value of imports in the EU economy (5 percentage points compared to the corresponding quarter of 2019).

An analysis of differences and similarities in the volumes of imports per capita in the EU member states leads to the following generalizations. The strongest similarities in imports were observed between the following pairs of countries: Malta and the Netherlands, Greece and Romania, Spain and Italy, the Czech Republic and Germany, Latvia and Lithuania, Denmark and Austria, and Estonia and Hungary. In the dendrogram depicted in Figure 2.9, two smaller and two larger clusters of similarities can be distinguished. The first of the smaller clusters is formed by Belgium, Malta and the Netherlands. The second includes Denmark, Austria and Sweden, with an average value of imports of about EUR 7,000. A larger cluster is formed by Bulgaria, Greece, Romania, Croatia, Poland, Spain, Italy and Portugal. Another larger cluster includes the Czech Republic, Germany, Slovenia, Cyprus, Finland, Latvia and Lithuania, with an average value of imports in the years 2006–2020 amounting to about EUR 4,000 per capita.

The largest average values of imports per capita were recorded in the years 2006–2020 in Luxembourg (EUR 55,866.08), Ireland (EUR 12,648.66), Belgium (EUR 11,413.74), Malta (EUR 10,639.52), and the Netherlands (EUR 10,311.61). The lowest values of imports of goods and services were recorded in the same states that achieved the lowest values of exports. The lowest average values were recorded in the years 2006–2020 in Bulgaria (EUR 1,470.65), Romania (EUR 1,768.95), Croatia (EUR 1,797.33), Poland (EUR 1,851.14) and Greece (EUR 1,940.68); those economies also recorded the slightest decrease in imports, resulting from the restrictions imposed to control the spread of the SARS-CoV-2.

Maps 2.5(a) and 2.5(b) represent the spatial differentiation of imports of goods and services in the 26 European economies – in the second quarter of 2019 and in the second quarter of 2020. Eight economies changed their positions in the general ranking between the analyzed periods. Cyprus rose by three positions, and Slovenia fell by three positions, so that the two countries "swapped" their groups. Bulgaria, Malta and Poland each rose in the

Impact on macroeconomic variables 41

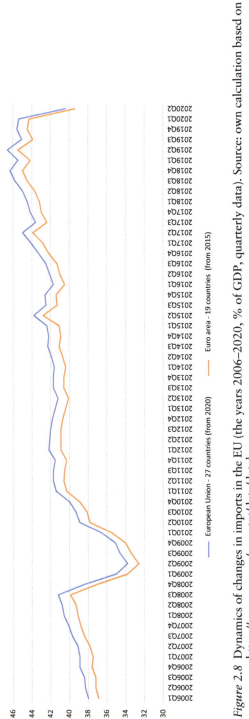

Figure 2.8 Dynamics of changes in imports in the EU (the years 2006–2020, % of GDP, quarterly data). Source: own calculation based on https://ec.europa.eu/eurostat/data/database.

42 *Monika Bolińska et al.*

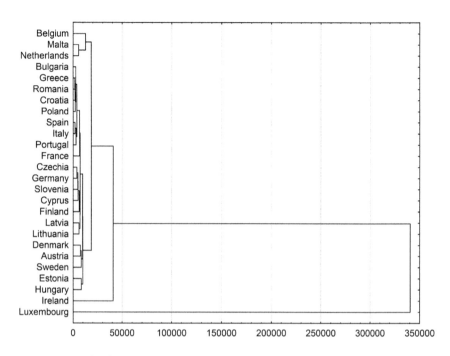

Figure 2.9 A dendrogram of similarities in imports (the years 2006–2020, Euclidean distance). Source: own calculation based on https://ec.europa.eu/eurostat/data/database.

general ranking by one position. A drop in the ranking of imports of goods and services in the EU states was recorded in the case of the Netherlands, Romania and Spain (by one position). Spain was reclassified from the group characterized by low values to the group with the lowest values of imports of goods and services per capita and was replaced by Poland.

All member states of the European Union recorded reductions in imports of goods and services in the second quarter of 2020 compared to the corresponding period in 2019 due to the imposed restrictions. The sharpest decreases affected Ireland (by EUR 10,278.69 per capita), Luxembourg (EUR 5,425.82), the Netherlands (EUR 2,152.84) and Belgium (EUR 2,076.84). The group of states that recorded the slightest decreases in imports includes Croatia (EUR 578.74), Greece (EUR 521.06), Romania (EUR 509.50) and Bulgaria (EUR 462.43).

2.7 Conclusions

An analysis of the impact of the COVID-19 pandemic on the differentiation of selected macroeconomic variables characterizing the EU economies over a short period leads to the following generalizations.

Impact on macroeconomic variables 43

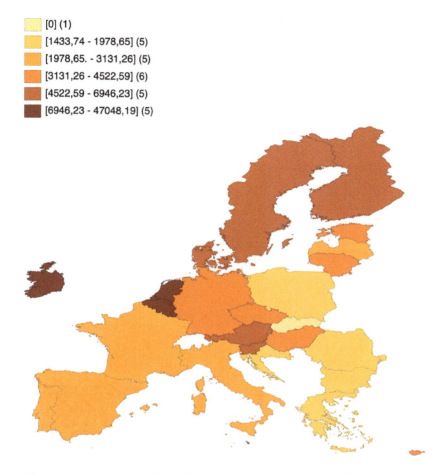

Map 2.5a Imports per capita in the second quarters of 2019 in the member states of the European Union (in EUR, constant prices from Q2 of 2020). Source: own calculation based on https://ec.europa.eu/eurostat/data/database.

First, the sharpest decrease in the absolute value of GDP per capita between Q2 of 2019 and Q2 of 2020 was recorded in the countries that in the years 2006–2019 belonged to the group with medium, high and highest values of average citizen's wealth. The depth of decreases in GDP (and consequently GDP per capita) in the second quarter of 2020 was unprecedented in the post-war history of the member states of the former European Communities and the current European Union.

Second, this variety of responses of labor markets to the supply and demand shock in Q2 of 2020 can be interpreted from various perspectives. The causes of such diversity should be sought in the varying scenarios of the implementation of lockdown measures.

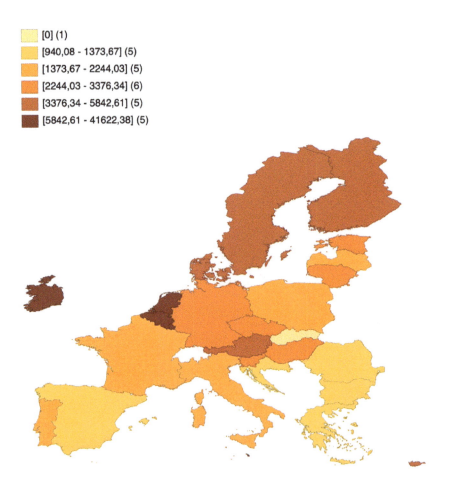

Map 2.5b Imports per capita in the second quarters of 2020 in the member states of the European Union (in EUR, constant prices from Q2 of 2020) Source: own calculation based on https://ec.europa.eu/eurostat/data/database.

Third, all analyzed EU economies recorded a clear reduction in the per-capita expenditures on property and plant equipment bought or produced. The highest absolute values of decrease were characteristic of Ireland, Luxembourg, Cyprus, Belgium and France. The slightest decrease affected Denmark, Romania, Portugal, Bulgaria and Greece.

Fourth, all member states of the EU recorded a sharp decrease in both exports and imports of goods and services in the second quarter of 2020 compared to the corresponding period in 2019 due to the imposed restrictions.

References

Atkeson, A. (2020). What will be the economic impact of COVID-19 in the US? Rough estimates of disease scenarios. NBER Working Paper, No. 26867. http://www.nber.org/papers/w26867 (accessed December 15, 2020).

Baumeister, Ch., Guérin, P. (2020). A comparison of monthly global indicators for forecasting growth. NBER Working Paper, No. 28014. http://www.nber.org/papers/w28014 (accessed December 15, 2020).

Brock, W., Xepapadeas, A. (2020). The economy, climate change and infectious diseases: Links and policy implications. *Environmental and Resource Economics*, 76, 811–824. https://doi.org/10.1007/s10640-020-00442-z (accessed December 15, 2020).

Dieppe, A. (2020). *Global productivity: Trends, drivers, and policies*. Advance Edition. Washington, DC: World Bank.

Forsythe, E., Kahn, L.B., Lange, F., Wiczer, D.G. (2020). Searching, recalls, and tightness: An interim report on the Covid labor market. NBER Working Paper, No. 28083. http://www.nber.org/papers/w28083 (accessed January 02, 2020).

IMF – International Monetary Fund (2020). *World economic outlook: A long and difficult ascent*. Washington, DC: International Monetary Fund.

IMF (2020). *World economic outlook*. April 2020: The Great Lockdown. https://www.imf.org/en/Publications/WEO/Issues/2020/04/14/weo-april-2020 (accessed December 15, 2020).

Lik Ng, W. (2020). To lockdown? When to peak? Will there be an end? A macroeconomic analysis on COVID-19 epidemic in the United States. *Journal of Macroeconomics*, 65, 103230.

Ludvigson, S.C., Ma, S., Ng, S. (2020). COVID-19 and the macroeconomic effects of costly disasters. NBER Working Paper No. 26987. https://www.nber.org/papers/w27784 (accessed December 15, 2020).

OECD (2020). *OECD economic outlook, volume 2020, issue 2: Preliminary version*. Paris: OECD Publishing. https://doi.org/10.1787/39a88ab1-en (accessed December 15, 2020).

3 Fiscal interventions in 2020

A comparative analysis of EU states' policies

Michał Włodarczyk, Rafał Wisła, and Monika Bolińska

3.1 Introduction

More than a decade after the outbreak of the 2008 crisis, the world economy faced again the risk of global instability. The lockdowns, restrictions on spatial mobility of workers and interrupted supply chains resulted in the sharpest drop in the gross domestic product (GDP) since World War II (Kose, Naotaka, 2020).

Like in 2008, some governments intensified their interventionism, increasing again money supply, budget deficits and public debt. The difference between 2008 and 2020 lies in the capability of maintaining long-term macroeconomic stability. The ratio of public debt to GDP in the eurozone amounted to 64.9% in 2008. By the end of 2009, it had risen to 75.7%. The government debt of the eurozone rose until 2014, to reach 86.6% of GDP. Thereafter, that debt dropped over five years to 77.6% in 2019 (Trading Economics, 2020).

By the end of Q2 in 2020, the government debt of the eurozone had risen to 95.1%, and in the entire European Union to 87.8% (Eurostat 2020). That growth was driven principally by extensive fiscal stimulus packages implemented over the period surveyed.

Demertzis et al. (2020) were among the first to assess plans adopted by the European Commission in the spring of 2020 to support the economies of member states: the Coronavirus Response Investment Initiative[1] (CRII; EUR 25 billion) and EU Solidarity Fund.[2] Klose and Tillmann (2020) observed, in their panel survey into fiscal responses of the EU member states, a short-term phenomenon of a rise in return on treasury securities in the states characterized by a high incidence of COVID-19. The return rate rose on the dates of the announcement of subsequent fiscal assistance packages.

In the eurozone, Germany was best prepared for a large unplanned fiscal intervention, as a country that reduced its public debt by 20 percentage

---

1 https://ec.europa.eu/commission/presscorner/detail/en/IP_20_440.
2 https://ec.europa.eu/regional_policy/en/funding/solidarity-fund/.

DOI: 10.4324/9781003211891-3

points in the years 2013–2019 by implementing a balanced budget policy. This made fiscal interventions on a large scale possible in Germany (Busetto, Dufour & Varotto, 2020). The countries from the High Indebted Euro Countries (HIDC) group, with debts exceeding 100% of GDP, face the risk of serious macroeconomic instability. The group includes, among others, Italy and Spain (Briceno, Perote, 2020). Italy, despite implementing its fiscal stimulus package, experienced in H1 of 2020 the sharpest drop in GDP in the entire European Union. The concept of government assistance was criticized by experts. They argued that more attention should have been paid to society than to reductions in taxes. A major role was played by the lobby of entrepreneurs who are heavily taxed in Italy (Pietro, Marattin & Minetti 2020).

Post-pandemic recovery financed by governments will accelerate the pace of growth of the green economy in the European Union. The fiscal stimulus packages reveal that emphasis is put on research and development (R&D) in advanced power generation sectors, on buildings' energy upgrades and on the prevention of climate change (Hepburn et al., 2020). The International Monetary Fund (IMF) announced that between June and December 2020 the G20 countries implemented fiscal stimulus packages worth USD 9 trillion. This facilitated goal-oriented actions and cooperation (McKibbin, Vines, 2020).

The context outlined in the first and second chapters determines the objective of this chapter, which aims to make a comparative analysis of fiscal responses of the EU member states and of the United Kingdom to the outbreak of the COVID-19 pandemic in the spring of 2020. This study covers the period between January and November 2020. One lockdown or two lockdowns took place in that period in most of the discussed 28 economies. The lockdown measures caused liquidity problems in businesses and entailed insolvency procedures, interruptions in supply chains, suspension of business activity and increases in unemployment. To contain the consequences of the downturn, governments put together subsequent fiscal stimulus packages that were expanded and modified as the pandemic evolved. Separate assistance packages for the eurozone and the member states of the European Union were announced by the European Central Bank and the European Commission. This chapter discusses fiscal packages launched in the 27 member states of the European Union and in the United Kingdom in 2020. The European Union is divided into the eurozone and the group of other states in the below analyses.

3.2 Eurozone states

The European Council announced on 21 July 2020 that a special EU recovery fund was established, branded Next Generation EU, with a budget of EUR 750 billion. The fund is financed using debt issue, a digital levy, a carbon border adjustment mechanism and tax on plastics. The funds distributed among the member states are divided into subsidies (EUR 390 billion) and loans (EUR 360 billion). All funds will be distributed by the end of 2023, and 70% of them by the end of 2022. Next Generation EU, together with the Multiannual Financial Framework 2021–2027, represents the principal instrument of public intervention aimed to reconstruct the EU economies, with total funds amounting to EUR 1.8 trillion (IMF 2020). More than 50% of funds from the EU budget will be allocated to research and innovation, via Horizon Europe, to energy transition (via the Just Transition Fund) and digitalization (Digital Europe). Thirty percent of funds will be allocated to fighting climate change. Initiatives planned include REACT-EU (supporting employment; EUR 47.5 billion), RescEU (supporting the Civil Protection Mechanism; EUR 1.9 billion) and InvestEU (filling a gap in investments; EUR 5.6 billion) (see Table 3.1 in the appendix).

The Coronavirus Response Investment Initiatives (CRII and CRII+) aim to simplify and make flexible the procedures of using EU funds. They focus on public investments aimed to fight the pandemic, worth EUR 54 billion (European Commission, 2020a).

The Support to Mitigate Unemployment Risks in an Emergency (SURE) instrument, announced on 24 August 2020, is aimed to protect employees and their jobs. The amount of assistance was increased on 16 November from EUR 87.9 billion to EUR 90.3 billion. The funds were raised by issuing social bonds (EUR 17 billion). The money will be made available as loans to 18 EU countries that are particularly affected by the pandemic (European Commission, 2020b) (see Table 3.2 in the appendix).

Table 3.1 Objectives of the Multiannual Financial Framework 2021–2027 and Next Generation EU and their financing

Objective	2021–2027 Framework	Next Generation EU	Total
Single market, innovation and digital	EUR 132.8 billion	EUR 10.6 billion	EUR 143.4 billion
Cohesion, resilience and values	EUR 377.8 billion	EUR 721.9 billion	EUR 1,099.7 billion
Natural resources and environment	EUR 356.4 billion	EUR 17.5 billion	EUR 373.9 billion
Migration and border management	EUR 22.7 billion	-	EUR 22.7 billion
Security and defence	EUR 13.2 billion	-	EUR 13.2 billion
Neighborhood and the world	EUR 98.4 billion	-	EUR 98.4 billion
European public administration	EUR 73.1 billion	-	EUR 73.1 billion
Total	EUR 1,074.3 billion	EUR 750 billion	EUR 1,824.3 billion

Source: European Commission, *Recovery plan for Europe*, https://ec.europa.eu/info/strategy/recovery-plan-europe_en (accessed 14 December 2020).

Considering the currency union, the member states of the European Union will be divided into one group comprising the 19 members of the eurozone, and the second group of other states (including the United Kingdom). The European Stability Mechanism (via Enhanced Conditions Credit Line) will provide the eurozone states with assistance amounting up to 2% of their GDP (EUR 240 billion in total allocated to expenses on health). The European Investment Bank received a capital injection of EUR 25 billion, allocated to provide small and medium-sized enterprises (SMEs) with assistance in the form of government guarantees (up to EUR 200 billion) (IMF, 2020).

The European Central Bank modified the monetary policy for the eurozone by liquidity injection (improving the liquidity of banks and businesses). Assets worth EUR 120 billion were purchased. The Temporary Pandemic Emergency Purchase Programme (PEPP) was developed, wherein the ECB will purchase securities worth EUR 750 billion in 2020. The requirements for collaterals requested by banks were relaxed and periods for refinancing were extended (ILO, 2020).

3.2.1 Austria

The economy of Austria was first locked down between 16 March and 13 April 2020. (The lockdown was introduced again on 3 November.) The Austrian fiscal package, with the value of funds amounting to EUR 38 billion (9.5% of GDP), was announced on 15 March 2020. The sum of EUR 4 billion was allocated to entities in the healthcare sector, to the preservation of jobs and to supporting companies in which employees contracted COVID-19. The tourism industry and exporters were provided with government guarantees amounting to EUR 9 billion. Corporate Income Tax (CIT) payments were postponed by three months (a cost of EUR 10 billion) and the tax rate was reduced from 25% to 20%. Hours of work could be reduced by 10% and pay to 80–90% of the former level. Households and SMEs were offered a three-month moratorium on loan repayment (IMF, 2020).C

The assistance package was increased to EUR 50 billion in mid-June (13% of GDP). The package was aimed to support non-profit organizations (EUR 700 million) and research projects (EUR 22 million) and to introduce fiscal relief in the hospitality industry (EUR 500 million). Companies received EUR 2,000 per apprentice to preserve employment. The unemployed received EUR 450 as a one-off allowance, and a children's bonus of EUR 360 per child (also a one-off benefit) (ILO, 2020).

3.2.2 Belgium

The lockdown in Belgium was in force between 18 March and 4 May. (The lockdown was introduced again on 2 November.) The value of assistance provided to the economy was set to EUR 17.5 billion (3.9% of GDP). The value of the total fiscal package, including loans for businesses, amounted to EUR 52 billion (12% of GDP). The funds were allocated to supporting healthcare, people fired due to the pandemic, the self-employed and to postponing the payment of corporate taxes. Employees who lost their jobs received 70% of their wages (up to EUR 1,450). The assistance measures were targeted at the industries severely affected by the pandemic: taxi companies, cultural, entertainment, hospitality and tourist businesses (KPMG, 2020). Payments of VAT for December 2020 were suspended to improve the liquidity of businesses. The value of donations and gifts made by companies and deductible from income tax was increased. Non-government and volunteer organizations were also supported. A temporary allowance of EUR 126.94 per month for teleworking was introduced. The allowance covered additional costs of heating and electricity (IMF, 2020).

A package of EUR 4.3 billion was allocated to the Flemish Region for investments in digitalization, sustainable growth, education, healthcare, R&D and 5G. Allowances were granted for house reconstruction and repair. Investment deductions were increased for projects implemented between March and December 2020. Deductions of costs incurred on events and catering were increased from 50% to 100%, to prevent the mass postponement of events until 2021 (ILO, 2020).

3.2.3 *Cyprus*

The economy was locked down between 24 March and 13 April. The value of the fiscal support package amounted to EUR 899 million (4.5% of GDP), including EUR 100 million allocated to the healthcare sector. Households were provided with assistance, people who lost their jobs received subsidies (up to 70%) and the tourism industry was supported (IMF, 2020). The VAT rate was reduced, and its payment was postponed by up to two months. State guarantees were introduced as a measure of domestic assistance provided to businesses and the self-employed, worth in total EUR 2 billion (70% of which was covered by the government and 30% by banks). SMEs were provided with guarantees or credit financing (EUR 1.7 billion) from the Pan-European Guarantee Fund. Parents employed in the private sector could obtain an allowance for the care of children (aged up to 15 years). Employees who could not work due to contracting the disease received a benefit of EUR 800 monthly (KPMG, 2020).

The central bank provided liquidity injection (EUR 100 million). It also simplified documentation requirements for new short-term loans with favorable interest rates. A moratorium on loan repayment was introduced until the end of December 2020 (ILO, 2020).

3.2.4 *Estonia*

The lockdown in Estonia was in force between 13 March and 1 May. Its fiscal package, worth EUR 2 billion (7% of GDP), included support provided to businesses and employees, and purchases of materials supplied to hospitals. As part of the fiscal package, assistance was provided to the unemployed (EUR 250 million), health insurance premiums were paid (EUR 200 million), liquidity of companies was ensured (EUR 500 million in loans), loans and guarantees were granted (EUR 1 billion), rural areas were given loans (EUR 200 million), the local government received support (EUR 130 million) and investment loans were granted to companies (EUR 50 million). Payments to the pillar II pension funds were suspended and compensation was paid for cancelled cultural and sporting events (EUR 3 million) (ILO, 2020).

The value of short-term treasury notes issued rose by EUR 600 million compared to 2019 (EUR 1 billion in total). A loan amounting to EUR 750 million was obtained from Nordic Investment (repayable over 15 years).

Eesti Pank (the central bank) reduced the systemic risk buffer for the commercial banks from 1% to 0%. This freed up resources (EUR 110 billion) for loan losses or new loans. Of the central bank's 2019 profits, 75% (EUR 18.9 million) were allocated to supporting the state budget in the wake of COVID-19 (IMF, 2020).

3.2.5 Finland

The government of Finland introduced the lockdown between 16 March and 4 May. An amount of almost EUR 15 billion was allocated to healthcare, public security and border controls. A grant of EUR 1 billion was allocated to research into a vaccine for COVID-19, the development of methods for rapid diagnostics and an expanded knowledge base of the disease. Pension premiums were reduced until the end of 2020 (EUR 1.05 billion) and tax payments were postponed (EUR 4.5 billion). Parental allowance, social assistance and unemployment insurance were expanded (EUR 3 billion). SMEs and the self-employed obtained access to subsidies (EUR 650 million), and the Finnair airlines received a capital injection (EUR 500 million) (ILO, 2020).

In May 2020, the assistance program was extended by allocating an additional EUR 700 million (0.3% of GDP) to share acquisitions in state ownership steering, support provided to restaurant and catering businesses (EUR 123 million) and purchases of vaccines (EUR 16 million). The total increase in government guarantees amounted to EUR 1.68 billion (0.7% of GDP). The employment fund received EUR 880 million (from SURE and the European Investment Bank). In June 2020, the assistance package was expanded by adding EUR 1.2 billion (for households and businesses), public investments (EUR 1 billion) and relief in the form of adjusted VAT payments (EUR 750 million) (KPMG, 2020).

The Bank of Finland supported liquidity on the bank market by purchasing short-term corporate securities (EUR 1 billion). This increased Finnish banks' lending capacity by an estimated sum of EUR 52 billion. Maritime transport companies were granted guarantees (EUR 600 million) and exporters were given loans (EUR 14.2 billion) (IMF, 2020).

3.2.6 France

Restrictions were imposed on the French economy between 17 March and 11 May (the second lockdown began on 30 October). A fiscal assistance package, with funds amounting to EUR 135 billion (6% of GDP), and a package of public guarantees of EUR 327 billion (15% of GDP) were announced in the spring of 2020. The funds were allocated to health insurance for the sick, an increase in expenses on healthcare and capital injections or nationalizations of companies in difficulty (IMG, 2020). SMEs, micro-enterprises and the self-employed received assistance in the form of suspended rents, social insurance and facility bill payments. Refund of tax credits was accelerated; payment of CIT and VAT was postponed. The government co-financed 60% of gross wages received by employees. The hardest-hit sectors (automotive and aerospace industries) were provided with green investment support (KPMG, 2020).

In September 2020, the government announced a new fiscal package aimed to support the recovery of the economy (Plan de Relance) with funds amounting to EUR 100 billion. The plan focused on the ecological transformation of the economy, increasing the competitiveness of French firms, and supporting social and territorial cohesion (ILO, 2020).

3.2.7 Germany

The lockdown was introduced between 23 March and 20 April (and again as of 2 November). Two fiscal assistance packages were announced, one in March with funds amounting to EUR 156 billion (4.9% of GDP), and one in June with funds amounting to EUR 130 billion (4% of GDP). The packages included spending on medical equipment, investments in hospitals, research into a vaccine for COVID-19 and support for green energy and digitalization. SMEs and the self-employed obtained access to grants (EUR 50 billion), short-term subsidies were paid to maintain employment, duration of unemployment insurance and parental leave benefits was expanded and taxes were postponed until the end of 2020. The cultural sector was supported by way of investments projects implemented by cultural institutions (EUR 250 million), protection of SMEs (EUR 480 million), protection of the music, festival and theater sector (EUR 300 million) and digitization of museum collections (Museum 4.0) (EUR 150 million) (ILO, 2020).

VAT rates were reduced (from 19% to 16% and from 7% to 5%). The government established Economic Stabilisation Funds (Wirtschaftsstabilisierungsfonds (WSF)) amounting in total to EUR 757 billion (24% of GDP). Funds support bigger companies and supplement the German development bank's (Kreditanstalt für Wiederaufbau (KfW) special programme.

Local governments supported their economies directly (EUR 141 billion) and by state-level loan guarantees (EUR 70 billion). Exporters were offered credit guarantees and subcontractors of German companies received credit collaterals (EUR 30 billion). The self-employed could obtain a one-off support of EUR 5,000 plus EUR 1,000 for employees in geriatric care. A reduction in hours of work by 10% was made possible, and employee wages continued to be co-financed by the government (70–75%, depending on the company size). SMEs were offered assistance in employee training (EUR 500 million) (KPMG, 2020).

The Bundesbank supported short-term liquidity (EUR 100 billion), purchased equity in large companies by way of capital contributions (EUR 100 billion) and introduced a three-month moratorium on consumer loans repayable by people affected by the COVID-19 crisis (IMF, 2020).

3.2.8 Greece

The first lockdown in Greece was introduced between 24 March and 4 April, and the second began on 3 November. Its fiscal assistance package of EUR 24 billion (14% of GDP) was financed using domestic and EU funds. Expenditures on healthcare were increased by EUR 88 million (hiring of 3,300 doctors and nurses, procurement of medical supplies, and bonuses to health sector workers) (ILO, 2020).

Suspended employees received EUR 535 monthly. Businesses were supported in the tourism, transport, construction and power generation and distribution industries (EUR 450 million). Businesses that reduced hours of work down to 50% were offered short-term support amounting to up to 60% of net pay (through the SYN-ERGASIA program). Businesses affected by the pandemic were offered credit guarantees, interest payment subsidies, a reduction in rents, deferred payment of taxes and of social insurance premiums. The VAT rates on critical products needed for COVID-19 protection, and transport and hospitality services were reduced (KPMG, 2020).

Banks launched a loan moratorium for household and corporate borrowers until the end of 2020. Greece is eligible for the liquidity facility Pandemic Emergency Longer-Term Refinancing Operations (PELTRO) (IMF, 2020).

3.2.9 Ireland

The lockdown was introduced between 12 March and 18 May, and announced again as of 21 October. The Irish fiscal package of EUR 24.5 billion (7% of GDP) consisted of direct support (EUR 20.5 billion) and credit guarantees, a stabilization and recovery fund and taxation measures, i.e., warehousing and deferrals. The health sector capacity was enhanced (EUR 2 billion), and the labor market was supported (EUR 11.4 billion). If revenues of a business dropped by more than 30%, the business was offered a subsidy of EUR 203 per employee. Workers who lost their jobs due to the pandemic received EUR 350 per week (until April 2020). Employee wages were subsidized in a maximum proportion of 70% (up to EUR 410 per week) (ILO, 2020).

The Restart Fund (EUR 250 million) made capital contributions in micro and small businesses. SMEs received EUR 2 billion in six-year loans. The government offered guarantees, financed employee training (EUR 200 million) and financed new businesses (EUR 550 million). VAT was reduced from 23 to 21% for six months. E-commerce received co-financing amounting to EUR 7.6 million (KPMG, 2020).

The Bank of Ireland introduced a moratorium on repayment of mortgage loans (six months) and a moratorium on eviction (six months) and released the countercyclical capital buffer (IMF, 2020).

3.2.10 Italy

The first lockdown was introduced between 9 March and 4 April, and the second began on 4 November. The value of the "Cura Italia" emergency package adopted in March amounted to EUR 25 billion (1.6% of GDP). The funds were allocated to strengthening the healthcare system (EUR 3.2 billion), preserving jobs (EUR 10.3 billion), deferrals of tax and fee payment by businesses affected by the pandemic (EUR 6.4 billion), subsidizing 80% of wages (up to EUR 1200 monthly paid to people working under contracts of employment and EUR 600 EUR paid to the self-employed). Loan supply was supported (EUR 5.1 billion) and the poor without income received EUR 300 from municipalities (KPMG, 2020).

Additional state guarantees were granted in April (EUR 400 billion; 25% of GDP). The total value of assistance backed by government guarantees increased to EUR 750 billion, allocated to improve the liquidity of businesses and households. The package was expanded in May by an additional EUR 55 billion (3.5% of GDP) allocated to support for families (14.5 billion), healthcare (3.3 billion), SMEs (EUR 16 billion). The sum of EUR 25 billion (1.6% of GDP) was allocated in August to support for employees (EUR 12 billion), income support for families, a suspension of social security contributions and a moratorium on SMEs' debt repayment. Another package of EUR 5.4 billion (0.3% of GDP) was adopted in October to provide relief to the sectors affected by the pandemic and award grants to 460 thousand SMEs and the self-employed (ILO, 2020).

As part of "Cura Italia", the Bank of Italy supported bank lending aimed to provide SMEs with new loans (via Cassa Depositi e Prestiti) and allowed banks to operate with selected ratios below the capital and liquidity requirements. IVASS (the insurance supervision authority) recommended that insurance companies exercise caution in dividend payment (IMF, 2020).

3.2.11 Latvia

The economy of Latvia was shut down between 13 March and 12 May. The value of the fiscal package amounted to EUR 3.4 billion (12% of GDP). The package included loans and guarantees for businesses affected by the pandemic (EUR 1.2 billion) (KPMG, 2020). Support is targeted at the air and transport industry, healthcare, education and infrastructure sectors (EUR 875 million). About 4,500 health care workers received a bonus (20%). A wage subsidy of 75% (up to EUR 700) for employees suffering from COVID-19 was introduced. The sum of EUR 50 million was allocated to support large companies (ILO, 2020).

The interest rate on loans obtained by SMEs in the tourism sector was reduced by 50%. The supplementary capital of Finance Development Institution Altum was increased by EUR 100 million to raise its capacity to provide companies with support through loans and guarantees. Altum issued bonds worth EUR 20 million (IMF, 2020).

3.2.12 Lithuania

The lockdown was introduced between 16 March and 18 June and again as of 7 November. A fiscal package of EUR 2.5 billion (5% of GDP) was adopted in March to assist the healthcare system (EUR 500 million), to ensure care for the sick (EUR 250 million), pay wage subsidies for employees (EUR 250 million) and to co-finance climate change investment projects. The government expanded guarantee schemes to EUR 1.3 billion (2.6% of GDP). A business support fund was established to preserve the liquidity of SMEs with resources amounting to EUR 1 billion (2.1% of GDP) (IMF, 2020).

The assistance program was expanded in May by EUR 1 billion (2% of GDP). Wage subsidies for people returning from unemployment were granted (EUR 380 million), job search allowances paid (EUR 200 million), vocational training financed (EUR 15.6 million).

An investment plan was approved in June, comprising EUR 6.3 billion (13% of GDP). The sum of EUR 2.2 billion was allocated to new projects and the remaining funds to accelerating the existing ones. The plan included investments in human capital, digital economy, innovation, research, infrastructure, projects addressing climate changes and power generation. Subsidies to wages were increased (to a maximum of 90% of pay, not more than EUR 607) in SMEs that retained at least 50% of jobs. Subsidies in large companies could reach a maximum of 70% (and not more than EUR 910) (ILO, 2020).

3.2.13 Luxembourg

The lockdown was in force between 15 March and 4 May, and then mass tests were performed in the population for COVID-19. The EUR 2.3 billion (3.6% of GDP) fiscal package was adopted and liquidity support was provided to businesses and the self-employed in the amount of EUR 8.1 billion (12.8% of GDP). The funds were allocated to purchases of medical equipment (EUR 194 million), sick leave benefits (EUR 106 million), parental leave benefits (EUR 226 million) and unemployment benefits (EUR 1 billion) (ILO, 2020).

Micro-enterprises and the self-employed received non-refundable financial assistance in the form of a one-off transfer of EUR 5,000 (EUR 250 million) and guarantees for start-ups (EUR 2.5 billion). The government subsidized up to 80% of wages. A moratorium on payment of taxes and social insurance premiums was introduced (EUR 4.6 billion) (IMF, 2020).

The fiscal assistance program was expanded in May by EUR 800 million (1.3% of GDP). The funds were allocated to affected businesses in the hospitality, tourism and sales sectors. The government introduced fiscal incentives to support investments in green recovery (KPMG, 2020).

3.2.14 Malta

The partial lockdown was in force between 28 March and 4 May. A fiscal package was adopted, with funds amounting to EUR 520 million (4% of GDP), to support the healthcare sector (EUR 130 million), businesses and households (subsidies to rents, benefits, a moratorium on loan repayment). Subsidies to employee wages amounted to a maximum of EUR 800 monthly. A direct grants scheme was approved to support investment in research and development related to the coronavirus outbreak (EUR 5.3 million) (KPMG, 2020).

The assistance program was expanded in June by EUR 900 million (7% of GDP). The funds were allocated to infrastructure investments (EUR 400 million), a moratorium on tax payments (200 million), tourist cash vouchers, reduced fuel prices and a tax refund for workers. Teleworkers received a one-off benefit (EUR 400) (ILO, 2020).

The Malta Development Bank established a guarantee fund of EUR 350 million (2.7% of GDP) available to businesses affected by the pandemic. The value of guaranteed loans reached EUR 780 million (6% of GDP). A six-month moratorium for borrowers was introduced (IMF, 2020).

3.2.15 The Netherlands

The lockdown was introduced between 15 March and 11 May and announced again as of 14 October. Two fiscal packages were approved (in March and in May) with funds amounting to EUR 33 billion (4.2% of GDP). The government compensated up to 90% of labor costs in businesses that lost more than 20% of income, and also paid compensations in affected sectors (hospitality, travel, agriculture, culture). Unemployment benefits were raised and subsidies for SMEs, the self-employed and start-ups were introduced (ILO, 2020).

Deferred taxes payable by businesses amounted to EUR 16.6 billion (2.1% of GDP). A program of public guarantees for SMEs to the sum of EUR 61 billion (7.8% of GDP) was adopted. Expanding sectors were offered support of labor mobility and training programmes (IMF, 2020).

3.2.16 Portugal

Portugal introduced the lockdown between 19 March and 17 April. A fiscal package was adopted to support the economy (EUR 5.2 billion); the government granted credit guarantees (EUR 3 billion) and deferred payment of taxes and social insurance premiums (EUR 1 billion). The assistance program included additional expenses on healthcare, digitalization of education (EUR 538 million), digitalization of public finance (EUR 1.65 billion), incentives for people resuming business activity (EUR 1.3 billion) and benefits for people forced to stay home to care for children. Government subsidies to wages amounted to a maximum of 70% (KPMG, 2020).

The government offered SMEs credit guarantees worth EUR 13 billion (6.8% of GDP) and loans (EUR 200 million). The support package targeted at small and micro-enterprises was expanded in November by subsidies (EUR 0.8 billion) and credit guarantees (EUR 0.8 billion), to strengthen businesses affected by the pandemic (ILO, 2020).

Banco de Portugal relaxed its macroprudential measures for consumer credit and postponed loan repayment (owed by businesses and households) until September 2020, rescheduled on-site inspections and the stress test exercise. Lines of credit were granted to restaurants (EUR 600 million), tourist agencies (EUR 200 million), the hospitality industry (EUR 900 million), and the garment industry (EUR 1.3 billion) (IMF, 2020).

3.2.17 Slovakia

The economy was shut down between 16 March and 22 April. The government performed national tests for COVID-19. Unemployment benefits, sickness and nursing benefits were raised, the labor market was supported with EUR 197 million, the government introduced subsidies to rents and compensations for businesses and the self-employed (including deferrals of social insurance premiums). Businesses were offered subsidies amounting to a maximum of 80% of employee wages, depending on the decrease in their revenues (EUR 180 to 540) (KPMG, 2020). The poor without income were offered a one-off benefit of EUR 210 during the state of emergency. Quarantined people were eligible for 55% of their wages paid by the government. SMEs and large companies were offered government guarantees amounting to EUR 4 billion (4.3% of GDP) (ILO, 2020).

The Bank of Slovakia permitted banks to temporarily operate below the defined level of capital, temporarily exempted banks from full compliance with the LCR (liquidity coverage ratio) (IMF, 2020).

3.2.18 Slovenia

The lockdown was introduced between 20 March and 15 May and announced again as of 16 October. The authorities adopted a fiscal package of EUR 1 billion (2.2% of GDP) in March; the package included support for entrepreneurs, subsidies for suspended workers (EUR 50 million), a one-off transfer to pensioners and students, a reduction in prices for electricity by one-third, deferrals of tax and social insurance premium payments. The government also made available its guarantees amounting to EUR 600 million (ILO, 2020).

The assistance program was expanded in April by EUR 5 billion of credit lines, guarantees and subsidies to wages. The additional sum of EUR 1 billion was allocated in May to vouchers for tourism (EUR 200 per adult and EUR 50 per child) and liquidity loans for businesses. The government assistance program was expanded in November by EUR 1 billion used to subsidize wages (up to 80%), exempt renters from rent payment and pay compensation to businesses that were losing revenue (KPMG, 2020).

The Bank of Slovenia reduced the maximum level of permitted bank account fees and allowed banks to temporarily exclude income declines caused by the pandemic when calculating creditworthiness and to defer bank loan repayments for up to 12 months (IMF, 2020).

3.2.19 Spain

The lockdown was in force between 14 March and 9 May. The adopted fiscal package of EUR 42 billion (3.8% of GDP) was used to assist healthcare (EUR 1.4 billion), medical services (EUR 2.9 billion), pay unemployment benefits (EUR 18 billion), sick benefits (EUR 1.4 billion), support industry (EUR 375 million) and education (EUR 40 million). The government subsidized up to 70% of wages received by people affected by COVID-19. Capital contributions were made to the State Housing Plan 2018–21 (EUR 450 million). People in need had access to funds (EUR 300 million) and children were offered meals (EUR 25 million). A minimum income scheme was implemented (EUR 3 billion). The scheme included 850,000 families (2.3 million people). The extent of poverty was to be reduced by that measure by 80%. The lowest rate amounted to EUR 462 per adult and EUR 139 per child. A family could receive a maximum of EUR 1,015 monthly (ILO, 2020).

The self-employed who suspended their business activity received assistance (EUR 5.5 billion). A group was exempted from payment of social insurance premiums (EUR 2.7 billion). Businesses were offered a moratorium on tax and social insurance premium payments (EUR 533 million). Tax on digital publications was reduced from 21% to 4% (EUR 5 million). Transitioning to low-emission vehicles was subsidized (MOVE II; EUR 250 million) (KPMG, 2020).

The Bank of Spain announced a moratorium for mortgage borrowers for three months, guarantees for exporters (EUR 2 billion), guarantees and loans for businesses (EUR 100 billion) and a rescue fund to support strategic business (EUR 10 billion). Instituto de Crédito Oficial launched credit guarantees to support investments in digitalization and sustainable growth (EUR 40 billion) (IMF, 2020).

3.3 States with separate currencies

3.3.1 Bulgaria

The lockdown in Bulgaria was in force between 13 March and 15 June. An assistance package was adopted in that country (BGN 4.5 billion). The value of government guarantees was increased, the VAT rate was reduced (from 20% to 9%), the government introduced subsidies to wages in the industries affected by the pandemic (up to 60% of pay), paid doctors and nurses a bonus of BGN 1,000 and distributed vouchers for tourism (BGN 210 per person). The operational program "Human Resources Development" was launched to assist people over 65 (BGN 45 million) (ILO, 2020).

The government provided assistance to SMEs and large companies that lost more than 20% of their revenues. Businesses in the tourism, healthcare and transport sectors received BGN 290 monthly per job retained (KPMG, 2020).

The central bank of Bulgaria implemented liquidity support measures for banks to the value of BGN 13.7 billion (6% of GDP), cancelled the increase in the countercyclical capital buffer and reduced foreign exposures of commercial banks (IMF, 2020).

3.3.2 Croatia

The lockdown was in force between 18 March and 27 April. An assistance package was adopted, with the value of HRK 30 billion. Subsidies to wages were introduced to preserve jobs. Croatian micro-businesses could obtain support for 20% of their employees. Up to 10% of employees were supported in medium-sized enterprises. Grants amounted to HRK 2,000 to 4,000 monthly per employee, depending on the extent of income lost. Local governments were given low-interest loans. EU funds have been partly reallocated to micro-loans (ILO, 2020).

The Bank of Croatia supported liquidity of domestic banks. Short-term notes were issued for HRK 3.8 billion, the reserve requirement ratio was reduced (from 12% to 9%), a three-month moratorium on obligations to banks was introduced and securities were purchased in the secondary market (HRK 17.9 billion). The Croatian Bank for Reconstruction and Development launched export guarantees and liquidity loans. In October

2020, the European Investment Bank (EIB) approved a financial package (EUR 200 billion) for faster recovery of Croatian SMEs (IMF, 2020).

3.3.3 Czech Republic

The lockdown was introduced between 13 March and 12 April, and announced again as of 3 November. A fiscal package was adopted with funds amounting to CZK 273 billion (EUR 10.4 billion; 4.9% of GDP). The government subsidized 80% of wages paid to quarantined employees until the end of 2020 (up to CZK 39,000), 60% of wages paid to people with reduced hours of work (up to CZK 29,000) and 100% of wages paid to people who lost their jobs due to the lockdown. The VAT rate was reduced (from 15 to 10%) in hotels, in the cultural and sports sector, and subsidies were paid (CZK 2 billion). One-off support for pensioners (CZK 5000) and support for welfare workers (CZK 16.6 billion) were announced (ILO, 2020).

During the second phase of lockdown, affected sectors received assistance (CZK 7.7 billion), SMEs and the self-employed obtained grants (CZK 500 daily), and state subsidies were introduced (CZK 500 billion; 9% of GDP). Rural areas were supported (CZK 3.3 billion) to stimulate food production (KPMG, 2020).

The Czech National Bank reduced the policy rate (down to 0.25%), decreased the countercyclical capital buffer rate (down to 0.5%) and announced a moratorium on loan repayment (for six months) (IMF, 2020).

3.3.4 Denmark

The lockdown was in force between 13 March and 13 April. The fiscal assistance package (DKK 131 billion; 5.7% of GDP) was allocated to supporting businesses, the medical sector and the self-employed. Payment of taxes was deferred and government guarantees were announced. The value of another package amounted to 5.1% of GDP (KPMG, 2020).

Businesses affected by the pandemic were reimbursed for 25–80% of their fixed costs. The self-employed who lost more than 30% of their revenues were reimbursed for up to 90% of lost revenues. The government introduced subsidies to employee wages (up to 75%; not more than DKK 30,000 monthly per employee). Monthly support per person in start-ups amounted to a maximum of DKK 23,000. The Scandinavian airlines were subsidized (DKK 6 billion) (ILO, 2020).

The Bank of Denmark raised the policy rate to –0.6% (from –0.75%), opened a line of credit for banks and announced government guarantees covering 70% of corporate debt caused by the pandemic. Standing swap lines with ECB (EUR 24 billion) and FED (USD 30 billion) were activated (IMF, 2020).

3.3.5 Hungary

The lockdown was in force between 28 March and 16 June. The adopted assistance package of HUF 1.34 billion (3.2% of GDP) was used to alleviate the fiscal burden on businesses (800,000 SMEs), support the tourism sector (HUF 600 billion) and employees of the healthcare sector (HUF 500,000) and introduce subsidies to wages of fired and suspended workers (up to 70% of average pay). An Anti-Epidemic Protection Fund and an economy protection fund were established to protect jobs (HUF 450 billion). Exporters received subsidies from the Eximbank state bank (HUF 800,000). The MFB bank offered a package of financial support instruments for companies (HUF 1.49 billion): three loan products, two guarantee products and four capital products.

The purchase of bank bonds issued during the crisis (HUF 150 billion) was announced in May when also government guarantees and low-interest loans for SMEs were expanded (ILO, 2020).

The central bank (MNB) supported the liquidity of businesses by regular swaps, the expansion of eligible collateral, long-term lines of credit. The base rate was reduced to 0.6%. The MNB purchased government bonds (50% of the issued value) and corporate bonds (purchases for HUF 793 billion out of 2 trillion planned) (IMF, 2020).

3.3.6 Poland

The lockdown was in force between 13 March and 20 April. The initial assistance program consisted of a fiscal package of PLN 116 billion (5.2% of GDP), credit guarantees and micro-loans for businesses amounting to PLN 74 billion (3.3% of GDP). The assistance program was expanded in May by PLN 212 billion (9% of GDP). The healthcare sector was supported (PLN 7.5 billion), the unemployment benefit was raised by 39%, a solidarity benefit was paid to people fired due to the pandemic and a voucher for tourism was introduced (PLN 500 per child). The government subsidized 40% of employee wages (50–90% of the minimum wage) in enterprises that recognized a drop in revenues exceeding 30% (ILO, 2020).

The Polish Development Fund gave loans (PLN 100 billion) to support liquidity of SMEs that were exempted from repaying 70% of their resultant debt. Also, a three-month moratorium on payment of taxes, loan instalments and social insurance premiums was announced. The Governmental Fund for Local Investments was established (PLN 12 billion) to support investments with a value exceeding PLN 400 thousand. Companies managing airports received support amounting to PLN 1 billion. Measures of protection against hostile takeovers were adopted (to protect businesses that achieved revenues exceeding EUR 10 million) (KPMG, 2020).

The central bank (NBP) reduced the policy rate (to 0.1%) and required reserve ratio (from 3.5 to 0.5%) and repealed the systemic risk buffer (3%). The NBP also purchased treasury securities for PLN 105.5 billion (4.6% of GDP) (IMF, 2020).

3.3.7 Romania

The lockdown was in force between 25 March and 15 May. The state assistance program consisted of a fiscal package (RON 20 billion), grants provided to SMEs for digitalization (RON 15 billion) and government guarantees (RON 15 billion). The government paid people fired due to the pandemic up to 75% of average wage. The expenses on pensions were increased by 14% while the hours of work were reduced to 4 days a week (ILO, 2020).

The businesses affected by the lockdown could receive support for procurement of work equipment (RON 1.5 billion), discounts in paying corporate income tax, deferral in payment of tax on real property and suspension of enforced debt collection (KPMG, 2020).

The central bank reduced the policy rate (to 1.5%) and requested commercial banks to announce a moratorium on loan repayment by businesses and households. Treasury notes were purchased for RON 39.5 billion (IMF, 2020).

3.3.8 Sweden

Sweden is the only EU country that did not implement any lockdown measures. Merely some restrictions were imposed and recommendations given. Fiscal assistance of SEK 803 billion (16% of GDP) included subsidies paid to the affected sectors (sport, education, culture, media), raised unemployment benefits and grants received by municipalities (SEK 5.5 billion). The government financed up to 75% of wages while employers added 15% (employees received in total up to 90% of their wages). People from the risk group received compensations (SEK 257 billion) (ILO, 2020).

SMEs were offered loans, deferred tax payments (SEK 13 billion) and capital injections (SEK 3 billion). The self-employed also received support (SEK 5 billion). Export credits (SEK 200 billion) and government guarantees (SEK 500 billion; 9.6% of GDP) were made available. Infrastructure investments were announced, regional public transport companies and regional airports were provided with support. The state also provided the SAS airlines with capital injections. The European Investment Bank allocated an additional SEK 250 billion to Swedish businesses. Subsequent fiscal packages were planned (SEK 105 billion in 2021 and SEK 85 billion in 2022) (KPMG, 2020).

The Bank of Sweden (Riksbank) reduced interest rates on loans and facilitated lending to businesses (up to SEK 500 billion). The Bank eased countercyclical capital buffer and purchased securities (SEK 500 billion). A swap facility was established between the Riksbank and Federal Reserve (FED)(IMF, 2020).

3.3.9 United Kingdom

The lockdown was introduced between 23 March and 13 May, and announced again as of 5 November. The assistance package included additional funding for the National Health Service and public services (GBP 48.5 billion), protection of jobs (GBP 1,000 per retained job), a quarantine allowance (GBP 130) and expenditures on improved energy efficiency. Government subsidies to wages dropped from 80% (GBP 2,500) to 60% (GBP 1,875) of the original wage. Employers financed at least 20% (up to 80% of the initial wage) (ILO, 2020).

Businesses obtained support amounting in total to GBP 29 billion, a six-month deferral of the payment of income tax, VAT and social insurance contributions, subsidies to innovation (GBP 1 billion) and credit guarantees (up to GBP 5 million). The VAT rate on tourist services and accommodation was temporarily reduced (from 20% to 5%) (KPMG, 2020).

The Bank of England reduced the bank rate (to 0.1%), offered loans and guarantees (GBP 330 billion; 15% of GDP) and reduced the countercyclical buffer rate (to 0%). Treasury securities (GBP 450 billion) and corporate securities (GBP 200 billion) were purchased (IMF, 2020).

3.4 Conclusions

An analysis of the fiscal and monetary responses of the European Union member states and the United Kingdom to the COVID-19 pandemic (until December 2020) leads to the following conclusions.

First, all countries covered by this study (except Sweden) implemented certain lockdown measures (a state of emergency with limited mobility of employees, closed border checkpoints, a ban on certain business activities). Those lockdown measures were in force for periods between 20 and 94 days. Restrictions imposed on social functions and economic activities caused a reduction in GDP of the analyzed economies by a total of EUR 188.7 billion, i.e. −4.5% of EU GDP (between Q4 of 2019 and Q3 of 2020). The sharpest drops were observed in Croatia (−12%) and Greece (−11%). The most dramatic nominal falls were observed in Great Britain (EUR 53 billion) and Germany (EUR 33.6 billion). The "freeze" of the economy caused an increase in unemployment rates in the countries surveyed from

5.8% to 7.2% on average. The most dramatic increase was observed in Lithuania (by 4.4 percentage points) and in Estonia (by 3.4 percentage points.)

Second, emergency programs were launched and a record-breaking fund dubbed Next Generation EU (EUR 1.8 trillion) was established at the European Union level. A series of programmes were developed, aimed to stimulate growth in the member states, promote employment and innovation, and support implementation of the European Green Deal. The SURE instrument, designed for the preservation of employment, will disburse to the most affected EU countries the amount of EUR 90.3 billion. Special lending, guarantee and subsidy schemes for businesses were launched in the eurozone (up to EUR 200 billion), and the ECB purchased assets worth EUR 750 billion in 2020.

Third, the methods employed to support various European economies were consistent. Subsidies to employee wages and training were paid, tax rates reduced, and temporary moratoriums introduced (on taxes, loan repayment, social insurance contributions) with the aim of preserving employment. Businesses were supported by subsidies, allowances, co-financing of rents and credit guarantees (the measures were focused on SMEs in the sectors most affected by the pandemic, such as tourist, hospitality, cultural and transport businesses). In the area of monetary instruments, interest rates were reduced and treasury and corporate securities purchased which resulted in an increase in money supply.

Fourth, all support packages imposed heavy financial burdens on the budgets of the states covered by the survey. The total budget deficits amounted in Q2 of 2020 to EUR 473.98 billion. Consequently, government debt rose in the surveyed economies from 80% to 90.6% of GDP on average. The most dramatic increase was observed in Cyprus (by 19.2 percentage points), Belgium (by 16.6 percentage points) and France (by 16 percentage points). The states that recognized the greatest values of debt in the European Union (government debt exceeding 100% of GDP) were Greece (187.4%), Italy (149.4%), Portugal (126.1%), Belgium (115.3%), France (114.1%), Cyprus (113.2%) and Spain (110%).

Fifth, proportions of package values in GDP significantly vary. Fiscal packages (excluding guarantees) that exceeded 10% of GDP were adopted in Sweden (16%), Greece (14%), Austria (13%), Latvia (12%), Belgium (12%), France (10.4%). Fiscal packages with values below 4% of GDP were announced in Bulgaria (1.9%), Slovakia (2.7%), Portugal (2.7%), Hungary (3.2%) and Spain (3.8%).

Appendix

Table 3.2 Fiscal measures implemented in the European Union member states and in the United Kingdom in 2020

Country	Currency	Funds from SURE (in EUR)	Duration of the 1st lockdown (in days)	Government deficit (in EUR million) 2019 Q4	Government deficit (in EUR million) 2020 Q2	Government debt (% of GDP) 2019 Q4	Government debt (% of GDP) 2020Q2	GDP change (2019 Q4–2020 Q3) (in EUR million)	Unemployment rate change (in PP) (2020/01 -2020/09)
Austria	Euro	–	28	130.9	-14,456.1	70.5	82.6	-3,294.3	1
Belgium	Euro	7.8 bn	47	2,949.8	-10,555.7	98.7	115.3	-5,910.0	0.1
Bulgaria	Lev	511 mn	94	-318.6	-332.2	20.2	21.3	-583.8	1.9
Croatia	Kuna	1 bn	40	-334.2	-1,307.0	73.2	85.3	-1,681.7	2
Cyprus	Euro	479 mn	20	-259.4	-800.3	94	113.2	-341.9	2.9
Czech Rep.	Koruna	2 bn	27	-909.5	-3,708.7	P30.2	39.9	-3,064.8	0.8
Denmark	Krone	–	31	2,249.8	-2,521.6	33.3	41.4	-1,948.3	1.1
Estonia	Euro	–	49	-31.5	-469.2	8.4	18.5	-261.6	3.4
Finland	Euro	–	49	-1,062	-3,652	59.3	68.7	-800.0	1.5
France	Euro	–	55	8,977	-62,763	98.1	114.1	-16,943.0	1.1
Germany	Euro	–	28	2,438	-58,276	59.6	67.4	-33,649.0	1.1
Greece	Euro	2.7 bn	42	1,735	-4,780	176.6	187.4	-4,994.1	-0.1
Hungary	Forint	504 mn	80	-2,291.6	-2,804.2	65.4	70.3	-2,963.6	1
Ireland	Euro	2.5 bn	67	3,772.1	-6,619.6	57.4	62.7	2,152.7	2.3
Italy	Euro	27.4 bn	56	8,816.6	-37,991.8	134.7	149.4	-19,472.8	0.1
Latvia	Euro	192 mn	60	-470.9	-88.1	36.9	42.9	-249.5	1.2
Lithuania	Euro	602 mn	94	-73.4	-663.3	35.9	41.4	-232.6	4.4
Luxembourg	Euro	–	50	-299.8	-990.3	22	23.8	199.9	1
Malta	Euro	244 mn	37	26.1	-392.2	42.6	51.1	-294.1	0.2
The Netherlands	Euro	–	57	2,990	-23,883	48.7	55.2	-2,456.0	1.4
Poland	Zloty	11.2 bn	38	-6,774.5	-19,173.2	46	55.1	-2,430.9	0.4
Portugal	Euro	5.9 bn	29	-973.7	-4,858.2	117.2	126.1	-2,430.5	1.1
Romania	Leu	4 bn	51	-2,963.6	-5,256.8	35.3	41.1	-5,131.8	1.4
Slovakia	Euro	631 mn	37	-844.1	-1,551.7	48.3	60.2	-344.6	0.9
Slovenia	Euro	1.1 bn	56	94.2	-1,741.2	65.6	78.2	-449.5	0.6
Spain	Euro	21.3 bn	56	-18,181	-61,589	95.5	110.1	-28,322.0	2.8
Sweden	Krona	–	0	-1,717.8	-5,212.5	35.1	37.1	221.4	1.7
United Kingdom	Pound sterling	–	51	-26,336.6	-137,546.3	85.4	96.6	-53,020.7	1

Source: Own analysis based on https://ec.europa.eu/eurostat/data/database; https://ec.europa.eu/info/business-economy-euro/economic-and-fiscal-policy-coordination/financial-assistance-eu/funding-mechanisms-and-facilities/sure_pl.

References

Briceno, H. R., Perote, J. (2020). Determinants of the public debt in the Eurozone and its sustainability amid the Covid-19 pandemic. *Sustainability*, 12(16), 6456.

Busetto, F., Dufour, A., Varotto, S. (2020). COVID-19 and fiscal policy in the Euro Area. In Billio, M., Varotto, S. (eds.) *A new world post COVID-19 lessons for business, the finance industry and policy makers*. Edizioni Ca'Foscari, Venice, Italy.

Demertzis, M., Sapis A., Tagliapietra, S., Wolff, G.B (2020). *An effective economic response to the Coronavirus in Europe*. Policy Contribution, Breugel, 6.

Dynus, M. (2007). *Polityka fiskalna. Towarzystwo Naukowe Organizacji I Kierowania Stowarzyszenie Wyższej Użyteczności*. Dom Organizatora, Toruń, 1.

Działo, J. (2012). Dlaczego trudno jest prowadzić "dobrą" politykę fiskalną? *Gospodarka Narodowa*, 1–2(245–246), 25–40.

Eurostat (2020). Second quarter of 2020 compared with first quarter of 2020 Government debt up to 95.1% of GDP in euro area Up to 87.8% of GDP in EU [website]. https://ec.europa.eu/eurostat/documents/2995521/11442886/2-22102020-BP-EN.pdf/a21ffbf8-09c9-b520-8fa9-6e804146bf0f (accessed December 8, 2020).

Fedorowicz, Z. (1998). *Polityka fiskalna*. Wydawnictwo Wyższej Szkoły Bankowej w Poznaniu, Poznań.

Hepburn, C., O'Callaghan, B., Stern, N., Stiglitz, J., Zenghelis, D. (2020). Will COVID-19 fiscal recovery packages accelerate or retard progress on climate change? *Oxford Review of Economic Policy*, 36(S1), 359–381.

International Labour Organization (ILO) (2020). Country policy responses, [website]. https://www.ilo.org/global/topics/coronavirus/regional-country/country-responses/lang--en/index.htm#UN (accessed December 14, 2020).

International Monetary Fund (IMF) (2020). Policy responses to COVID-19, [website]. https://www.imf.org/en/Topics/imf-and-covid19/Policy-Responses-to-COVID-19#E (accessed December 14, 2020).

Klose, J., Tillmann, P. (2020). *COVID-19 and financial markets: A panel analysis for European Countries, joint discussion paper series in economics, 25–2020*. Philipps-Universität Marburg, Faculty of Business Administration and Economics, Department of Economics. https://www.uni-marburg.de/fb02/makro/forschung/magkspapers/paper_2020/25-2020_klose.pdf (accessed December 12, 2020).

Komisja Europejska (2020a). Plan odbudowy dla Europy [website]. https://ec.europa.eu/info/strategy/recovery-plan-europe_pl#finansowanie-dugoterminowego-budetu-ue-i-nextgenerationeu (accessed December 14, 2020).

Komisja Europejska (2020b). Instrument SURE [website]. https://ec.europa.eu/info/business-economy-euro/economic-and-fiscal-policy-coordination/financial-assistance-eu/funding-mechanisms-and-facilities/sure_pl (accessed December 14, 2020).

Kose, A., Naotaka, S. (2020). WorldBank blog [web blog] Understanding the depth of the 2020 global recession in 5 charts. https://blogs.worldbank.org/opendata/understanding-depth-2020-global-recession-5-charts (accessed December 8, 2020).

KPMG (2020). Government Response – Global landscape. An overview of government and institution measures around the world in response to COVID-19 [website]. https://home.kpmg/xx/en/home/insights/2020/04/government-response-global-landscape.html (accessed December 14, 2020).

McKibbin, W., Vines, D. (2020). Global macroeconomic cooperation in response to the COVID-19 pandemic: A roadmap for the G20 and the IMF. *Oxford Review of Economic Policy*, 36(S1), 297–337.

Pietro, M., Marattin, L., Minetti, R. (2020). Fiscal policies amid a pandemic: The response of Italy to the COVID-19 crisis. *National Tax Journal*, 73(3), 927–950.

Trading Economics. Euro area government debt to GDP [website]. https://tradingeconomics.com/euro-area/government-debt-to-gdp (accessed December 08, 2020).

4 Effect of the COVID-19 pandemic on selected economies in Eastern Europe

Olesia Chornenka, Oleksij Kelebaj, Monika Bolińska, Paweł Dykas, and Rafał Wisła

4.1 Introduction

The depth of fall in aggregate flow values (gross domestic product (GDP), investment, exports) in Q2 of 2020 in all analyzed economies of the EU was unprecedented in the post-war history of the current member states of the European Union. The pandemic also had an adverse effect on other developed economies of the world (World Bank, 2020). The 2020+ pandemic posed a much more serious challenge for the countries located in Eastern Europe. The most severe effects of the 2020+ pandemic were reported in the tourist and transport sectors and in the healthcare system. Initial assessments of the economic and social impact of the COVID-19 pandemic on the countries located in Eastern Europe were carried out already in 2020 among others by: Kulyts'kyy (2020a, 2020b), Drobot, Makarov, Nazarenko and Manasyan (2020), Zhalilo, Bazylyuk, Kovalivs'ka and Kolomiyets' (2020) or the World Bank (2020).

Kulyts'kyy (2020a) assessed the effect of the pandemic on the Ukrainian economy, by analyzing existing and forecast fluctuations in basic macroeconomic indicators in a short- and a long-time horizon in the context of general instability of the global economy caused by the 2020+ pandemic. He additionally (2020b) analyzed the impact of the 2020+ pandemic on the Ukrainian labor market. He observed the most severe short-term effect of the pandemic in the Ukrainian service sector.

The World Bank (2020) in its description of macroeconomic effects of the pandemic on Russia indicates a massive drop in economic activity in Q2 of 2020. Surveys conducted by the World Bank demonstrate that the crisis caused by the coronavirus pandemic severely affected small and medium-sized enterprises (SMEs) that are more sensitive to supply and demand shocks than larger companies. The 2020+ pandemic has deepened the economic crisis in Russia, caused among other factors by dramatic falls in prices for petroleum. The average price for Russian Urals oil brand was USD 41.73 per barrel in 2020. The value amounted in 2019 to USD 63.59,

DOI: 10.4324/9781003211891-4

i.e. it was 34% lower on average in 2020, exerting an adverse effect on both the state budget and trade balance.

Drobot, Makarov, Nazarenko and Manasyan (2020) assessed the effect of coronavirus spread on the condition of selected Russian industries. Their research demonstrates that, in the context of general adverse effects of the 2020+ pandemic on the Russian economy, selected industries reported growths in sales – of foodstuffs, chemicals, pharmaceuticals and medical instruments and equipment. Drobot, Makarov, Nazarenko and Manasyan (2020) construct two scenarios of overcoming the crisis of the Russian economy. Under an optimistic scenario (assuming a substantial rise in oil prices), Russia will reach the pre-crisis level of 2019 by mid-2021. Under a pessimistic scenario, the crisis in Russia caused by the pandemic and fall in prices for fossil fuels will not be overcome until 2023.

Zhalilo, Bazylyuk, Kovalivs'ka and Kolomiyets' (2020) carried out an in-depth analysis of the impact of the 2020+ pandemic on the Ukrainian economy, adopting macroeconomic, sectoral, social and spatial perspectives. The authors emphasize that the final containment of the COVID-19 virus spread will not mark the end of the recession in Ukraine. They observed a particularly strong effect of the 2020+ pandemic on the condition of unstable national economic systems. The effect of the coronavirus spread on an institutionally unstable economic system was also analyzed by the National Bank of Ukraine (2020). Attention was directed to an increased risk of short- and long-term internal (inflation) and external (strongly negative balance of payments) instability.

That synthetic review of pandemic effects on social and economic life demonstrates a varying impact of the 2020 health issue on relatively immature social and economic systems. As we focus in this book on European economies, and a sufficient set of statistical data (quarter-over-quarter) on institutionally unstable economic systems is not available, we limit our analysis and assessment of the effects of the 2020+ pandemic to two countries located in Eastern Europe.

This chapter aims to analyze and assess the impact of the COVID-19 pandemic on the economies of Russia and Ukraine in comparison to EU economies. The first section of this chapter contains an analysis of the GDP (per capita) index. The analysis covers a long (2006–2020) and a short period (Q2 of 2019 vs. Q2 of 2020). The second section of this chapter discusses spatial interactions between the European Union, the Russian Federation and Ukraine taking place in labor and product markets. The third section describes selected forms of fiscal intervention used by the governments of Ukraine and Russia in 2020. This chapter supplements the macro-analyses conducted in Chapter 2 by describing two countries from outside the European Union, but also builds a connection with Chapter 3 that discusses fiscal interventions in the EU member states.

4.2 Changes in GDP of Ukraine and Russia vs. the EU economy

The 1990s saw a deep economic recession in Ukraine. GDP per capita (at purchasing power parity (PPP), and fixed prices from 2017) fell from USD 15,700 in 1990 to USD 6,700 in 1999. By 2019, it had not yet returned to its 1990 level (World Bank, 2021). The situation in Ukraine was indirectly worsened by the Russian financial crisis of 1998. The social and economic situation in the first decade of Ukrainian independence was influenced not only by a revolutionary shock but also by a complete absence of market economy institutions.

The scenario of economic development in the last decade of the 20th century was almost the same in Russia and in Ukraine. A difference lay in the levels and not in the depth of the recession. Russian GDP per capita (at PPP, and fixed prices from 2017) fell from USD 21,500 in 1990 to USD 13,200 in 1999. But by 2019 it had reached USD 27,000 per capita (World Bank, 2021). Against that background, the economies of European Communities and then the European Union can be described as a space of stable economic growth. GDP per capita in the European Union (at PPP, and fixed prices from 2017) in 1990 amounted to USD 28,600 and after 30 years to USD 44,400 per capita.

Ukrainian real GDP per capita grew in 2000–2008 by almost 100%. The Russian financial crisis combined with the gas disputes with Russia led to a deep recession in Ukraine in 2009 (a fall by almost 15%), followed by the return of the Ukrainian economy in 2011/2012 to the growth path that continued until 2014. The accumulated real growth in GDP per capita amounted to 11.2% in that period. The growth trend discontinued after the Euromaidan movement (2013–2014), the annexation of Crimea by Russia, and fighting with pro-Russian separatists in eastern Ukraine. Ukrainian real GDP per capita fell in 2014–2015 by almost 10%. In 2020, Ukrainian GDP per capita was similar to small post-Soviet states such as Moldova, Georgia or Armenia.

Like in the 1990s, the curve of Russian economic development took on a similar shape to Ukraine in the first two decades of the 21st century. However, the levels are significantly higher. Considering the institutional aspect, Russia is capable of using resources and solutions that are unavailable in Ukraine. These include for example Russia's participation in a regional integration group (the Eurasian Customs Union) and its political stability (considerable power resting with the president).

Figures 4.1 (a), (b) and (c) offer a slightly different perspective on fluctuations in GDP per capita in Ukraine, Russia and the European Union (at PPP, and fixed prices from Q2 of 2020) in the years 2006–2020 quarter-over-quarter. The economic history of Ukraine, Russia and the European Union as a whole over the last 30 years provides evidence of diversified levels of institutional, political and economic stability in those three economic areas.

Effect on economies of Eastern Europe 71

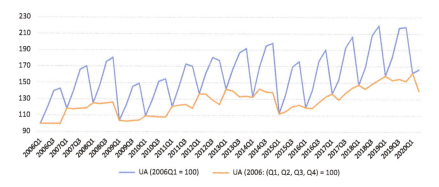

Figure 4.1a Changes in Gross Domestic Product per capita, at PPP, quarter-over-quarter (2006–2020, 2020 = 100) in (a) Ukraine. Source: own calculation based on http://www.ukrstat.gov.ua/ (accessed: 2021-01-30).

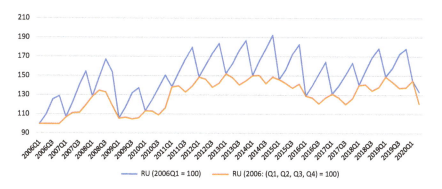

Figure 4.1b Changes in Gross Domestic Product per capita, at PPP, quarter-over-quarter (2006–2020, 2020 = 100) in (b) Russia. Source: own calculation based on https://eng.rosstat.gov.ru (accessed: 2021-01-30).

The same exogenous shocks produce similar short-term effects (and this is not surprising under the conditions of globalization), but their long-term consequences vary in form and time. The first decade of the 21st century in Ukraine saw economic growth following a decade of deep revolutionary recession in the 1990s. The growth wave in this phase of the economic cycle was abruptly discontinued in Q1 of 2009, due to an exogenous shock that firstly affected the United States in 2008 and then spread across the global economy. As a result, the Ukrainian economy slipped into a three-year recession. The years 2012–2014 saw a return to the growth path characteristic of the era preceding the 2008+ crisis. A series of protests in Ukraine provoked by Ukraine's decision to put off signing the association agreement with the

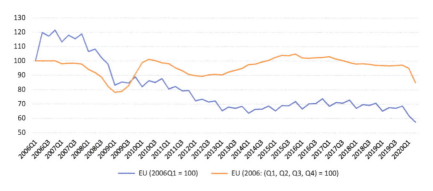

Figure 4.1c Changes in Gross Domestic Product per capita, at PPP, quarter-over-quarter (2006–2020, 2020 = 100) in (c) the European Union. Source: own calculation based on https://ec.europa.eu/eurostat/data/database (accessed: 2021-01-30).

European Union (beginning in November 2013), followed by demonstrations in many towns of eastern and southern Ukraine, including Donetsk, Luhansk, Kharkiv and Odessa, and growing separatist trends in Crimea, resulted in a repeated sudden reversal of growth trends in the Ukrainian economy. This time, it was a short-term recession.

The years 2015–2019 saw spectacular growth, followed by another dramatic and deep downturn caused by the global pandemic. Hence, the Ukrainian economy experienced three major demand and supply shocks. The Russian economy recorded a fall of 7.8% in 2009, when the oil prices dropped to the level of USD 40–50 per barrel. At that time of crisis, Russia possessed considerable foreign exchange reserves amassed in the years 2000–2008 due to high and rising prices for raw materials, including especially petroleum (2008/2009: about USD 140 per barrel).

The year 2009 marked the end of the longest era of uninterrupted dynamic economic growth in modern Russia, lasting from 2000 and reaching about 7% annually on average. Despite unfavorable macroeconomic and microeconomic indicators, Russians' real income continued to grow during the 2008+ crisis, due to considerable funds from foreign exchange reserves redirected to the domestic market (Łobuszewska, Kazimierska & Mańkowski, 2015: 20).

When the Russian financial market was affected by a crisis in mid-December 2014, the authorities of the Federation no longer possessed huge reserves that would enable them to promptly respond to falls; in addition, the Russian economy was to a large extent denied access to financing by foreign loans and investments (Menkiszak, Fischer, 2014). The sanctions imposed on Russia by the European Union and the United States following Russia's involvement in the conflict in eastern Ukraine, and the counter-measures implemented by Russia, seriously affected the inflow of foreign investment and consequently the entire Russian economy in 2014–2017. Structural reforms, the emergence of a more dynamic private sector, a reduced role of the state in economic processes and changes in taxation of the oil sector exercised a favorable influence on the Russian economy in 2018–2019.

The global financial and economic crisis led to a deep recession in the EU-27 in 2009, followed by a recovery in 2010. The real GDP growth rate in the EU was considerably diversified, both in time and between the member states. Following the economic recession that in 2009 affected all member states of the EU except Poland, 2010 saw a repeated economic growth trend in 23 member states and the situation continued in those 23 member states also in 2011. However, the trend was reversed in 2012 when only slightly more than half (14) of the member states reported economic growth, while the remaining member states saw a reduction in production. Eventually, a substantial majority of the member states recorded growth again. The group included 16 states in 2013, 23 states in 2014 and 26 states in 2015 and 2016. All 27 member states of the EU reported growth in 2017 for the first time since 2007. The trend continued in 2018 and 2019. The sole member state to record a drop in 2015 and 2016 was Greece (by 0.4% and 0.2% respectively), following a slight growth by 0.7% in 2014 and five successive reductions in economic output during the years 2009–2013 (Statistics Explained, 2020: 2).

In early 2020, the global economy, including the economies of Ukraine, the Russian Federation and the European Union, were exposed to a new and completely unforeseeable biological hazard that led to a severe downturn in economic growth and undermined the institutionally weak economic systems of Eastern European states. The enforced lockdown adversely affected the efficiency and effectiveness of social and economic systems (Zhalilo, Bazylyuk, Kovalivs'ka & Kolomiyets', 2020).

Figure 4.2 (a, b, c) presents quarter-to-quarter changes in Gross Domestic Product in Russia, Ukraine and in European Countries. The lockdown measures implemented in Ukraine in the spring of 2020 continued for almost two months; the government introduced a "weekend quarantine" in the autumn, meaning almost complete lockdown on public holidays. On the basis of figures 4.2 (a) we can state that GDP per capita in Q2 of 2020 dropped by 8% compared to Q2 of 2019. Another lockdown was imposed in January 2021 for almost three weeks. An assessment of the effects of those measures on the economy is ambiguous. The Ukrainian ministry of economy announced that inflation in 2020 reached 5%, principally due to a dynamic increase in revenues from retail sales and a rise in prices for energy sources on the global market that affected local expenses on public utility services, finally reducing the consumer demand.

The volume of cargo transport dropped in 2020 by 15% compared to the same period of 2019 while the passenger transport sector reached in 2020 only 46% of its revenues in the same period of 2019.

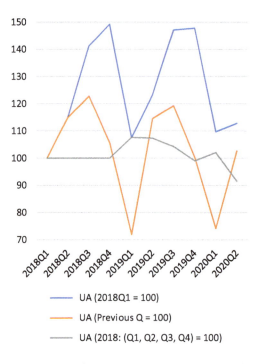

Figure 4.2a Changes in Gross Domestic Product per capita, at PPP, quarter-over-quarter (2019–2020) in (a) Ukraine. Source: own calculation based on http://www.ukrstat.gov.ua/; https://eng.rosstat.gov.ru; https://ec.europa.eu/eurostat/data/database (accessed: 2021-01-30).

Russia faced an extremely high mortality rate caused by the COVID-19 pandemic in 2020; the Russian population decreased by almost 700,000 people. It was the deepest annual decrease of the last 15 years. Non-residents invested three times less in the business enterprise sector in H1 of 2020 than in the same period of 2019.

The result was five times less in the entire year 2020 than in 2019. Hence, the 2020+ pandemic seems to be only one of the factors causing problems in the Russian economy. Low oil prices, structural problems (labor market, a shallow financial market) and geopolitical risk affect the current situation and will have a decisive effect on the condition of the Russian economy in the future.

Maps 4.1(a) and 4.1(b) represent spatial differentiation of GDP per capita subsequently in Q2 of 2019 and Q2 of 2020 in the EU economies, the Russian Federation and Ukraine. A detailed description of changes in the member states of the European Union is contained in Chapter 2, hence we focus here on the differences in changes that take place between the EU economies and the Russian Federation and Ukraine.

Effect on economies of Eastern Europe 75

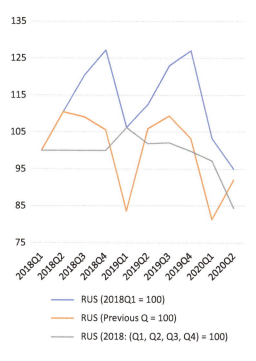

Figure 4.2b Changes in Gross Domestic Product per capita, at PPP, quarter-over-quarter (2019–2020) in (b) Russia. Source: own calculation based on http://www.ukrstat.gov.ua/; https://eng.rosstat.gov.ru; https://ec.europa.eu/eurostat/data/database (accessed: 2021-01-30).

The analyzed economies were divided into quintile groups characterized by the lowest (five), low (six), average (five), high (six) and the highest (five) values; Slovakia was classified in an additional group due to the absence of available statistics. Both in Q2 of 2019 and in Q2 of 2020, Ukraine recorded the lowest values of the analyzed variable among all countries – this confirmed its status as the poorest state in the group covered by our analysis. The difference between Ukraine and the state with the lowest values of GDP per capita in Europe, i.e. Bulgaria, amounted in Q2 of 2019 to USD 291.83 while that difference fell to USD 31.61 in the same period of the following year. This indicates that the fall in economic output flow was deeper in Bulgaria than in Ukraine. However, the value of GDP per capita fell in Ukraine by USD 272.27 between the analyzed quarters; it was the lowest value of decrease among all the countries. The Russian Federation retained its rank between Q2 of 2019 and Q2 of 2020 and remained in the group characterized by low values of GDP per capita.

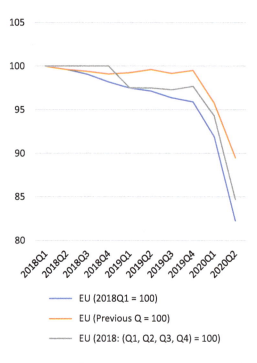

Figure 4.2c Changes in Gross Domestic Product per capita, at PPP, quarter-over-quarter (2019–2020) in (c) the European Union. Source: own calculation based on http://www.ukrstat.gov.ua/; https://eng.rosstat.gov.ru; https://ec.europa.eu/eurostat/data/database (accessed: 2021-01-30).

4.3 Spatial interactions taking place on labor and product markets between the European Union, Russian Federation and Ukraine

To identify the determinants of differences in labor productivity, we assume as our starting point the neoclassical Cobb-Douglas power production function (Cobb-Douglas, 1928):

$$Y = f(K,L) = A e^{gt} K^\alpha L^{1-\alpha} \tag{4.1}$$

where:
  Y – production,
  K – capital input,
  L – labor input,
  g – Hicks technical progress rate,
  A – total productivity of capital and labor input,
  α and $\alpha-1$ – output elasticity Y of capital K and labor L respectively (see Tokarski, 2008).

Effect on economies of Eastern Europe 77

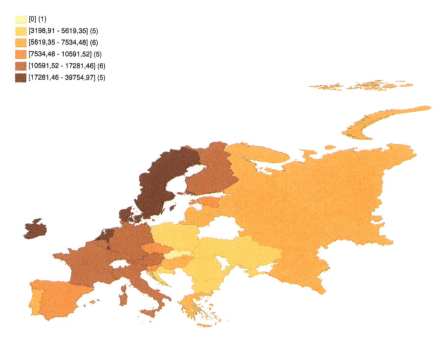

Map 4.1a Spatial differentiation of GDP per capita in Q2 of 2019 in the member states of the European Union, the Russian Federation and Ukraine (in USD, fixed prices from Q2 of 2020) Source: own calculations. based on https://ec.europa.eu/eurostat/data/database, http://www.ukrstat.gov.ua and https://rosstat.gov.ru.

After log transformation of both sides, we obtain the equation:

$$\ln(Y) = \ln(A) + gt + \alpha \ln(K) + (1-\alpha)\ln(L) \quad (4.2)$$

that facilitates transition from a power to a quasi-linear relation. Then the natural logarithm of the number of the employed is subtracted on both sides of equation (4.2) to obtain equation (4.3) that defines the natural logarithm of labor productivity.

$$\ln\left(\frac{Y}{L}\right) = \ln(A) + gt + \alpha \ln\left(\frac{K}{L}\right) \quad (4.3)$$

Equation (4.3) shows that labor productivity is determined by the technical progress rate, total productivity of inputs and capital–labor ratio. Based on equation (4.3), the parameters of equation (4.4) were estimated using data about the European Union, Russian Federation and Ukraine:

$$\ln\left(\frac{Y_{it}}{L_{it}}\right) = \alpha_0 + \alpha_1 t + \alpha_2 \ln\left(\frac{K_{it}}{L_{it}}\right) \quad (4.4)$$

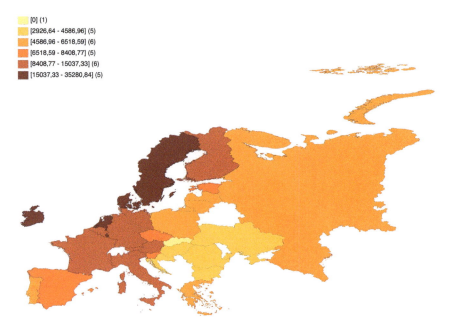

Map 4.1b Spatial differentiation of GDP per capita in Q2 of 2020 in the member states of the European Union, the Russian Federation and Ukraine (in USD, fixed prices from Q2 of 2020) Source: own calculations. based on https://ec.europa.eu/eurostat/data/database, http://www.ukrstat.gov.ua and https://rosstat.gov.ru.

where:

Y_{it} – GDP in object i (i = 1, 2, 3) in the year t (t = *1996, 1997..., 2019*),
L_{it} – number of the employed in object i in the year t,
K_{it} – gross value of property, plant, equipment in enterprises in object i in the year t,
α_0 – the logarithm of total productivity of inputs,
α_1 – a parameter that defines the effect of technical progress rate on labor productivity,
α_2 – elasticity of labor productivity relative to the capital–labor ratio.

A definition of the unemployment rate is now used to statistically analyze an increase in unemployment rates. Based on a definition of the unemployment rate, its increase can be made conditional on the unemployment rate in the preceding period and the output growth rate. We adopt the following definition for this purpose (Tokarski, 2005):

$$u(t) = \frac{U(t)}{U(t)+L(t)} = 1 - \frac{L(t)}{N(t)} \tag{4.5}$$

where:
$u(t)$ – unemployment rate,

$U(t)$ – number of the unemployed,
$L(t)$ – number of the employed,
$N(t)$ – labor supply.

By differentiating equation (4.5) in time t, we obtain an increase in the unemployment rate expressed by the derivative:

$$\dot{u}(t) = -\frac{\dot{L}(t)N(t) - L(t)\dot{N}(t)}{N^2(t)} = \frac{L(t)}{N(t)}\left[\frac{\dot{N}(t)}{N(t)} - \frac{\dot{L}(t)}{L(t)}\right]$$

The above relation and equation (4.5) indicate that an increase in the unemployment rate can be transformed into:

$$\dot{u}(t) = (1 - u(t))\left(\frac{\dot{N}(t)}{N(t)} - \frac{\dot{L}(t)}{L(t)}\right) \qquad (4.6)$$

An analysis of equation (4.6) leads to the conclusion that the rate of growth in the number of the employed $\frac{\dot{L}(t)}{L(t)}$ is an increasing function of the output growth rate (g). Hence, there is a mapping (f) so that $\frac{\dot{L}(t)}{L(t)} = f(g)$ and $\frac{df}{dg} > 0$; then, an increase in the unemployment rate is described using the following formula:

$$\dot{u}(t) = (1 - u(t))\left[\frac{\dot{N}(t)}{N(t)} - f(g)\right] \qquad (4.7)$$

An analysis of relation (4.7) leads to the conclusion that an increase in the unemployment rate is determined by the output growth rate (g), labor supply growth rate $\left(\frac{\dot{N}(t)}{N(t)}\right)$ and unemployment rate $(u(t))$. Additionally, an increase in the unemployment rate is a decreasing function of the output growth rate (g), and an increasing function of the labor supply growth rate $\left(\frac{\dot{N}(t)}{N(t)}\right)$. If the labor supply growth rate is greater (less) than the employed number growth rate, a rise in the unemployment rate is a decreasing (an increasing) function of the unemployment rate.

Based on the above theoretical discussion of the factors determining increases in unemployment rates (equation 4.7), the parameters of the following equation are estimated:[1]

$$\Delta u_{it} = \alpha_0 - \alpha_1 u_{it-1} + \alpha_2 d_{\Delta u} u_{it-1} - \alpha_3 \Delta \ln(Y_{it}) \qquad (4.8)$$

---

1 Equation (4.8) ignores the labor supply growth rate because fluctuations in labor supply were relatively insignificant compared to changes in unemployment in the years 1996–2019.

where:

$u_{it} = \dfrac{U_{it}}{U_{it} + L_{it}}$ – registered unemployment rate in economy i ($i = 1, 2, 3$) in the year t ($t = 1996, 1997..., 2019$);

$\Delta ln(Y_{it})$ – labor productivity growth rate in object i in the year t,

α_0 – a constant defining an increase in the unemployment rate that would be observed at a zero unemployment rate in the preceding period and zero labor productivity rate,

α_1 a variable defining the strength of effect exerted by the unemployment rate from the preceding period on the increase in the unemployment rate where that variable does not grow,

α_2 – a measure of the strength of effect exerted by the unemployment rate from the preceding period on the increase of that variable where the rate grows,

α_3 – describes the relation between the increase in the unemployment rate and the labor productivity growth rate,

$d_{\Delta u}$ – a dummy variable that takes on the value of 1 if the unemployment rate grows, and otherwise equals 0.

An interpretation of the parameters α_1 and α_2 is dictated by a dichotomous variable $d_{\Delta u}$. This is because that variable, in the equation describing an increase in unemployment rates, plays the role of a switching variable that adjusts the effect of the unemployment rate from the preceding period on a change in the current unemployment rate by including its growth or drop.

The seemingly unrelated regression (SUR) method as developed by Zellner (Zellner, 1962) was used in estimations of equations (4.4) and (4.8); the parameters of all equations were estimated simultaneously so that the parameters of each equation incorporate information about the other equations. This method leads to an improved efficiency of parameters estimated, by using additional information. With an increase in correlation between error vectors of the analyzed equations, in the number of observations and with a greater linear relationship between explanatory variables the efficiency of estimated parameters grows (Yahya et al., 2008). The SUR method is used to simultaneously estimate the parameters of all analyzed equations, considering correlations between them.

In equation (4.4), the logarithm of labor productivity is adopted as an endogenous variable in the models while the logarithm of capital–labor ratio and the technical progress growth rate represent exogenous variables. In equation (4.8), independent variables such as the unemployment rate from the preceding year and the logarithm of labor productivity explain an increase in the unemployment rate. The analysis covers the longest period for which sufficient data can be obtained: the years 1996–2019. Cash variables are converted into fixed prices from 2010. Statistical significance is indicated next to values using the following markings: confidence level < 0.01 as ***, confidence level < 0.05 as ** and confidence level < 0.1 as *;

also estimation errors are given in brackets. The tables also contain the coefficient of determination R^2, here understood as a percentage of variance of the dependent variable explained by variability of the dependent variables, and included for purely descriptive purposes, not as a coefficient of determination used in traditional econometrics.

Estimations of equations (4.4) and (4.8) using the SUR method are accompanied by a table of results containing the values of correlation coefficient of random components e_{it}. The correlation coefficient of random components is calculated for each pair of equations that are subsequently represented in a matrix of correlations of random variables. Additionally, the value of the statistic obtained in the Breusch-Pagan[2] test is given below the matrix to show whether there are correlations between random interferences in individual equations.

Tables 4.1 and 4.2 contain results of estimations of the parameters of equations (4.4) and (4.8). The estimates of structural parameters of regression equations that describe labor productivity in the analyzed economies proved to be statistically significant. The elasticity of labor productivity relative to the capital–labor ratio in the European Union and in Ukraine were similar while in the Russian Federation it was clearly higher. However, the estimated parameters defining technical progress rates are significantly different: in the European Union, the value of that rate is three times lower than in Ukraine and almost two times lower than in the Russian Federation.

Table 4.1 Estimates of the parameters of equation (4.4) for the European Union, Russian Federation and Ukraine

Regressors	European Union	Russian Federation	Ukraine
$\ln\left(\dfrac{K_{it}}{Y_{it}}\right)$	0.3960 *** (0.0204)	0.4251 *** (0.0210)	0.3861 *** (0.0437)
g	0.0066 *** (0.0027)	0.0111 *** (0.0013)	0.0198 *** (0.0022)
constant	−5.8624 *** (0.0455)	−15.7639 *** (2.3839)	−33.9315 *** (4.3949)
number of observations	24	24	24
R^2	0.9899	0.9938	0.9089
RMSE	0.0073	0.0191	0.0701
European Union	1.0000		
Russian Federation	0.3821	1.0000	
Ukraine	0.4948	−0.1795	1.0000
Breusch-Pagan test		chi2(3) = 10.154	Pr = 0.0173

Source: own calculation based on http://www.ukrstat.gov.ua/; https://eng.rosstat.gov.ru; https://ec.europa.eu/eurostat/data/database (accessed: 2021-01-30).

2 The test statistic is based on chi-squared distribution. The number of degrees of freedom in the test is given in brackets and equals $\dfrac{M(M-1)}{2}$, where M represents the number of equations in the model, estimated using the SURE method.

Table 4.2 Estimates of the parameters of equation (4.8) for the European Union, Russian Federation and Ukraine

Regressors	European Union	Russian Federation	Ukraine
u_{it-1}	−0.0013 *	0.2741 **	−0.1539 *
	(0.0012)	(0.1442)	(0.1055)
$d\Delta u_{it-1}$	0.0110 ***	0.0143 ***	0.0148 ***
	(0.1381)	(0.0029)	(0.0026)
$\Delta \ln Y_{it}$	−0.0093 *	0.0163 **	−0.0138 **
	(0.0203)	(0.0086)	(0.0053)
constant	0.0833 *	−0.1597 **	0.1055 **
	(0.2062)	(0.0800)	(0.0441)
number of observations	24	24	24
R^2	0.6490	0.6101	0.7105
RMSE	0.0041	0.0064	0.0059
European Union	1.0000		
Russian Federation	0.0727	1.0000	
Ukraine	0.2771	0.0143	1.0000
Breusch-Pagan test		chi2(3) = 1.975	0.5776

Source: own calculation based on http://www.ukrstat.gov.ua/; https://eng.rosstat.gov.ru; https://ec.europa.eu/eurostat/data/database (accessed: 2021-01-30).

The coefficient of correlation between the random components of the equations describing labor productivity in the European Union and Russian Federation and the European Union and Ukraine is positive. Only the equation for the Russian Federation and Ukraine responds otherwise to random interferences. The value p of the Breusch-Pagan test statistic clearly demonstrates that the relations between random components of equation pairs are statistically significant. Additionally, the estimated equations of the SUR model convincingly explain the variability of labor productivity in the discussed economies.

The estimates of structural parameters of the equations describing increases in unemployment rates in the SUR model for the European Union, Russian Federation and Ukraine are statistically significant but their signs are not always consistent with economic theory. The estimates of parameters for the Russian Federation seem to be inconsistent with economic theory (an exception is provided by the parameter defining the effect of unemployment from the preceding period under conditions of increase in that variable). Additionally, fluctuations in the unemployment rate in prior periods had a much stronger effect on the current increase in that variable in Ukraine than in the European Union. A similar, although slightly weaker relation, is observed in the value of elasticity of increase in current unemployment relative to labor productivity; the response of unemployment rates to changes in the labor productivity growth rate is about 50% weaker in the European Union.

The goodness of fit of the equations to empirical data, as measured by a quasi-coefficient "R^2", is lower than in the case of the equation describing labor productivity; it can also be concluded that the SUR model quite satisfactorily explains variability in the increase in the unemployment rate. However, the result of the Breusch-Pagan test did not confirm that there are statistically significant spatial interrelations between the European Union, Russian Federation and Ukraine.

Correlations between simultaneous random components are weak, and it can be concluded that objects constituting the aggregate are generally independent. That independence is understood as varying responses (meaning directions of development) of an increase in the unemployment rate to external factors. The result of Breusch-Pagan test did not confirm that there are statistically significant spatial interrelations between the European Union, Russian Federation and Ukraine. Correlations between simultaneous random components are weak, and it can be concluded that objects constituting the aggregate are generally independent. That independence is understood as varying responses (meaning directions of development) of an increase in the unemployment rate to external factors.

4.4 Fiscal interventions in Ukraine and Russia in 2020

The COVID-19 pandemic posed a considerable challenge to the global economy, principally because it did not represent a "classical" economic crisis or a local epidemic crisis (Zhalilo, Bazylyuk, Kovalivs'ka and Kolomiyets', 2020). Governments had to choose between protecting societies against the virus and maintaining the existing level of welfare. The principal method used to protect society was the implementation of lockdown measures with varying severity combined with public transfers, such as subsidies directed to selected economic sectors, co-financing of small and medium-sized businesses, reductions in (or partial exemption from) taxes, etc.

4.4.1 Ukraine

The decisions made by the Ukrainian government, aimed to limit the adverse impact of the COVID-19 pandemic on the Ukrainian economy, were not exceptional compared to measures taken in many other countries. Public aid included (KMU, 2020):

- loan moratoriums,
- tax allowances,
- support provided to small and medium-sized businesses,
- separate, dedicated support provided to agriculture,
- information assistance provided to businesses.

The Ukrainian central bank recommended that Ukrainian commercial banks offer borrowers debt restructuring plans (Decree no. 39 of 26 March 2020

(*Постанова НБУ №39 від 26 березня 2020 року*)) (NBU, 2020a). The central bank proposed two principal versions of debt restructuring:

- complete or partial exemption from repayment of principal loan amount for the quarantine duration with an extension of financing term,
- capitalization of interest.

Additionally, a ban was imposed on rises in interest rates on loans between 1 March and 30 November 2020. Also, a ban on fines and penalties for delays in loan repayment was imposed in that period. A long-term bank refinancing mechanism was launched and the algorithm for recognition of required reserves was changed (Zhalilo, Bazylyuk, Kovalivs'ka & Kolomiyets', 2020). The government adopted a series of fiscal measures:

- exemption from charges for land use for business purposes and from tax on real property (residential spaces) in March 2020,
- limitation of most fines imposed for tax offences,
- a moratorium on tax inspections (except inspection of refunded VAT),
- exemption from VAT of importers and suppliers of medications, medical devices, medical apparatus and other goods used to contain the spread of COVID-19 in the territory of Ukraine,
- increased annual income limits for groups 1, 2 and 3 of entrepreneurs,
- zero rate of excise tax for state enterprises manufacturing alcohol-based disinfectants,
- power to set tax rates for small businesses delegated to local government (Єдиний податок) (KMU, 2020).

Support provided to small and medium-sized businesses included principally subsidies to employee pay. Act no. 3275 (Закон України "*Про внесення змін до деяких законодавчих актів, спрямованих на забезпечення додаткових соціальних та економічних гарантій у зв'язку з поширенням коронавірусної хвороби (COVID-2019)*" (VRU, 2020)) introduced the concept of "partial unemployment" for the time of quarantine. The Act lays down the conditions for assistance provided to small and medium-sized enterprises in the form of benefits payable to partially unemployed personnel of those enterprises.

The agricultural sector is of key importance for the Ukrainian economy; almost 20% of the employed in Ukraine work in agriculture. The proportion of income from the agricultural sector in Ukrainian GDP is the largest in Europe (about 10%) (Bosak & Mustafaieva, 2019; SSSU, 2020). Ukraine allocated EUR 131 million to its farmer support programme. The government allocated an additional EUR 39 million to a reduction in debt of the agricultural sector. It is expected that the programme will contribute to the establishment of 100 new farms and agricultural-industrial complexes that will create 1,700 new jobs (KMU, 2020).

To assist entrepreneurs in their business activity during the quarantine, the government created several information platforms, providing data and enabling people to register a business and obtain online tax advice.

Due to a series of tax allowances granted, tax income of public sector institutions significantly dropped, e.g. receipts from social insurance premiums decreased (Єдиний соціальний внесок). An estimated reduction in tax receipts due to exemptions from payment of insurance premiums amounts to EUR 66 monthly (Zhalilo, Bazylyuk, Kovalivs'ka & Kolomiyets', 2020). Consequently, the budget deficit in 2020 was the largest in the 20 years of independent Ukraine. The budget deficit was compensated using new sovereign loans which translated into an increase in public debt as of the end of 2020 (Kulyts'kyy, 2020a).

4.4.2 Russia

The principal state intervention measures implemented in Russia in 2020 can be divided into general, social and economic. The set of general measures includes:

- restrictions imposed on spatial mobility of people (including administrative and criminal liability for failure to meet those conditions),
- various simplified regulations adopted to maintain continuity of social and economic functions, such as licences for the manufacture and sales of alcoholic drinks, provision of telecommunication services, detective and security guard activity extended until the end of 2020, simplified doctoral examinations, extended deadlines for payment of patent fees, etc.

Principal methods employed to support continued social functions include:

- medications and medical devices, including personal protective equipment, and materials for their manufacture and disinfectants used to contain the spread of coronavirus in the territory of Russia are exempted from customs duties,
- simplified registration procedure of medications and medical devices,
- exemption from VAT of imported medical goods transferred to healthcare centers treating patients with the coronavirus,
- simplified application for and granting of social benefits; parents of children aged below 16 and people who lost their jobs during the pandemic, and employees of the healthcare sector received additional support during the quarantine.

Tax holidays were granted in the sectors adversely affected by the COVID-19 pandemic, like in Ukraine:

- social insurance premiums payable by small and medium-sized enterprises were reduced,

86 *Olesia Chornenka et al.*

- a moratorium on state (including customs and tax) inspections was declared,
- entrepreneurs from selected sectors were exempted from certain taxes, enterprises of key importance for the Russian economy were granted the option to defer payment of their tax liabilities,
- electricity producers, banks, and car manufacturers obtained subsidies amounting to EUR 281 million in total, and airports received about EUR 122 million,
- interest rates on loans taken out by enterprises adversely affected by the pandemic were reduced, or interest on loans was cancelled to enable enterprises to give pays,
- a simplified procedure for agricultural enterprises requesting low-interest loans; a loan moratorium for small and medium-sized enterprises in the form of loan fees deferred for 6 months (RFG, 2020).

Russian state interventions affected the condition of the public finance sector, like in Ukraine. Adverse trends were also recorded in the Russian balance of payments, due to a reduced volume of exports from the energy sector (World Bank, 2020).

4.5 Conclusions

Russia possessed in 2008–2010 considerable foreign currency reserves, amassed in the years 2000–2008 due to high and rising prices for raw materials. Despite unfavorable macroeconomic and microeconomic indicators, Russians' real income continued to grow in that period, due to considerable funds from foreign exchange reserves redirected to the domestic market. The sanctions imposed on Russia by the European Union and the United States following Russia's involvement in the conflict in eastern Ukraine, and the counter-measures implemented by Russia, seriously affected the inflow of foreign investment and consequently the entire Russian economy in 2014–2017.

The Ukrainian economy was exposed to three major demand and supply shocks in 2008–2020 that increased institutional, economic and social instability in Ukraine. Generally, the 2020+ pandemic increased instability of the institutional and economic systems in Ukraine and Russia.

The global financial and economic crisis led to a deep recession in the EU-27 in 2009, followed by a recovery in 2010. Only 14 member states recorded economic growth in 2012, the remaining reported a decrease in production. All 27 member states of the EU recognized economic growth in 2017 for the first time since 2007.

In early 2020, the global economy, including the economies of Ukraine, Russia and the European Union, were exposed to a new and completely unforeseeable biological hazard that led to a severe downturn in economic growth. The Ukrainian ministry of economy announced that inflation in

2020 reached 5%, principally due to a dynamic increase in revenues from retail sales and a rise in prices for energy sources on the global market that affected local expenses on public utility services, finally reducing the consumer demand. The passenger transport sector achieved in 2020 only 46% of its revenues earned in the same period of 2019. Russia faced an extremely high mortality rate caused by the COVID-19 pandemic in 2020; the Russian population decreased by almost 700,000 people. It was the deepest annual decrease of the last 15 years. Non-residents invested in the business enterprise sector in 2020 5 times less capital than in 2019. The 2020+ pandemic seems to be only one of the factors causing problems in the Russian economy.

Estimates of the structural parameters of equations describing increases in unemployment rates in the SURE model for the European Union, Russian Federation and Ukraine lead to ambiguous results. Generally, fluctuations in the unemployment rate in prior periods had a much stronger effect on the current increase in that variable in Ukraine than in the European Union. A similar, although slightly weaker relation, is observed in the value of elasticity of increase in current unemployment relative to labor productivity; the response of unemployment rates to changes in the labor productivity growth rate is about 50% weaker in the European Union (exogenous shocks in 2008–2020).

References

Bosak, A., Mustafaieva, L. (2019). Current status and prospects for agricultural development: Search of new markets of acquisition, Naukovyy visnyk UzhNU. *Seriya: Mizhnarodni ekonomichni vidnosyny ta svitove hospodarstvo*, 24, 48–54.

Cobb C. W., Douglas P. H. (1928). A theory of production. *American Economic Review*, 18, 139–165.

Drobot, Y., Makarov, I., Nazarenko, V., Manasyan, S. (2020). Vliyaniye pandemii COVID-19 na real'nyy sektor ekonomiki. *Ekonomika, predprinimatel'stvo i pravo*, 8, 2135–2150.

KMU (2020). Prohramy pidtrymky biznesu. https://COVID19.gov.ua/prohramy-pidtrymky-biznesu (accessed January 30, 2021).

Kulyts'kyy, S. (2020a). Problemy rozvytku ekonomiky Ukrayiny, obumovleni pandemiyeyu koronavirusu COVID-19 u sviti, ta poshuk shlyakhiv yikh rozv'yazannya. *Ukrayina: podiyi, fakty, komentari*, 9, 47–53.

Kulyts'kyy, S. (2020b). Ukrayins'kyy rynok pratsi pid vplyvom pandemiyi COVID-19: Stan ta otsinka perspektyv rozvytku. *Ukrayina: podiyi, fakty, komentari*, 12, 43–57.

Łobuszewska, A. (ed.), Kazimierska, K., Mańkowski, W. (2015). *Kryzys gospodarczo-finansowy w Rosji. Uwarunkowania, przejawy, perspektywy*. Ośrodek Studiów Wschodnich, Warszawa.

Menkiszak, M., Fischer E. (2014, 17 December). *Kryzys putinowskiego modelu gospodarki w Rosji*, osw.waw.pl, http://www.osw.waw.pl/pl/publikacje/analizy/2014-12-17/kryzys-putinowskiego-modelu-gospodarki-w-rosji (accessed January 30, 2021).

NBU (2020a). Inflyatsiynyy zvit. Zhovten' 2020 roku. https://bank.gov.ua/admin_uploads/article/IR_2020_Q4.pdf?v=4 (accessed January 30, 2021)

NBU (2020b). Postanova № 39. https://bank.gov.ua/ua/legislation/Resolution_26032020_39 (accessed January 30, 2021).

RFG (2020). Plan preodoleniya ekonomicheskikh posledstviy novoy koronavirusnoy infektsii. http://static.government.ru/media/COVID19/plans/9Wdz2EDiAKsn7rjQWFkg5eRvHYLtDhee/PlanRF.pdf (accessed January 30, 2021).

SSSU (2020). Agriculture of Ukraine. http://www.ukrstat.gov.ua/druk/publicat/kat_u/2020/zb/09/zb_sg_Ukr_2019.pdf (accessed January 30, 2021).

Statistics Explained (2020, 30 November). National accounts and GDP. https://ec.europa.eu/eurostat/statisticsexplained/ (accessed January 30, 2021).

Tokarski, T. (2005). *Statystyczna analiza regionalnego zróżnicowania wydajności pracy, zatrudnienia i bezrobocia w Polsce*. Wydawnictwo PTE, Warszawa.

Tokarski, T. (2008). Oszacowanie regionalnych funkcji produkcji. *Wiadomości Statystyczne*, 10, 38–53.

VRU (2020). Zakon Ukrayiny "Pro vnesennya zmin do deyakykh zakonodavchykh aktiv Ukrayiny, spryamovanykh na zabezpechennya dodatkovykh sotsial'nykh ta ekonomichnykh harantiy u zv"yazku z poshyrennyam koronavirusnoyi khvoroby (COVID-19)". https://zakon.rada.gov.ua/laws/show/540-20?lang=en#Text (accessed January 30, 2021).

World Bank (2020). *Russia economic report, no. 43, July 2020: Recession and growth under the shadow of a pandemic*. World Bank, Washington, DC. https://openknowledge.worldbank.org/handle/10986/34219License:CCBY3.0IGO (accessed January 30, 2021).

World Bank (2021). International Comparison Program, World Bank. World Development Indicators database, World Bank. Eurostat-OECD PPP. https://data.worldbank.org/indicator/NY.GDP.PCAP.PP.KD?locations=UA-RU&view=chart (accessed June 30, 2021).

Yahya, W. B., Adebayo, S. B., Jolayemi, E. T., Oyejola, B. A., Sanni, O. O. M. (2008). Effects of non–orthogonality on the efficiency of seemingly unrelated regression (SUR) models. *InterStat Journal*, 1, 1–29.

Zellner, A. (1962). An efficient method of estimating seemingly unrelated regressions and tests for aggregation bias. *Journal of the American Statistical Association*, 57, 348–368.

Zhalilo, Y., Bazylyuk, Y., Kovalivs'ka, S., Kolomiyets', O. (2020). *Ukrayina pislya koronakryzy-shlyakh oduzhannya*. Natsilnal'nyy Instytut Stratehichnykh Doslidzhen', 304.

5 Modelling the social and economic impact of an epidemic

*Monika Bolińska, Paweł Dykas,
Tomasz Tokarski, and Rafał Wisła*

5.1 Introduction

The methods of analytical description of the spread of contagious diseases have been widely discussed in the scientific literature (see Murray, 2003; Ruan, 2007; Xiao, Ruan 2007; Fei-Ying, Wan-Tong & Zhi-Cheng, 2015; Jardón-Kojakhmetov, Kuehn, Pugliese & Sensi, 2021) that adopts the epidemiological model known as SIR (Susceptible–Infected/Infectious–Recovered/Removed), proposed by Kermack and McKendrick in 1927. The original SIR model ignores restrictions imposed on social and economic life to contain the spread of an epidemic and economic consequences of the epidemic and of those restrictions imposed to contain its spread. Bärwolff (2020) expanded the SIR model to include analyses of epidemic spread and subsidence. According to Bärwolff, the government introduces additional restrictions on socio-economic life when the number of people infected in the population exceeds the threshold set by the government. It also assumes that the introduction of stronger restrictions will slow the spread of the pandemic. However, he argues that a lockdown leads only to a displacement of the climax of the pandemic, but not really to an efficient flattening of the curve representing the number of infected people.

The effects of a rapid spread of a pandemic on economic growth were not analyzed in mainstream economic research in the past. The economic effects of HIV/AIDS in Asia (Bloom, Lyons, 1993) and in selected countries of Europe, Africa, North America and South America (Bloom, Mahal, 1995; Kambou, Devarajan, Over, 1992) were analyzed in the last two decades of the 20th century. For example, Bloom and Mahal, in their studies published in 1995 and 1997, argue that the HIV/AIDS epidemic had no material effect on the rate of growth of income per capita in 51 developed and industrialized countries of the world in the years 1980–1992. After two decades, Cuesta (2010) came to a similar conclusion about Honduras, the country most severely affected by the HIV/AIDS epidemic in South America.

The current scale and rate of spread of the COVID-19 pandemic, caused by a coronavirus, entails serious disturbances in social and economic life. The pandemic of 2020 represents the worst global health crisis since the

DOI: 10.4324/9781003211891-5

Spanish flu that struck in 1918. In response to the chain of events observed, several measures are being presently considered. Alvarez, Argente and Lippi (2020) and Atkeson (2020) address the problem of optimization of the severity level of a lockdown. They use the SIR model under conditions of changing the economic activity of the population and enterprises. The importance of social distance is emphasized by Lik Ng (2020) who indicates adverse effects of a lockdown policy treated as the principal method preventing the spread of the pandemic. Research into trade-offs in public choices was also initiated in 2020. Aum, Lee and Shin (2020) analyze a trade-off between gross domestic product (GDP) and public health under pandemic conditions. They argue that a lockdown not only limits the spread of the pandemic but also mitigates the accumulated GDP loss in the long run. If no lockdown measures are taken during a pandemic, mass quarantining is necessary, leading to adverse economic effects. The self-employed who achieve relatively low income form the group exposed to the most severe consequences of a lockdown. Brock and Xepapadeas (2020) adopt an even wider perspective. They argue that continuous growth of consumption activities, capital accumulation and climate change could increase the exposure of society to the risk of infection. In their opinion, a policy preventing the spread of an epidemic should consist of two components. The first component includes short-term measures. The second component includes economic policies aimed at changing consumption patterns and addressing climate change.

Research projects described in the scientific literature also include studies into the effects of an epidemic on economic growth, employing neoclassical growth models. Cuddington (1993) used the Solow growth model (1956) to analyze the growth path of per-capita GDP in the context of the HIV/AIDS epidemic and its demographic consequences. The model used by him indicated a material risk of reduction in the GDP growth rate in Tanzania by the year 2010. Cuddington and Hancock (1994) adopted the same methodological approach to assess the effect of HIV/AIDS on the economy of Malawi. Delfino and Simmons (2005) identify significant empirical links between the health structure of the population and the productive system of an economy that is subject to infectious disease, in particular tuberculosis. Another neoclassical model of economic growth used in research into the effects of the spread of HIV on economic growth was proposed by Mankiw, Romer and Weil (1992). Lovasz and Schipp (2009) used that model to assess the effects of educational and health capital, and of the pace of epidemic spread on aggregate macroeconomic indicators. The effect of HIV is not the same in all countries, and even within individual countries. The economies characterized by developed healthcare infrastructures are capable of providing means that aim to prevent a rapid spread of an epidemic in its early phase. Additionally, Lovasz and Schipp, when analyzing the problem of accumulation of human capital under epidemic conditions, argue that a loss of human capital due to an epidemic does not always entail the same consequences.

The education level and number of skilled workers and their outflow from manufacturing processes due to an epidemic affects the GDP growth rate to a varying extent. Similarly, the social capital stock is interrelated with economic growth under epidemic conditions.

The above outline of main topics of research into the impact of an epidemic on economic growth provides foundations to the epidemiological-economic model proposed in this chapter. The proposed model incorporates restrictions imposed by the government on social and economic life in two alternative versions: in a gradual, continual manner as a function of the proportion of infected people in the population, and as a strict lockdown adopted abruptly by the government. The value of aggregate production is affected by the capital stocks, the rising percentage of infectious people that reduces investment and the rate of capital accumulation, and the scale of lockdown restrictions. The model proposed in this chapter is not strictly related or limited to the COVID-19 pandemic, as it is useful in analyzing the effects of any epidemic that leads to material social damage (a high percentage of infected and dead people, limited interpersonal contacts due to lockdown measures implemented) and economic losses (a drop in production caused by a collapse of aggregate demand and a reduction in the supply capacity of the economy, and consequently in the rate of capital accumulation).

5.2 An epidemiological-economic model

The epidemiological-economic model described below represents a compilation of the SIR (Susceptible–Infectious/Infected–Removed/Recovered) epidemiological model proposed by Kermack and McKendrick (1927) and the neoclassical model of economic growth proposed by Solow (1956).

The original SIR model does not include restrictions imposed on social and economic activity in response to the spread of an epidemic. For this reason, an analysis of the process of spread and subsidence of an epidemic was made using the SIR model as modified by Bärwolff (2020). Bärwolff assumes that governments impose restrictions on social and economic life when an epidemic begins to spread out of control (once the percentage of infected people exceeds a certain critical level defined in an arbitrary manner by the government). Bärwolff also assumes that the more restrictive the lockdown introduced, the slower the pace of epidemic spread.

Bärwolff's study is based on the assumption that the state introduces lockdown measures rapidly in an arbitrary manner (within a period or at certain time intervals). In our epidemiological-economic model, we assume that the level of lockdown severity is defined using a specific functional rule. Namely, we assume that the severity index of a lockdown is an analytical function of the percentage of the infected. If the percentage grows, the government does not use arbitrary criteria but follows the rule described by the function when imposing restrictions on social and economic life.

5.2.1 The epidemiological module

We consider two scenarios when analyzing the spread and subsidence of an epidemic. Like in the original SIR model, we consider a scenario wherein the government has no access to a vaccine (preventing the disease spread) and a scenario wherein the government has a vaccine.

In the scenario with the government having no access to a vaccine, we assume that the spread of epidemic is described by the following differential equations:

$$\begin{cases} \Delta S_t = -\beta \kappa_t S_{t-1} I_{t-1} \\ \Delta I_t = \beta \kappa_t S_{t-1} I_{t-1} - \gamma I_{t-1} \\ \Delta H_t = \gamma h I_{t-1} \\ \Delta D_t = \gamma (1-h) I_{t-1} \end{cases} \quad (5.1)$$

where $S_t \in (0,1)$ represents the percentage of susceptible people on day t (for $t = 1, 2, \ldots$), $I_t \in (0,1)$ represents the percentage of the infected, $H_t \in (0,1)$ represents the percentage of the recovered (the recovered are not eventually included in the group of the susceptible), and $D_t \in (0,1)$ represents the percentage of the dead.[1] We also assume that β, $h \in (0,1)$, $\gamma \in (0,\beta)$ and $\kappa_t \in [0,1]$ in consecutive days $t = 1, 2, \ldots$. The parameter β in the system of equations (5.1) describes the pace of epidemic spread, γ represents the percentage of infected people who either recover or die, and h represents the mortality rate among the infected. The parameter κ_t that can vary in its value in time (like in the original study of Bärwolff from 2020) represents an indicator of restrictions imposed on social and economic life on consecutive days of epidemic duration. If the parameter equals 1, the government does not impose any restriction on social and economic life in response to the epidemic. If $\kappa_t = 0$, a full lockdown is imposed. The lower the value of the κ_t indicator, the stricter the lockdown imposed. Additionally, the lower the value of that indicator, the slower the spread of epidemic.

It follows from the first equation in the system (5.1) that a reduction in the percentage of the susceptible (that is $-\Delta S_t$) is directly proportional to the indicator of restrictions imposed on social and economic life (κ_t), the percentage of the susceptible ($-\Delta S_{t-1}$) and the percentage of the infected (I_{t-1}). The second equation in the system (5.1) is interpreted so that an increase in the percentage of the infected (that is ΔI_t) equals the difference between a reduction in the percentage of the susceptible (that is $-\Delta S_t$) and the percentage of the infected who recover or die (γI_{t-1}). Equations three and four in the system (5.1) imply that h part of the infected recover and $1 - h$ part of them die. Additionally, it follows from the second equation in the above system that the percentage of the infected I_t rises as long as the

---

[1] Certainly, on each day t the equation is true: $S_t + I_t + H_t + D_t = 1$.

percentage of the susceptible S_t is greater than the expression $\frac{\beta \kappa_t}{\gamma}$. Hence, restrictions imposed on social and economic life by the government (and described by a dropping value of the parameter κ_t) lead to a postponement of the initial day of a fall in the percentage of the infected. In the vaccination scenario, the SIR model is reduced to the following system of differential equations that represents an extension of the system of equations (5.1):

$$\begin{cases} \Delta S_t = \begin{cases} -\beta \kappa_t S_{t-1} I_{t-1} \: for \: t < \tau + 21 \\ -\beta \kappa_t S_{t-1} I_{t-1} - \varepsilon \rho \pi_{t-21} S_{t-21} \: for \: t \geq \tau + 21 \end{cases} \\ \Delta I_t = \beta \kappa_t S_{t-1} I_{t-1} - \gamma I_{t-1} \\ \Delta H_t = \gamma h I_{t-1} \\ \Delta D_t = \gamma (1-h) I_{t-1} \\ \Delta P_t = \begin{cases} 0 \: for \: t < \tau + 21 \\ \varepsilon \rho \pi_{t-21} S_{t-21} \: for \: t \geq \tau + 21 \end{cases} \end{cases} \quad (5.2)$$

$P_t \in (0,1)$ in the system of equation (5.2) represents the percentage of effectively vaccinated people (that is people who are no longer susceptible to infection after their vaccination), τ represents the first day of vaccination, $\varepsilon \in (0,1)$ represents an indicator of vaccine effectiveness (that is the percentage of the vaccinated population that will not contract the disease), $\rho \in (0,1)$ represents the percentage of those who wish to receive the vaccine, and $\pi_t \in (0,1)$ (for consecutive days $t = \tau, \tau + 1...$) represents the percentage of those who wish to receive the vaccine and are vaccinated until day t. We also assume that people effectively vaccinated develop immunity to the disease in 21 days after vaccination.

A modification in the system of differential equation (5.2) compared to the system of equation (5.1) can be reduced to the conclusion that beginning on day 21 after the first day of vaccination, the percentage of the susceptible is reduced by the percentage of effectively vaccinated people (that is by $\varepsilon \rho \pi_{t-21} S_{t-21}$).

When analyzing models without vaccination and with vaccination, we adopt two alternative scenarios of changes in the severity indicator of restrictions imposed on social and economic life κ_t. We assume that

$$\kappa_t = 1 - I_{t-1}^\sigma \quad (5.3)$$

or:

$$\kappa_t = \begin{cases} 1 & for \: \bar{I}_{Gt} < \iota \\ \theta & for \: \bar{I}_{Gt} \geq \iota \end{cases} \quad (5.4)$$

where $\bar{I}_{Gt} = \prod_{i=1}^{14} I_{t-i}$ represents a geometric moving average of the percentage of the infected in the most recent two weeks. Regarding the parameters θ, σ and ι in the equations (5.3) and (5.4), we assume that: $\theta, \iota \in (0,1)$, and $\sigma > 0$.

We assume in equation (5.3) that if the percentage of the infected I_t rises from 0 to 1, the restriction severity indicator κ_t drops from 1 to 0, and if $\sigma \in (0,1)(\sigma > 1)$, subsequent falls in the indicator κ_t, corresponding to identical rises in the percentage of the infected I_t, are increasingly bigger (smaller).[2] Equation (5.4) implies that we consider a scenario wherein the government does not impose any restriction on social and economic life, if the geometric moving average of the percentage of the infected over the most recent two weeks does not exceed the percentage ι. When that percentage is exceeded, the government imposes a lockdown and the indicator κ_t drops abruptly from 1 to θ.

The indicator of immunization coverage π_t is described by the following equation:

$$\pi_t = \frac{at}{b+t}$$

where $a, b > 0$, and t represents consecutive days of vaccination. That indicator of vaccination coverage (at t increasing from 0 to $+\infty$) rises with a decreasing pace from 0 to a.[3]

5.2.2 The economic module

We adopt the following assumptions about developments of basic macroeconomic variables in our economic module:[4]

1) The value of production on day t (that is Y_t) is described by a modified Cobb-Douglas production function (1928) expressed by the formula:

$$Y_t = \kappa_t K_t^\alpha L_t^{1-\alpha} \qquad (5.5)$$

---

[2] This is because we obtain from a continuous function $f(x) = 1 - x^\sigma$: $f'(x) = -\sigma x^{\sigma-1}$ and $f''(x) = (1-\sigma)\sigma x^{\sigma-2}$, and consequently for $\sigma > 0$: $\forall x \in (0,1) f'(x) < 0$, $\sigma \in (0,1) \Rightarrow f''(x) > 0 \wedge \sigma > 1 \Rightarrow f''(x) < 0$.

[3] This is because we obtain from a continuous function $f(x) = \frac{at}{b+t}$: $f(0) = 0$, $\lim_{t \to +\infty} f(t) = a$, $f'(t) = \frac{ab}{(b+t)^2} > 0 \wedge f''(t) = -\frac{2ab}{(b+t)^3} (\forall t > -b)$.

[4] Assumptions (1) and (2) refer directly to the model proposed by Solow in 1956, and assumptions 3) and 4) extend that model to include basic variables describing the functions of the labor market.

where $\sigma \in (0,1)$ represents output elasticity Y_t of capital input K_t. In function (5.5), we take into account both supply and demand factors affecting the value of production. The supply component (like in the original Cobb-Douglas production function) is described by the expression $K_t^\alpha L_t^{1-\alpha}$, hence if the epidemic did not strike, the value of production (like in the Solow model) would amount to[5] $K_t^\alpha L_t^{1-\alpha}$. We also assume that if the government imposes a lockdown and reduces the indicator of social and economic activity from 1 to $\kappa_t \in (0,1)$, the value of aggregate demand falls and (due to Keynesian multiplier effects) the volume of production also falls from a level of $K_t^\alpha L_t^{1-\alpha}$ to $\kappa_t K_t^\alpha L_t^{1-\alpha}$. Hence, a relative reduction in the volume of production caused by a fall in δ. Like in the original model proposed by Solow, capital accumulation (daily, in a discrete time) is described by a differential equation in the following form:

$$\Delta K_t = s \frac{Y_{t-1}}{365} - \delta \frac{K_{t-1}}{365} \qquad (5.6)$$

where $s \in (0,1)$ represents the savings-investment rate, and $\delta \in (0,1)$ represents the capital depreciation rate.

2) The value of demand for labor (and the number of currently employed people) is described by:

$$L_t = \omega (1 - I_t - D_t) \left(\frac{Y_t}{Y^*} \right)^\phi \qquad (5.7)$$

where $\omega, \phi \in (0,1)$, and $Y^* > 0$ represents the value of production in the Solow long-run steady state (that is at $\Delta K_t = 0$). The parameter ϕ represents elasticity of demand for labor relative to the volume of production. I_t and D_t in equation (5.7) represent (like in the epidemiological module of the proposed model) percentages of the infected and those who died of the epidemic.

It follows from equation (5.7) that in our model, if the epidemic did not strike, at production rising from $Y_t < Y^*$ to Y^*, the percentage of the employed would rise from a level of $\omega \left(\frac{Y_t}{Y^*} \right)^\phi$ to ω. In the time of epidemic, the percentage of the employed represents $(1 - I_t - D_t)$ part of the demand for labor, because the infected and dead (certainly) do not work.

3) The unemployment rate u_t is (by definition) described by the formula:

$$u_t = 1 - \frac{L_t}{w} \qquad (5.8)$$

---

[5] To simplify notation, we assume that the total factor productivity on each day t, described by the formula $\frac{Y_t}{K_t^\alpha L_t^{1-\alpha}}$, equals 1. This has no effect on the scope of applicability of the below discussion.

where $w \in (0,1)$ represents the percentage of the professionally active. We assume implicitly that on day $t = 1$ the population amounted to 1, and on consecutive days equalled $1 - D_t$ while the number of professionally active people amounted to $w(1 - D_t)$.

It follows from equations (5.5–5.8) that in the Solow long-run steady state (i.e. at $\Delta K_{t=0}$): $L^* = \omega$, $K^* = \omega \left(\dfrac{s}{\delta}\right)^{\frac{1}{1-\alpha}}$, $Y^* = \omega \left(\dfrac{s}{\delta}\right)^{\frac{\alpha}{1-\alpha}}$ and $u^* = \dfrac{w - \omega}{w}$, where asterisks next to consecutive variables indicate their values in the steady state of the economic growth model analyzed here.

The following system of differential equations is obtained from equation (5.5)-(5.8):

$$\begin{cases} Y_t = \kappa_t K_t^\alpha L_t^{1-\alpha} \\ \Delta K_t = s \dfrac{Y_{t-1}}{365} - \delta \dfrac{K_{t-1}}{365} \\ L_t = \omega (1 - I_t - D_t) \left(\dfrac{Y_t}{Y^*}\right)^\phi \\ u_t = 1 - \dfrac{L_t}{w} \\ U_t = \sqrt[4]{(1 - I_t) \kappa_t \dfrac{u_{Nt}}{u_t} \dfrac{Y_t}{Y_{Nt}}} \end{cases} \qquad (5.9)$$

where u_N and Y_N represent (respectively) an unemployment rate and a production value that would be recorded if the epidemic did not strike (that is in a scenario wherein on each day $t = 1, 2, \ldots$ the percentage of the susceptible S_t would equal 1).

The last equation in system (5.9) describes the social utility function U. The function represents a geometric average of the indicator of social and economic activity κ, the percentage of the susceptible $1 - I$, the ratio of the unemployment rate under non-epidemic to that rate under epidemic conditions (u_N/u) and the ratio of production under non-epidemic conditions to production under epidemic conditions (Y/Y_N). The function of social utility $U_t = \sqrt[4]{(1 - I_t) \kappa_t \dfrac{u_{Nt}}{u_t} \dfrac{Y_t}{Y_{Nt}}}$ takes into account both social (described by the indicator κ_t) and health $(1 - I_{tt})$, and economic $(u_{Nt}/u_t$ and $Y_t/Y_{Nt})$ consequences of the epidemic.

Additionally, the social utility function U_t assumes values from the interval [0;1]. If the epidemic did not strike, $\kappa_t = 1 - I_t = \dfrac{u_{Nt}}{u_t} = \dfrac{Y_t}{Y_{Nt}} = 1$, and hence $U_t = 1$. The lower values are assumed by function U, the higher

Modelling the impact of an epidemic 97

are aggregate social, health and economic costs of the epidemic. During a full lockdown (that is at $\kappa = 0$), the value of social utility function falls to 0.

5.3 Calibrated model parameters

5.3.1 Parameters of the epidemiological module

We assume that the infection lasts for 14 days on average. Hence, the parameter γ in the epidemiological module is selected at the level of $\gamma = 1/14 \approx 0.071429$.

The parameter β is calibrated so that peak incidence, if the government does not impose any lockdown, falls on day 365 of the epidemic. Hence the parameter equals 0.1066 in consecutive versions of numerical simulations.

We also assume that the mortality rate among the infected amounts to 2%, hence $h = 0.98$. We assume that one person per million was infected on day one of the epidemic, that is $I_1 = 10^{-6}$.

When analyzing the equation of social and economic activity indicator $\kappa_t = 1 - I_t^\sigma$, we assume σ equals 0.5 (if the government imposes severe restrictions to contain the epidemic) or 1 (if a liberal approach is adopted).

When we use the function $\kappa_t = \begin{cases} 1 & \text{for } \bar{I}_{Gt} < \iota \\ \theta & \text{for } \bar{I}_{Gt} \geq \iota \end{cases}$ to describe restrictions imposed by the government to contain the epidemic, we assume that the government adopts a lockdown when the geometric moving average of the percentage of the infected $\bar{I}_{Gt}$ exceeds $\iota = 0.5‰$ and then social and economic activity will be reduced by 15% (that is $\theta = 0.85$). If the government adopts a liberal approach to the epidemic, we assume $\iota = 1‰$ and $\theta = 0.95$.

When analyzing the models with vaccination, we assume that vaccines are administered as of day 300 of the pandemic. We also assume that a percentage $\rho = 48\%$ of the population wish to receive the vaccine and the effectiveness of vaccination ε equals 95%.

We make two alternative assumptions about the dynamics of daily immunization coverage in the population π_t:

- first, we assume that the parameters a and b in the indicator of immunization coverage are such that the indicator equals 1‰ on day 7 of vaccination and 2‰ on day 100. Hence, we obtain: $\dfrac{7a}{b+7} = 0.001$ and $\dfrac{100a}{b+100} = 0.002$ which gives (in line with the Cramer's rule): $a = \dfrac{93 \cdot 0.001 \cdot 0.002}{100 \cdot 0.001 - 7 \cdot 0.002} \approx 0.00216$ and $b = \dfrac{700 \cdot (0.002 - 0.001)}{100 \cdot 0.001 - 7 \cdot 0.002} \approx 8.140$. The scenarios are referred to below as scenarios with slow progress in immunization coverage of the population;

- second, we assume that $\pi_7 = 0.001$ and $\pi_{100} = 0.006$. In this case, the Cramer's formula produces: a≈0.00962 and b≈60.345. The scenarios are referred to below as scenarios with rapid progress in immunization coverage.

5.3.2 Parameters of the economic module

The elasticity α of Cobb-Douglas production function (5.5) is calibrated at the level of 0.5. We also assume a 20% savings-investment rate s and a 5% capital depreciation rate δ. The long-run capital output ratio K^*/Y^* at the values of those parameters set as above equals 4.

We assume the indicator of economic activity of the population $w = 46\%$, that is similar to the value recorded in the EU states.

The parameter ω in the function of demand for labor (5.7) is calibrated at the level of 0.44, and consequently the long-run unemployment rate equals about 4.35% at $w = 0.46$. The parameter ϕ is selected so that under non-epidemic conditions, in an economy with an initial capital input K_1 representing 40% of capital in the Solow long-run steady state (that is K^*), the unemployment rate equals 10%. Then, the elasticity of demand for labor L_t relative to production Y_t equals about 0.106.

5.4 Scenarios and numerical simulation results

The numerical simulations discussed below include 12 scenarios of epidemic development. The first four of those scenarios give the government no access to a vaccine, and a vaccine is available in the remaining eight scenarios (see the statement in Table 5.1).

In the scenarios wherein the government has no access to a vaccine (scenarios I–IV), we assume that the government reduces the intensity of social and economic activity gradually, in line with a functional formula (5.3) (scenarios I and II) or that activity is restricted abruptly (scenarios III and IV). In scenarios I and III, the government imposes severe restrictions to contain the spread of the epidemic; in scenarios II and IV, the government adopts a liberal approach.

The scenarios with vaccination (V–XII) can be divided into those with slow progress (scenarios V–VIII) and those with rapid progress (IX–XII) in immunization coverage of the population. Scenarios V and IX assume that the government adopts a lockdown like in scenario I; scenarios VI and X assume a lockdown as in scenario II, etc.

The results of numerical simulations of epidemiological indicators in the extended SIR model (systems of equations (5.1–5.2)) in consecutive scenarios are contained in Table 5.2. Figures 5.1–5.4 represent curves of analyzed epidemiological variables.[6]

---

6 All epidemiological simulations are carried out for a five-year period while macroeconomic simulations for a three-year period. This is because curves of macroeconomic variables stabilize after three years.

Table 5.1 Scenarios of epidemic development

Scenario	κ_t	Vaccine	Notes
I	$1-\sqrt{I_{t-1}}$	None	–
II	$1-I_{t-1}$		
III	$\kappa_t = \begin{cases} 1 & \text{for } \bar{I}_{Gt} < 0.0005 \\ 0.85 & \text{for } \bar{I}_{Gt} \geq 0.0005 \end{cases}$		
IV	$\kappa_t = \begin{cases} 1 & \text{for } \bar{I}_{Gt} < 0.001 \\ 0.95 & \text{for } \bar{I}_{Gt} \geq 0.001 \end{cases}$		
V	$1-\sqrt{I_{t-1}}$	First vaccinations on day 300 of the epidemic following the formula: $$\pi_t = \frac{0.00216t}{8.14+t}$$ where t is the consecutive day of vaccination	Slow progress in immunization coverage. About 17.2% of those wishing to receive the vaccine are immunized within 100 days
VI	$1-I_{t-1}$		
VII	$\kappa_t = \begin{cases} 1 & \text{for } \bar{I}_{Gt} < 0.0005 \\ 0.85 & \text{for } \bar{I}_{Gt} \geq 0.0005 \end{cases}$		
VIII	$\kappa_t = \begin{cases} 1 & \text{for } \bar{I}_{Gt} < 0.001 \\ 0.95 & \text{for } \bar{I}_{Gt} \geq 0.001 \end{cases}$		
IX	$1-\sqrt{I_{t-1}}$	First vaccinations on day 300 of the epidemic following the formula: $$\pi_t = \frac{0.00962t}{60.345+t}$$	Rapid progress in immunization coverage. About 39.8% of those wishing to receive the vaccine are immunized within 100 days
X	$1-I_{t-1}$		
XI	$\kappa_t = \begin{cases} 1 & \text{for } \bar{I}_{Gt} < 0.0005 \\ 0.85 & \text{for } \bar{I}_{Gt} \geq 0.0005 \end{cases}$		
XII	$\kappa_t = \begin{cases} 1 & \text{for } \bar{I}_{Gt} < 0.001 \\ 0.95 & \text{for } \bar{I}_{Gt} \geq 0.001 \end{cases}$		

Source: own assumptions.

100 Monika Bolińska et al.

Table 5.2 Epidemiological indicators in consecutive scenarios

Scenario	Variable						
	κ_m	S_m	I_M	H_M	D_M	P_M	T
I	0.8347	0.5762	0.0273	0.4153	0.0085	-	391
II	0.9475	0.4566	0.0525	0.5326	0.0109	-	365
III	0.85	0.6043	0.0246	0.3878	0.0079	-	456
IV	0.95	0.4728	0.0490	0.5167	0.0105	-	383
V	0.8380	0.1485	0.0263	0.3374	0.0069	0.5072	381
VI	0.9480	0.1122	0.0520	0.4927	0.0101	0.3850	363
VII	0.85	0.1650	0.0189	0.2650	0.0054	0.5646	428
VIII	0.95	0.1181	0.0473	0.4649	0.0095	0.4075	378
IX	0.8389	0.0014	0.0260	0.2885	0.0059	0.7042	377
X	0.9481	0.0010	0.0519	0.4632	0.0095	0.5264	363
XI	0.85	0.0016	0.0167	0.1939	0.0040	0.8006	408
XII	0.95	0.0011	0.0468	0.4259	0.0087	0.5643	376

The subscript *m* indicates the minimum value of a variable, *M* – its maximum value. *T* – day of the greatest percentage of the infected.
Source: own calculations.

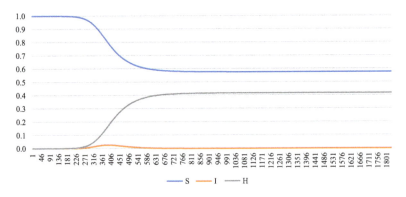

Figure 5.1a Curves of S, I, H and P in scenarios I, V and IX (at $\kappa_t = 1 - \sqrt{I_{t-1}}$) Scenario I. Source: own calculations.

The simulation results contained in Table 5.2 and Figures 5.1–5.4 lead to the following conclusions:

- if the government did not adopt any lockdown measures and had no access to a vaccine, the greatest percentage of the infected would be recorded (as already indicated) on day 365 of the epidemic. If the government has no access to a vaccine and imposes a severe lockdown, the peak will be postponed to day 391 (scenario I) or 456 (scenario II) of the epidemic. If a mild lockdown is imposed, the greatest number of the infected will be recorded on day 365 (scenario II) or 383 (scenario IV);

Modelling the impact of an epidemic 101

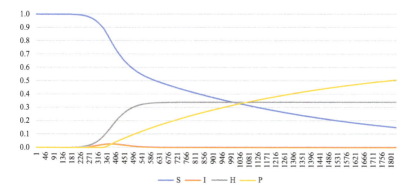

Figure 5.1b Curves of S, I, H and P in scenarios I, V and IX (at $\kappa_t = 1 - \sqrt{I_{t-1}}$) Scenario V. Source: own calculations.

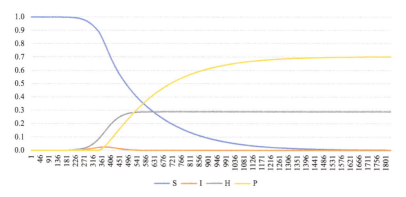

Figure 5.1c Curves of S, I, H and P in scenarios I, V and IX (at $\kappa_t = 1 - \sqrt{I_{t-1}}$) Scenario IX. Source: own calculations.

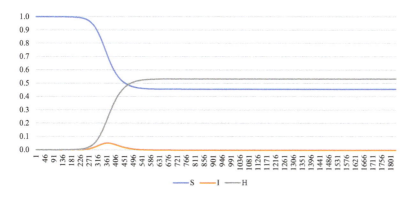

Figure 5.2a Curves of S, I, H and P in scenarios II, VI and X (at $\kappa_t = 1 - I_{t-1}$) Scenario II. Source: own calculations.

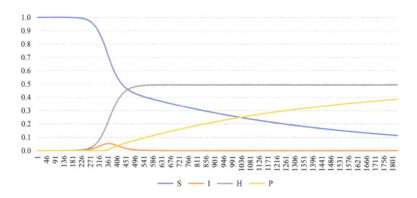

Figure 5.2b Curves of S, I, H and P in scenarios II, VI and X (at $\kappa_t = 1 - I_{t-1}$) Scenario VI. Source: own calculations.

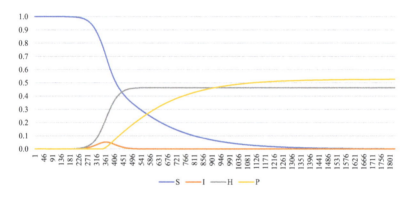

Figure 5.2c Curves of S, I, H and P in scenarios II, VI and X (at $\kappa_t = 1 - I_{t-1}$) Scenario X. Source: own calculations.

- at slow progress in immunization coverage of the population (scenarios V–VIII), the greatest number of the infected is recorded between days 381 and 428 of the epidemic (if severe restrictions are imposed in response to the epidemic) or between days 363 and 378 (if a liberal approach to the epidemic is adopted). On the other hand, rapid progress in immunization coverage results in a postponement of epidemic peak to a date between days 377 and 408 of the epidemic (if severe restrictions are imposed in response to the epidemic), or between days 363 and 376 (if a liberal approach to the epidemic is adopted);
- in the scenarios wherein the government has no access to a vaccine, a maximum limitation of social and economic activity (at the peak of the epidemic) can reach 15–16.5% under conditions of a severe lockdown or 5–6.5% under conditions of a mild lockdown. The scenarios wherein

Modelling the impact of an epidemic 103

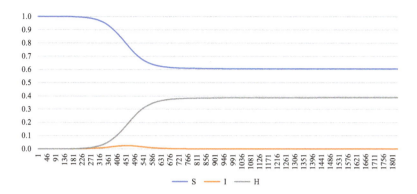

Figure 5.3a Curves of S, I, H and P in scenarios III, VII and XI, at $\kappa_t = \begin{cases} 1 \, dla \, \overline{I}_{Gt} < 0.0005 \\ 0.85 \, dla \, \overline{I}_{Gt} \geq 0.0005 \end{cases}$ Scenario III. Source: own calculations.

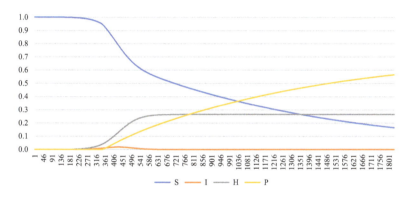

Figure 5.3b Curves of S, I, H and P in scenarios III, VII and XI, at $\kappa_t = \begin{cases} 1 \, dla \, \overline{I}_{Gt} < 0.0005 \\ 0.85 \, dla \, \overline{I}_{Gt} \geq 0.0005 \end{cases}$ Scenario VII. Source: own calculations.

the government uses vaccination (i.e. scenarios V–XII) have no significant effect on that parameter;
- if no vaccine is administered, the maximum percentage of infected people will reach 2.5–2.7% (severe restrictions in scenarios I and III) or 4.9–5.3% (liberal scenarios II and IV). In the case of slow progress in immunization coverage, that percentage will drop to about 1.9–2.6% under conditions of a severe lockdown or to 4.7–5.2% if a liberal approach is adopted. In the case of rapid progress in immunization coverage, that percentage will slightly fall;

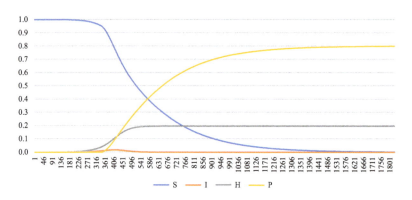

Figure 5.3c Curves of *S*, *I*, *H* and *P* in scenarios III, VII and XI, at $\kappa_t = \begin{cases} 1\,dla\,\overline{I}_{Gt} < 0.0005 \\ 0.85\,dla\,\overline{I}_{Gt} \geq 0.0005 \end{cases}$ Scenario XI. Source: own calculations.

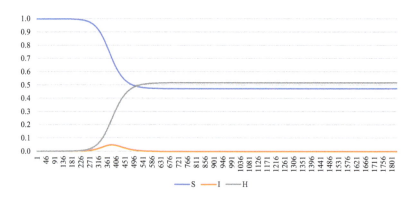

Figure 5.4a Curves of *S*, *I*, *H* and *P* in scenarios IV, VIII and XII, at $\kappa_t = \begin{cases} 1\,dla\,\overline{I}_{Gt} < 0.001 \\ 0.95\,dla\,\overline{I}_{Gt} \geq 0.001 \end{cases}$ Scenario IV. Source: own calculations.

- in the scenarios without vaccination, the percentage of the susceptible (uninfected) will reach after the epidemic about 57.6–60.4% under conditions of a severe lockdown or 45.7–47.3% under conditions of a mild lockdown;
- if the government has access to a vaccine but progress in immunization coverage is slow, the percentage of uninfected population (understood then as $S_m + P_M$) will reach 65.6–73.0% under conditions of a severe lockdown or 49.7–52.6% if a liberal approach is adopted;
- rapid progress in immunization coverage leads to an increase in those indicators to 70.6–80.2% (a severe lockdown) or 52.7–56.5% (a mild lockdown);

Modelling the impact of an epidemic 105

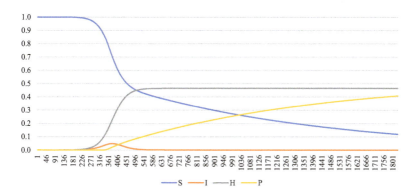

Figure 5.4b Curves of *S*, *I*, *H* and *P* in scenarios IV, VIII and XII, at $\kappa_t = \begin{cases} 1 \, dla \, \bar{I}_{Gt} < 0.001 \\ 0.95 \, dla \, \bar{I}_{Gt} \geq 0.001 \end{cases}$ Scenario VIII. Source: own calculations.

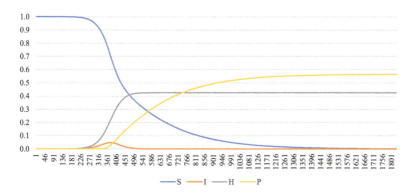

Figure 5.4c Curves of *S*, *I*, *H* and *P* in scenarios IV, VIII and XII, at $\kappa_t = \begin{cases} 1 \, dla \, \bar{I}_{Gt} < 0.001 \\ 0.95 \, dla \, \bar{I}_{Gt} \geq 0.001 \end{cases}$ Scenario XII. Source: own calculations.

- if no vaccine is administered, 7.9–8.5‰ of the population will die of the epidemic under conditions of a severe lockdown imposed by the government or 10.5–10.9‰ under conditions of a mild lockdown. Slow progress in immunization coverage will reduce those indicators to 5.4–6.9‰ (a severe lockdown) or 9.5–10.1‰ (a liberal approach). Rapid progress in immunization coverage will reduce the rate of mortality caused by the epidemic to 4.0–5.9‰ of the population (a severe lockdown) or 8.7–9.5‰ (a mild lockdown).

An analysis of the epidemic effect on the values of principal macroeconomic indicators (in the real economy sector) includes the scenarios described

106 *Monika Bolińska et al.*

above in two versions. We consider values of those indicators in an economy conventionally termed "poorly developed" (with capital input K_1 representing 40% of the value of that variable in the Solow long-run steady state) and in a strongly developed economy (with $K_1 = 0.9K^*$)7.

Selected results of numerical simulations are contained in Tables 5.3 (a poorly developed economy) and 5.4 (a strongly developed economy). Figures 5.5–5.7 depict curves of the social utility function U_t in consecutive scenarios both in a poorly developed and in a strongly developed economy.

The simulation results contained in Tables 5.3–5.4 lead to the following conclusions:

- in a poorly developed economy that has no access to a vaccine, falls in production at peak incidence (measured by the indicator $\min_t \left\{ \dfrac{Y_t}{Y_{Nt}} \right\}$, where Y_{Nt} represents the value of production that could be achieved if the epidemic did not strike) will reach 18.6–19.9% under conditions of a severe lockdown or 10.7–10.9% if a liberal approach is adopted. In a strongly developed economy, the falls are slightly smaller and reach (respectively) 18.3–19.7% or 10.4–10.6%;
- slow progress in immunization coverage of the population combined with severe restrictions imposed in response to the epidemic will reduce falls in production to 17.9–19.5% in a poor economy or 17.7–19.3% in a wealthy economy. If a liberal approach to the epidemic is adopted, falls in production will reach (respectively) 10.5–10.6% or 10.2–10.3%;
- rapid progress in immunization coverage has no material effect on falls in production at peak incidence;
- if severe restrictions are imposed in response to the epidemic, without vaccination, accumulated falls in the value of production will reach over 3 years about 6.8–9.8% in a poorly developed economy or 6.7–9.6% in a strongly developed economy. If a liberal approach to the epidemic is adopted, the falls will reach 2.3–3.5% in a poor economy and 2.2–3.3% in a wealthy economy;
- slow progress in immunization coverage of the population combined with severe restrictions imposed in response to the epidemic will lead to accumulated falls in production by 5.5–8.1% in a poorly developed economy or by 5.4–7.9% in a strongly developed economy. A liberal approach to the epidemic will lead to accumulated falls in production by 2.1–3.2% in a poor economy or 2.0–3.1% in a wealthy economy;
- a rapid pace of progress in immunization coverage of the population will reduce falls in production in a poor economy to 4.7–6.6% (severe

---

7 Those economies are also termed below "poor" and "wealthy".

Table 5.3 Economic indicators in consecutive scenarios at $K_1/K^*=0.4$ (a poorly developed economy)

Scenario	$\min_t\left\{\dfrac{Y_t}{Y_{Nt}}\right\}$	$\dfrac{\sum_t Y_t}{\sum_t Y_{Nt}}$	$\min_t\left\{\dfrac{K_t}{K_{Nt}}\right\}$	$\dfrac{\sum_t K_t}{\sum_t K_{Nt}}$	$\max_t\left\{\dfrac{u_t}{u_{Nt}}\right\}$	$\dfrac{\bar{u}_G}{\bar{u}_{GN}}$	$\min_t U_t$	$\bar{U}_G$
	from monthly data						from daily data	
I	0.801	0.932	0.987	0.993	1.212	1.068	0.855	0.951
II	0.891	0.977	0.996	0.998	1.112	1.023	0.901	0.974
III	0.814	0.902	0.982	0.990	1.197	1.100	0.866	0.936
IV	0.893	0.965	0.994	0.996	1.109	1.034	0.903	0.969
V	0.805	0.945	0.990	0.994	1.208	1.055	0.858	0.961
VI	0.894	0.979	0.996	0.998	1.108	1.021	0.902	0.978
VII	0.821	0.919	0.985	0.991	1.190	1.082	0.869	0.947
VIII	0.895	0.968	0.994	0.996	1.107	1.031	0.905	0.973
IX	0.806	0.953	0.991	0.994	1.206	1.046	0.859	0.967
X	0.895	0.980	0.996	0.998	1.107	1.020	0.902	0.981
XI	0.824	0.934	0.988	0.992	1.186	1.066	0.870	0.956
XII	0.896	0.971	0.995	0.997	1.106	1.029	0.905	0.976

The subscript N indicates non-epidemic conditions, G – geometric average.
Source: own calculations.

Table 5.4 Economic indicators in consecutive scenarios at $K_1/K^* = 0.9$ (a strongly developed economy)

Scenario	$\min_t \left\{ \dfrac{Y_t}{Y_{Nt}} \right\}$	$\dfrac{\sum_t Y_t}{\sum_t Y_{Nt}}$	$\min_t \left\{ \dfrac{K_t}{K_{Nt}} \right\}$	$\dfrac{\sum_t K_t}{\sum_t K_{Nt}}$	$\max_t \left\{ \dfrac{u_t}{u_{Nt}} \right\}$	$\dfrac{\bar{u}_G}{\bar{u}_{GN}}$	$\min_t U_t$	$\bar{U}_G$
	from monthly data						from daily data	
I	0.803	0.933	0.990	0.995	1.436	1.135	0.819	0.938
II	0.894	0.978	0.997	0.998	1.225	1.044	0.865	0.960
III	0.817	0.904	0.986	0.992	1.404	1.198	0.831	0.922
IV	0.896	0.967	0.995	0.997	1.219	1.067	0.866	0.954
V	0.807	0.946	0.992	0.995	1.428	1.108	0.823	0.950
VI	0.897	0.980	0.997	0.998	1.218	1.041	0.866	0.967
VII	0.823	0.921	0.989	0.993	1.389	1.160	0.834	0.936
VIII	0.898	0.969	0.996	0.997	1.215	1.061	0.868	0.962
IX	0.808	0.954	0.994	0.996	1.425	1.091	0.824	0.957
X	0.898	0.981	0.997	0.998	1.215	1.038	0.867	0.971
XI	0.826	0.935	0.991	0.994	1.382	1.129	0.835	0.947
XII	0.899	0.972	0.996	0.998	1.213	1.056	0.869	0.966

The subscript N indicates non-epidemic conditions, G – geometric average.
Source: own calculations.

Modelling the impact of an epidemic 109

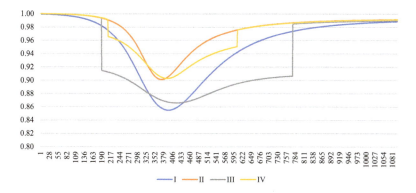

Figure 5.5a Curves representing social utility in scenarios I–IV. A poorly developed economy. Source: own calculations.

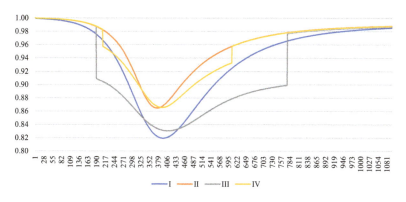

Figure 5.5b Curves representing social utility in scenarios I–IV. A strongly developed economy. Source: own calculations.

restrictions imposed) or 2.0–2.9% (a liberal approach), and in a wealthy economy to 4.6–6.5% or 1.9–2.8%;
- a more general conclusion can be reached: the introduction and rapid administration of a vaccine will have a stronger effect on accumulated falls in production than on the depth of the recession. In addition, both accumulated falls in production and the depth of recession will be slightly greater in a poorly developed economy than in a strongly developed economy;
- both one-off (at the epidemic peak) and accumulated falls in capital stock are significantly smaller than falls in production. Whether the government has access to a vaccine or not, whether severe restrictions are imposed or a liberal approach to the epidemic is adopted, accumulated falls in capital stock in both analyzed types of economy, that is $\dfrac{\sum_t K_t}{\sum_t K_{Nt}}$, will not exceed 1%;

110 *Monika Bolińska et al.*

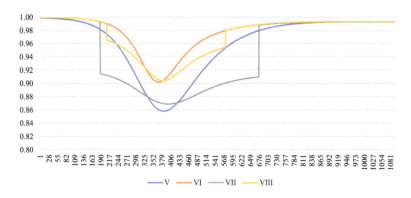

Figure 5.6a Curves representing social utility in scenarios V–VIII. A poorly developed economy. Source: own calculations.

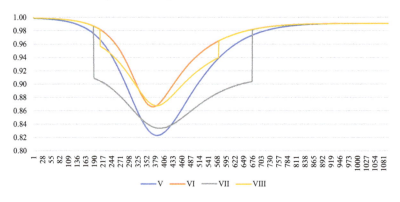

Figure 5.6b Curves representing social utility in scenarios V–VIII. A strongly developed economy. Source: own calculations.

- relative increases in the unemployment rate (understood as $\max_{t}\left\{\frac{u_t}{u_{Nt}}\right\}$) at peak incidence in a poor economy without vaccination will reach about 20% if severe restrictions are imposed in response to the epidemic, or about 10–11% if a liberal approach is adopted. In a wealthy economy the indicators will reach 40–44% or 22–23%;[8]

---

8 The parameters of the macroeconomic module of the proposed model are calibrated so that the initial unemployment rate in a poorly developed economy amounts to about 5%, and in a strongly developed economy to about 10%. Hence, the value of indicator $\max_{t}\left\{\frac{u_t}{u_{Nt}}\right\}$ amounting e.g. to 1.1 means that the unemployment rate rises from 5% to 5.5% in a wealthy

Modelling the impact of an epidemic 111

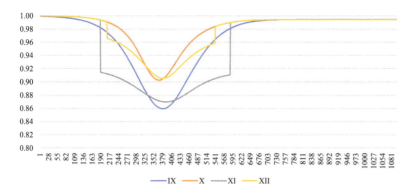

Figure 5.7a Curves representing social utility in scenarios IX–XII. A poorly developed economy. Source: own calculations.

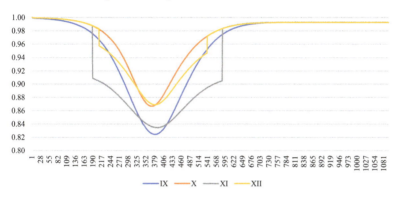

Figure 5.7b Curves representing social utility in scenarios IX–XII. A strongly developed economy. Source: own calculations.

- the indicators only slightly fall with slow or rapid progress in immunization coverage;
- the average unemployment rates over a three-year period (and more precisely the products $\dfrac{\bar{u}_G}{\bar{u}_{GN}}$) will be higher in the scenarios of severe restrictions imposed by the government in response to the epidemic and will decrease with an increase in the pace of immunization coverage of the population. Those products will also be higher in a wealthy economy. However, it must be emphasized that the geometric average of

---

economy or from 10% to 11% in a poor economy. The indicator $\dfrac{\bar{u}_G}{\bar{u}_{GN}}$ is to be similarly interpreted.

112 *Monika Bolińska et al.*

the unemployment rate $\bar{u}_{GN}$ is significantly lower in a wealthy economy than in a poor economy due to the model design;
- Figures 5.5–5.7 (depicting curves of the social utility function in consecutive scenarios in a poor and in a wealthy economy) lead to the following conclusions. First, falls in social utility U in both types of economy, in scenarios of severe restrictions imposed in response to the epidemic (the scenarios marked with odd Roman numerals) are significantly greater than in scenarios of a liberal approach (the scenarios marked with even numbers). Second, the sooner a vaccine is administered, the smaller are falls in social utility. Third, falls in social utility are slightly smaller in a poor economy, because expressions $\dfrac{u_{Nt}}{u_t} \dfrac{Y_t}{Y_{Nt}}$ are higher in that type of economy.

5.5 Conclusions

Chapter 5 discusses the effect of an epidemic on economic growth. The analysis is conducted using a model of economic growth under epidemic conditions. The epidemiological module introduces an indicator that shows restrictions imposed on social and economic life during the epidemic. The indicator is defined in two versions; in the first version, it changes continually on consecutive days of the epidemic as a function of the percentage of infections, and in the second version, it changes discretely when the government abruptly imposes a lockdown. The epidemiological section also includes a scenario wherein a vaccine (against the spreading disease) is available to the government and a population vaccination programme is implemented. In the section of the model discussion that is dedicated to the economy, it is assumed that the production process is described by a neoclassical Cobb-Douglas production function; accumulation of fixed capital, like in the original Solow model of 1956, is defined as the difference between investment and the depreciated value of that capital. Also, a social utility function is introduced, defined as a geometrical average of the indicator of social and economic activity, the percentage of the uninfected, the ratio of unemployment rate under non-epidemic conditions to that rate under epidemic conditions and the ratio of production during the epidemic to production under non-epidemic conditions.

The chapter also discusses scenarios of epidemic development depending on the availability of a vaccine to the government. In the scenarios wherein the government has no access to a vaccine, it was assumed that the government imposes restrictions on social and economic activity following certain functional relations or abruptly. The scenarios with vaccination are divided into those with slow and those with rapid progress in immunization coverage of the population. Those scenarios also include a lockdown imposed by the government, like in the scenarios without vaccination.

Falls in production in an economy without access to a vaccine reach, at peak incidence, 18.3% to 19.9% if severe restrictions are imposed in response to the epidemic, or 10.4% to 10.9% if a liberal approach is adopted. Slow progress in immunization coverage of the population combined with severe restrictions imposed in response to the epidemic will reduce falls in production by 17.7% to 19.5%. If a liberal approach to the epidemic is adopted, falls in production will reach (respectively) 10.2–10.6%. Additionally, rapid progress in immunization coverage has no material effect on falls in production at peak incidence.

If the government imposes severe restrictions in response to the pandemic and has no access to a vaccine, accumulated falls in the value of production will reach, over three years, about 6.7–9.8%, and if a liberal approach to the epidemic is adopted, the falls will reach 2.2–3.5%. Slow progress in immunization coverage of the population combined with severe restrictions imposed in response to the pandemic will lead to accumulated falls in production of 5.4–8.1% while a liberal approach to the pandemic will lead to accumulated falls in production of 2.0–3.2%. A rapid pace of progress in immunization coverage of the population reduces accumulated drops in production to about 4.6–6.6%, if severe restrictions are imposed, or to 1.9–2.9%. Consequently, the introduction of vaccination and rapid progress in immunization coverage will have a stronger effect on accumulated falls in production than on the depth of recession. Additionally, whether the government has access to a vaccine or not, falls in the capital stock will be significantly smaller than falls in production and will not exceed 1%.

Relative increases in the unemployment rate at peak incidence in a poor economy without vaccination will reach about 20–44% if severe restrictions are imposed in response to the epidemic, or about 10–23% if a liberal approach is adopted. The introduction and acceleration of vaccination entails a minor reduction in relative rises in the unemployment rate at peak incidence. Additionally, average unemployment rates over a three-year period will be higher in the scenarios of severe restrictions imposed by the government in response to the epidemic and will decrease with an increase in the pace of immunization coverage of the population.

Falls in social utility will be significantly greater in scenarios of severe restrictions imposed in response to the epidemic than in scenarios of a liberal approach. Implementation of a vaccination programme will result in a reduced depth of fall in social utility, and the faster is progress in immunization coverage of the population, the relatively smaller are falls in social utility.

References

Alvarez, F., Argente, D., Lippi, F. (2020). *A simple planning problem for COVID-19 lockdown*. NBER Working Paper, No. 26981. http://www.nber.org/papers/w26981 (accessed February 16, 2021).

Atkeson, A. (2020). *What will be the economic impact of COVID-19 in the US? Rough estimates of disease scenarios*. NBER Working Paper, No. 26867. http://www.nber.org/papers/w26867 (accessed February 16, 2021).

Aum, S., Lee, S., Shin, Y. (2020). *Inequality of fear and self-quarantine: Is there a trade-off between GDP and public health?* NBER Working Paper, No. 27100. http://www.nber.org/papers/w27100 (accessed February 16, 2021).

Bärwolff, G. (2020). Mathematical modeling and simulation of the COVID-19 pandemic. *Systems*, 8(3), 1–12. https://doi.org/10.3390/systems8030024 (accessed February 16, 2021).

Bloom, D., Lyons, J. (Eds.) (1993). *Economic implications of AIDS in Asia*, United Nations Development Programme, New York.

Bloom, D., Mahal, A. (1995). *Does the AIDS epidemic really threaten economic growth?* National Bureau of Economic Research working paper No. 5148, NBER, Cambridge, MA. https://doi.org/10.1016/S0304-4076(96)01808-8 (accessed February 16, 2021).

Bloom, D., Mahal, A. (1997). Does the AIDS epidemic really threaten economic growth? *Journal of Econometrics*, 77(1), 105–124.

Brock, W., Xepapadeas, A. (2020). The economy, climate change and infectious diseases: Links and policy implications. *Environmental and Resource Economics*, 76, 811–824. https://doi.org/10.1007/s10640-020-00442-z (accessed February 16, 2021).

Cuddington, J. (1993). Modeling the macroeconomic effects of AIDS, with an application to Tanzania. *The World Bank Economic Review*, 7, 173–789.

Cuddington, J., Hancock, J. (1994). Assessing the impact of aids on the growth path of the Malawian economy. *Journal of Development Economics*, 43(2), 363–368.

Cuesta, J. (2010). How much of a threat to economic growth is a mature AIDS epidemic? *Applied Economics*, 42(24), 3077–3089.

Delfino, D., Simmons, P. (2005). Dynamics of tuberculosis and economic growth. *Environment and Development Economics*, 10(6), 719–743. https://doi.org/10.1017/S1355770X05002500 (accessed February 16, 2021).

Fei-Ying, Y., Wan-Tong, L., Zhi-Cheng, W. (2015). Traveling waves in a nonlocal dispersal SIR epidemic model. *Nonlinear Analysis: Real World Applications*, 23, 129–147.

Jardón-Kojakhmetov, H., Kuehn, Ch., Pugliese, A., Sensi, M. (2021). A geometric analysis of the SIR, SIRS and SIRWS epidemiological models. *Nonlinear Analysis: Real World Applications*, 58, 103220.

Kambou, G., Devarajan, S., Over, M. (1992). The economic impact of AIDS in an African country: Simulations with a computable general equilibrium model of Cameroon. *Journal of African Economies*, 1, 109–130.

Kermack, W. O., McKendrick, A. G. (1927). A contribution to the mathematical theory of epidemics. *Royal Society*, 115(772), 700–721.

Lik Ng, W. (2020). To lockdown? When to peak? Will there be an end? A macroeconomic analysis on COVID-19 epidemic in the United States. *Journal of Macroeconomics*, 65, 103230.

Lovasz, E., Schipp, B. (2009). The impact of HIV/AIDS on economic growth in Sub-Saharan Africa. *South African Journal of Economics*, 77(2), 245–256.

Mankiw, N. G., Romer, D., Weil, D. N. (1992). A contribution to the empirics of economic growth. *Quarterly Journal of Economics*, 107(2), 407–437.

Murray, J. D. (2003). Mathematical biology, II, spatial models and biomedical applications, in *Interdisciplinary applied mathematics*, 3rd ed., vol. 18, Springer-Verlag, New York.

Ruan, S. (2007). Spatial–temporal dynamics in nonlocal epidemiological models, in Y. Takeuchi, K. Sato, Y. Iwasa (Eds.), *Mathematics for life science and medicine*, Springer-Verlag, Berlin, pp. 99–122.

Solow, R. M. (1956). A contribution to the theory of economic growth, *Quarterly Journal of Economics*, 70(1), 65–94.

Xiao, D., Ruan, S. (2007). Global analysis of an epidemic model with nonmonotone incidence rate, *Mathematical Biosciences*, 208, 419–429.

6 Simulations of the pandemic propagation patterns on the example of Poland and Ukraine

Paweł Dykas, Katarzyna Filipowicz, Olesia Chornenka, Oleksij Kelebaj, and Tomasz Tokarski

6.1 Introduction

The COVID-19 pandemic in Poland, as well as in Ukraine, started in March 2020. The first measures to limit the spread of the SARS-CoV-2 virus were implemented as early as the beginning of 2020. In Poland, preventive measures were introduced well before the first case of the SARS infection was registered (4 March 2020, in Zielona Góra) and the first person died because of it (14 March 2020). As early as 25 January 2020, Warsaw Chopin Airport introduced special security procedures for passengers arriving from China (Lotnisko Chopina w Warszawie, 2020). On 31 January 2020, the National Institute of Hygiene in Poland began laboratory testing of people with suspected SARS infection (Medonet, 2020). In Ukraine, on the other hand, the National Security and Defence Council at its meeting on 25 February 2020 decided to introduce temperature screening for all persons entering the territory of Ukraine (Ukrinform, 2020), and the public was informed about the risks and health hazards related to this virus infection and the recommended precautions.

In Ukraine, the first person infected with SARS-CoV-2 was registered on 3 March 2020, in the Chernivtsi region of western Ukraine, and the first death caused by the virus was registered on 13 March 2020 (Indexminfin, 2021). Following the KMU Decree,[1] the so-called lockdown (defined as a national quarantine) was introduced in Ukraine on 12 March 2020. The decree provided for the introduction of a quarantine in the entire territory of Ukraine from 12 March to 3 April 2020 involving mainly a number of restrictions including, among others, the closure of all educational institutions and a ban on all mass gatherings for more than 200 people[2] (KMU, 2020a).

---

1 KMU Decree no 211 of 11 March 2020.
2 With the exception of the meetings necessary to ensure the work of public authorities and local governments.

DOI: 10.4324/9781003211891-6

The situation was very similar in Poland, where the epidemiological status[3] was introduced 16 days after the first infection (Serwis Rzeczypospolitej Polskiej, 2020a). In Poland, the following measures were introduced: an obligatory 14-day quarantine for persons entering the territory of Poland,[4] a ban on the circulation of certain protective goods, restrictions on the functioning of certain educational and cultural institutions and workplaces, and a ban on gatherings for more than 50 people. As of 25 March 2020, when the total number of infected people fluctuated around 1,050, further restrictions were introduced (Serwis Rzeczypospolitej Polskiej, 2021). Despite these restrictions, the number of infections continued to rise dramatically, with 2,311 infections and 33 deaths recorded in Poland at the end of March, so the government introduced further restrictions as of 1 April 2020 under which, among others, persons under 18 were not allowed in public spaces without an adult guardian, parks, forests and beaches were closed to visitors and the activity of hairdressing and beauty salons was suspended. In shops and service outlets, there were restrictions on the number of customers served at the same time.

As part of Ukraine's national quarantine, border checkpoints were partially closed (only 49 out of 219 remained open), while educational and cultural institutions were forced to operate online. As of 16 March 2020 (when there were seven infected individuals in Ukraine), a ban on foreigners entering the territory of Ukraine was introduced. On the following day, international air, bus and rail traffic was suspended. Similar restrictions were applied on 18 March within Ukrainian regions and cities, preventing people without their own transport from travelling outside their places of residence. Due to the increasing rate of infections in Ukraine (on 1 April, the total number of infections in Ukraine amounted to 794 and 20 people died), on 2 April the Ukrainian government adopted another decree,[5] which extended the national quarantine until 24 April 2020 and introduced even more restrictions for Ukrainian citizens (e.g. the restriction of movement in groups of more than two persons, obligatory covering of the mouth and nose in public places, a ban on visiting parks and forests, the suspension of the activity of catering and sports facilities). Just like in Poland, administrative and criminal liability for non-compliance with quarantine rules was introduced (VRU, 2020).

After four weeks of quarantine in Poland, the total number of infected persons was 9,593 and 380 persons died due to SARS-CoV-2 infection. At this time, the lockdown easing started as part of stage one out of four stages of restriction relaxation. The number of customers in shops was increased while parks and forests were opened. The next stage involved the opening

---

3 Pursuant to the Resolution of the Health Minister of 20 March 2020.
4 With the exception of some categories of people.
5 Decree no 255 of 2 April 2020.

of shops with construction materials on weekends as well as hotels and cultural institutions. In the third stage, hairdressing and beauty salons, catering facilities and shops in shopping malls were opened.[6] Sporting events could be attended by no more than 50 people,[7] and nurseries and kindergartens, as well as schools for children from classes 1–3, were opened. The final stage of the quarantine abolition involved the opening of sports and recreational facilities, as well as theatres and cinemas (Serwis Rzeczypospolitej Polskiej, 2020b).

In April, the Health Ministry of Ukraine announced its intention to lift some of the restrictions. Just like in Poland, the process was extended over several stages. At the beginning of May 2020, when the total number of infected persons was around 15 thousand, the Ukrainian government introduced the first stage of the national quarantine relaxation, which resulted in parks and forests being opened and non-food shops, dental and cosmetology surgeries resuming their economic activity (Glavcom, 2020). On 22 May 2020, when the total number of infections was 20,148, people could resume using public transport (KMU, 2020b). Further steps in the quarantine abolition in Ukraine involved the opening of cultural and sports institutions in June 2020, and on 15 June 2020 international air traffic was partially restored (Unian, 2020).

The total number of infected persons in Poland at the end of May 2020 fluctuated around 24,000 (more than 1,000 deaths were also registered), and as early as the end of August the number had almost tripled and amounted to 67,372 persons (and 2,039 deaths). Although in the first two months of the summer season the situation in Poland relatively normalized and the daily number of newly infected persons fluctuated around 350, by August this number had almost doubled. In September, the rate of infections increased even more and at the end of the month the number of new infections was over 1,300 per day.

The situation was similar in Ukraine, with an average of 700 newly infected persons per day (and 15 deaths per day) in June and 800 persons per day (and 17 deaths per day) in July. In August, however, the number of infected persons began to increase dramatically and by the end of the month already exceeded 2,000 persons per day, which is why the Ukrainian government decided to introduce another restriction, i.e. a ban on entry for foreigners from 28 August 2020 to 28 September 2020 (MSZU, 2020).

In autumn, both Poland and Ukraine reported increasing infection rates. In October 2020, the number of newly infected persons in Poland fluctuated around 8,500 persons and in Ukraine the number was 6,000. The number of deaths per day, in both countries, averaged around 100, so by the end of October the total number of infections in Ukraine was 387,481 and there

---

6 With sanitary restrictions.
7 Without the participation of the audience and in open space.

had been 7,196 deaths, while in Poland these numbers were (respectively) 362,731 and 5,631.

Due to the dramatically rapid increase in the number of infections,[8] the governments of both countries were forced to introduce further restrictions. In Ukraine it was done in November 2020 when the Ukrainian government introduced the so-called weekend quarantine from 13 November to 30 November 2020 (KMU, 2020c). The restrictions primarily involved a ban on services provided by cultural institutions, sports and catering facilities during the weekend. However, as the Ukrainian government later admitted, the weekend quarantine did not have the desired effect and by the end of November 2020, the total number of infected persons was 732,625.

In Poland, the aforementioned restrictions took effect as of 24 October 2020. Restrictions on movement and the operation of schools (including universities) were reintroduced, the business activity of sports venues and catering facilities was suspended (allowing only takeaway options) and the number of customers in shops was limited (Portal miasta Gdańsk, 2020).

At the end of the period analyzed in this chapter, i.e. on 3 December 2020, the total number of infected persons was 772,760 and 12,960 people had died in Ukraine, while for Poland these numbers were, respectively, 1,028,610 and 18,828. Due to the rapid rate of SARS-CoV-2 propagation and the high risk of health system collapse, in early December the governments of both countries announced the possibility of introducing another lockdown during the holiday season. According to the announcement of December 2020, it was to last until the end of January 2021.

6.2 The epidemiological model and calibrations of its parameters

The empirical analyses of the epidemiological situation in Poland and Ukraine in Chapter 6 are based on the extended SIR (Susceptible–Infected–Removed) model of Kernack, McKendrick (1927), which was presented in Chapter 5. This model is based on the conjunction of the following increments:

$$\begin{cases} \Delta S_t = -\beta \kappa_t S_{t-1} I_{t-1} - \delta_t \varepsilon \rho \pi S_{t-21} & (6.1) \\ \Delta I_t = \beta \kappa_t S_{t-1} I_{t-1} - \gamma I_{t-1} & (6.2) \\ \Delta H_t = \gamma h I_{t-1} & (6.3) \\ \Delta D_t = \gamma (1-h) I_{t-1} & (6.4) \\ \Delta P_t = \delta_t \varepsilon \rho \pi S_{t-21} & (6.5) \end{cases}$$

---

[8] In late October, the number of cases per day exceeded 20,000 people in Poland and 8,000 in Ukraine.

where:

S_t – percentage of uninfected individuals,
I_t – percentage of infected individuals,
H_t – percentage of convalescent individuals,
D_t – percentage of deaths,
P_t – percentage of the vaccinated population.

Parameter β describing the rate of the epidemic spread was chosen numerically, so that the proportion of the population determined by the model on day 275 of the epidemic was equal to the empirical value of this proportion on 3 December 2020. As a result of numerical analyses, the value of β for Poland was adopted at the level of 0.1015 and for Ukraine at 0.1053. Just like in Chapter 5, it is assumed that the average duration of an infection caused by SARS-CoV-2 is 14 days, hence the value of parameter γ obtained is 0.071429. In numerical analyses, it is assumed that the average percentage of convalescent persons h is 0.985, which means that the mortality rate of infected persons is at the level of 1.5%. In further deliberations, it is also assumed that on the first day of the epidemic the proportion of infected persons was one per one million inhabitants.

This model introduces the indicator describing the degree of socioeconomic activity. This kind of approach can be found in the works of Bärwolff (2020) or Atkeson (2020), among others. In this chapter, it is assumed that the socioeconomic activity index κ_t in both countries is achieved by means of the following relationship:

$$\kappa_t = \theta \cdot \eta_t, \tag{6.6}$$

where variable η_t is a dichotomous variable taking the value of 1 when restrictions are introduced on a given day and 0 when there are no socioeconomic life restrictions on a given day. In Poland, the value of parameter θ was assumed at the level of 0.804; in Ukraine it was 0.792. Just like in the case of parameter β, the values of parameter θ were chosen in such a way that the proportion of infected individuals resulting from the model coincided with the empirical proportion.

In the model described by equations (6.1–6.5), dichotomous variable δ_t takes the value of 1 when a vaccination programme was introduced on a given day and 0 when there were no vaccinations. In further analyses, it is assumed that in Poland vaccination starts on 28 December 2020, i.e. on day 300 of the pandemic, and in Ukraine on day 335 of the pandemic. It is also assumed that in Poland 50% of the population declares the willingness to be vaccinated ($\rho = 0.5$), while for Ukraine this indicator is 60% ($\rho = 0.6$), but in the scenario analysis it is assumed that the values of this parameter in both countries deviate by ±50% from the adopted values. Furthermore, in further considerations it is assumed that vaccine efficacy ε is 95% and daily vaccination rate π for those declaring their willingness to be vaccinated equals 2‰ in both countries.

6.3 Results of numerical simulations

Numerical simulations were conducted in four scenarios. Scenario one, called the baseline scenario, assumes that the epidemic spreads naturally, without any state intervention. In subsequent scenarios, it is assumed that the state introduces restrictions on socioeconomic life. In scenario A, it is assumed that restrictions are maintained until the proportion of infected individuals falls below half of the empirical proportion on day 275 of the epidemic. Scenario B assumes that the lockdown restrictions are gradually lifted starting from day 321 after the outbreak; furthermore, the rate of restriction easing in this scenario is 5% per week. In scenario C, all restrictions will be lifted on day 321 of the epidemic. Each scenario includes four variant options. In variant 1 there is no vaccination, while the subsequent variant options include a vaccination programme. In variants 2–4, it is assumed that in the case of Poland 50%, 75% and 25% of the population declare their willingness to be vaccinated (respectively). In the case of Ukraine, the proportions are 60%, 90% and 30%.

6.3.1 Results of numerical simulations for Poland

The baseline scenario assumes that the pandemic spreads freely, without any government intervention. This scenario will serve as a reference for the other scenarios. In the hypothetical situation considered, the peak of the epidemic would occur on day 311 since its beginning (i.e. about 8 January 2021[9]) with the maximum proportion of infected individuals at the level of 4.94%. The cumulative death rate would be 7.9‰, i.e. about 303,000 people[10] would die in Poland. The epidemic in Poland would end 968 days after its outbreak and convalescent individuals would make 52.12% of the population (cf. Figure 6.1).

In scenario A, it is assumed that socioeconomic life restrictions will be maintained until the proportion of infections falls below 4.73‰ (i.e. half of the empirical percentage on day 275 of the epidemic). In option A_1 (without a vaccine), the lockdown would end on day 544 of the epidemic, i.e. on 29 August 2021. The maximum proportion of infections would be recorded on day 363 of the epidemic and it would be equal to 1.24% (i.e. 3.7 percentage points lower than in the baseline scenario). After the lifting of restrictions, the proportion of infections would rise again slightly to the level of 7.21‰ on day 672 of the epidemic, decreasing in the following months (on day 1,500 of the epidemic the number of infected people in Poland would be

---

9 It is assumed that the first day of the epidemic is the day of the first confirmed case of the virus infection, i.e. 4 March 2020 in Poland.
10 Calculated on the basis of the data provided by the Chief Statistical Office (GUS). According to GUS, Poland's population in September 2020 was 38,351,000 people: https://stat.gov.pl/podstawowe-dane/.

122 *Paweł Dykas et al.*

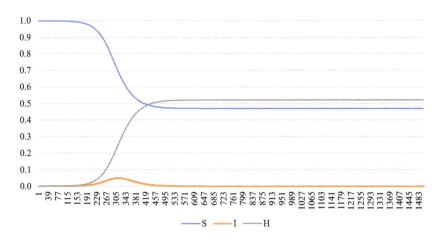

Figure 6.1 Trajectories of proportions *S*, *I* and *H* for the baseline scenario. Source: the author's own study.

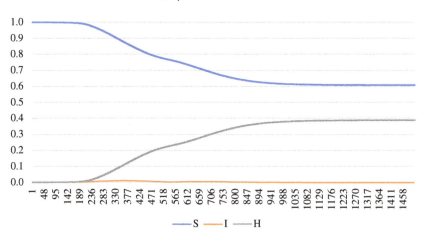

Figure 6.2 Trajectories of proportions *S*, *I* and *H* for scenario A_1 (without a vaccine). Source: the author's own study.

about 313). In this scenario, 38.7% of the Polish population would make the group of convalescents. The cumulative death rate would amount to 5.9‰, i.e. about 226,000 persons would die (about 77,000 fewer than in the baseline scenario, cf. Figures 6.2 and 6.6, Table 6.1).

The next three variants of scenario A (A_2 – 50% vaccinated, A_3 – 75% vaccinated, A_4 – 25% vaccinated) focus on the spread of the epidemic in the situation when the vaccination process has begun. It is assumed that on 18 January 2021 (i.e. on day 321 of the epidemic), the first individuals with post-vaccination immunity will appear in the population (thus reducing

Table 6.1 Minimum proportion of uninfected persons (S_m), maximum proportion of infected persons (I_M), maximum proportion of vaccinated persons (P_M), maximum proportion of convalescents (H_M) and the deceased (D_M), day of the epidemic with the highest number of infections (T) for scenario A with different variants

variants	S_m	I_M	H_M	D_M	P_M	T
A_1	0.6077	0.0124	0.3865	0.0059	0	362
A_2	0.2567	0.0121	0.2204	0.0034	0.5195	342
A_3	0.1537	0.0120	0.1957	0.0030	0.6476	338
A_4	0.4176	0.0122	0.2665	0.0041	0.3119	349

Source: the author's own study.

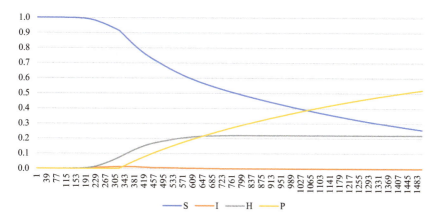

Figure 6.3 Trajectories of proportions S, I, H and P for scenario A_2 (50% of the population vaccinated). Source: the author's own study.

the proportion of the population at the risk of infection). In scenario A_2 it is assumed that 50% of the Polish population will be willing to be vaccinated. In this hypothetical situation, socioeconomic restrictions would be maintained until June 14, 2021. The epidemic peak would occur on day 342 of the epidemic with an infection rate of 1.21% (slightly lower than in variant A_1). The cumulative death rate would be 3.4‰, i.e. about 130,000 people would die (96,000 fewer than in variant A_1 and 173,000 fewer than in the baseline scenario). It is also worth mentioning that, in contrast to scenario A_1, the lockdown abolition combined with an ongoing vaccination process does not actually cause an increase in the proportion of infections (six days after the lockdown easing this proportion falls again). The epidemic would end on day 1,084 after its onset. On the day of its end, the proportion of the convalescent population would be about 22% and about 40% of the Polish population would be vaccinated (cf. Figures 6.3 and 6.6, Table 6.1).

124 *Paweł Dykas et al.*

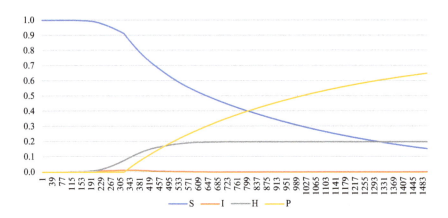

Figure 6.4 Trajectories of proportions S, I, H and P for scenario A$_3$ (75% of the population vaccinated). Source: the author's own study.

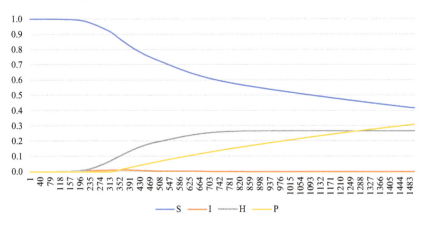

Figure 6.5 Trajectories of proportions S, I, H and P for scenario A$_4$ (25% of the population vaccinated). Source: the author's own study.

Variants A$_3$ and A$_4$ are, in turn, optimistic and pessimistic predictions concerning the vaccination of Polish citizens. In the first one, it is assumed that 75% of the population will be interested in vaccinations, in the second only 25%.

In the optimistic variant, the lockdown would end on 27 May 2021. The peak of the epidemic would occur on day 338 with the maximum proportion of infected individuals at 1.2% (a similar value to the one in options A$_1$ and A$_2$).

The cumulative proportion of deaths would be 3‰, i.e. about 115,000 people (15,000 people fewer than in variant A$_2$). The epidemic in Poland would end on day 960 after its beginning, with the proportion

Pandemic simulations on Poland and Ukraine 125

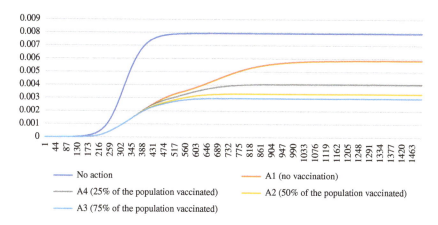

Figure 6.6 Trajectories of death rates for Scenario A. Source: the author's own study.

of vaccinated persons at the level of 48.0% and convalescents at 19.6% (Figures 6.4 and 6.6, Table 6.1).

In the pessimistic variant, assuming that the willingness to become vaccinated in Poland will be low, restrictions would be lifted on 12 July 2021. The maximum proportion of the infected persons would be 1.22% (similar to the value in the previous variants of scenario A) and it would take place on day 349 of the epidemic. After the lockdown abolition, the proportion of infected persons would again start to increase slightly until day 539 of the epidemic, i.e. 24 August 2021, when it would be equal to 5.1‰ (a similar increase after the lockdown easing could be observed under option A_1). The cumulative proportion of deaths would be 4.1‰, i.e. 157,000 people would die in Poland (42,000 more than in variant A_3). In Poland, the epidemic would end 1,321 days after its beginning, with the proportion of convalescents equal to 26.7% (7.1 percentage points more than in variant A_3) and the proportion of vaccinated persons equal to 27.6% (20.4 percentage points fewer than in variant A_3, cf. Figures 6.5 and 6.6 and Table 6.1).

The next scenario (B) assumes that the restrictions on socioeconomic life are gradually lifted as of 18 January 2021 (the 321st day of the epidemic). This scenario assumes that the rate of the lockdown easing is 5% per week and thus the restrictions are abolished entirely after four weeks, on day 349 of the epidemic. In variant B_1 of scenario B (without a vaccine), the maximum number of infected persons will fall on 6 May 2021 (day 429 of the epidemic, see Table 6.2). The proportion of those infected would then be 3.65%, 1.29 percentage points lower than in the baseline scenario (see Figures 6.1 and 6.7). In variant B_1 the proportion of deaths would be 7.5‰, which would translate into about 288,000 persons dying as a result of the epidemic. In this variant the number of deaths would decrease by about

126 *Paweł Dykas et al.*

Table 6.2 Minimum proportion of uninfected persons (S_m), maximum proportion of infected persons (I_M), maximum proportion of vaccinated persons (P_M), maximum proportion of convalescents (H_M) and the deceased (D_M), day of the epidemic with the highest number of infections (T) for scenario B with different variants

variants	S_m	I_M	H_M	D_M	P_M	T
B_1	0.5023	0.0365	0.4902	0.0075	0	429
B_2	0.2033	0.0260	0.3617	0.0055	0.4295	411
B_3	0.1242	0.0229	0.3159	0.0048	0.5551	402
B_4	0.3239	0.0301	0.4196	0.0064	0.2501	420

Source: the author's own study.

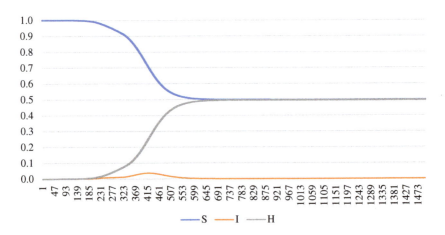

Figure 6.7 Trajectories of proportions S, I and H for scenario B_1 (without a vaccine).
Source: the author's own study.

15,000. Moreover, in variant B_1 the maximum proportion of convalescents would amount to 49.02% of the Polish population. On the 1,174th day of the epidemic the number of infected persons would fall below one, and on that day the proportion of those who recovered would be about 49.02% (cf. Figure 6.7).

In subsequent variants, similarly to Scenario A, the vaccination programme is taken into account.

In variant B_2 (50% of the population vaccinated), it is assumed that the declared proportion of the population that expresses the willingness to receive vaccinations is 50%. In this option, the maximum proportion of infected persons would fall on 18 April 2021, the 411th day of the epidemic, and it would be 2.6% of the population (28.8% lower than in option B_1 without a vaccine). The number of people who died as a result of the epidemic under this option would decrease by 77,000 compared to option B_1

Pandemic simulations on Poland and Ukraine 127

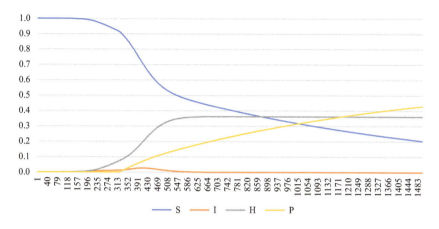

Figure 6.8 Trajectories of proportions S, I, H and P for scenario B$_2$ (50% of the population vaccinated). Source: the author's own work.

and would be about 211,000. With variant B$_2$, the epidemic would end on day 945, when there would be 29.5% of vaccinated persons and 36.2% of convalescents in the Polish population (see Figure 6.8).

Figure 6.9 illustrates the trajectories of proportions S, I, H and P resulting from numerical simulations for variant B$_3$, where the proportion of persons declaring the willingness to be vaccinated is 75% of the population. With this option, the maximum number of infected persons would occur 27 days earlier than with option B$_1$ and would be on 9 April 2021 (day 402 of the epidemic, see Table 6.2). The proportion of people infected on this date would be 2.29%, approximately 37.4% lower than for the no-vaccine option.

The proportion of deaths in variant B$_3$ decreased as compared to both variant B$_1$ and variant B$_2$ (by 36.0% and 12.7% respectively) and was 4.8‰. This would translate into approximately 184,000 people dying as a result of the epidemic. Moreover, on 7 August 2022, i.e. on the 887th day, the epidemic would end (counting from the onset) and on that day there would be 38.8% of vaccinated persons and 31.6% of convalescents in the Polish population.

The final, fourth variant (B$_4$) of scenario B assumes that only 25% of the Polish population declare their willingness to be vaccinated (variant B$_4$).

The maximum number of infected persons would then be recorded on 27 April 2021, i.e. on day 420 of the epidemic. The maximum proportion of infected persons in this variant would be 3.01% of the population and it would be 17.5% lower than in the variant without a vaccine and, respectively, 15.8% and 31.4% higher than in variants B$_2$ and B$_3$ (cf. Table 6.2).

In the variant B$_4$ the maximum proportion of deaths is 6.4‰ of the Polish population, which translates into about 245,000 dead people, and in comparison with the previous variants, it would increase the number of dead

128 *Paweł Dykas et al.*

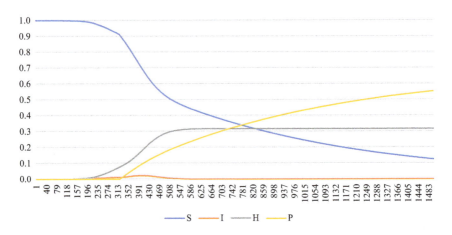

Figure 6.9 Trajectories of proportions S, I, H and P for scenario B_3 (75% of the population vaccinated). Source: the author's own study.

people by about 34,000 for variant B_2 and by about 61,000 for variant B_3 (compare Figure 6.11 and Table 6.2). The epidemic in Poland would end on day 1,026 when there would be 17.2% vaccinated persons and 41.9% convalescents in the Polish population (cf. Figure 6.10).

In the third scenario (C), the socioeconomic restrictions associated with the lockdown are to be lifted on 18 January 2021 (day 321 of the epidemic). In scenario C_1 (without a vaccine), the maximum number of infected persons would be recorded on 25 April 2021 (418th day of the epidemic).

The proportion of infected persons on that day would be 3.8% of the population and it would be 1.15 percentage points lower than in the baseline scenario (cf. Table 6.3). The maximum proportion of deaths would translate into over 291,000 people dying as a result of the epidemic, which is approximately 12,000 fewer than compared with the baseline scenario.

In Scenario C_1, the epidemic would be extinguished after 1,145 days and the proportion of convalescents on that date would be 49.6% (see Figure 6.12). In scenario C including a vaccination programme with a 50% vaccination coverage rate, the maximum number of infected persons (day 402 of the epidemic) is observed 16 days earlier as compared with scenario C without a vaccine (see Table 6.3). In variant C_2 (50% of the population vaccinated), the maximum proportion of deaths in the population would be 5.8‰, which would translate into approximately 222,000 deaths. What follows is that in scenario C with a vaccination programme and 50% of the population declaring their willingness to be vaccinated there will be a reduction in deaths due to the epidemic by about 69,000 people. Analyzing the trajectories of proportions S, I, H and P (cf. Figure 6.13) it can be seen that on 16 September 2022, after 927 days, the epidemic will have expired. Then

Pandemic simulations on Poland and Ukraine 129

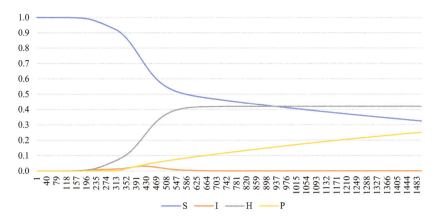

Figure 6.10 Trajectories of proportions S, I, H and P for scenario B_4 (25% of the population vaccinated). Source: the author's own study.

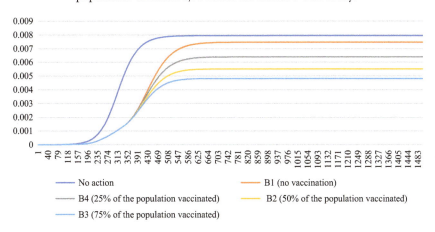

Figure 6.11 Trajectories of death rates for Scenario B. Source: the author's own study.

Table 6.3 Minimum proportion of uninfected persons (S_m), maximum proportion of infected persons (I_M), maximum proportion of vaccinated persons (P_M), maximum proportion of convalescents (H_M) and the deceased (D_M), day of the epidemic with the highest number of infections (T) for scenario C with different variants

variants	S_m	I_M	H_M	D_M	P_M	T
C_1	0.4966	0.0379	0.4958	0.0076	0	418
C_2	0.1976	0.0293	0.3787	0.0058	0.4180	402
C_3	0.1202	0.0264	0.3357	0.0051	0.5390	394
C_4	0.3171	0.0330	0.4318	0.0066	0.2445	410

Source: the author's own study.

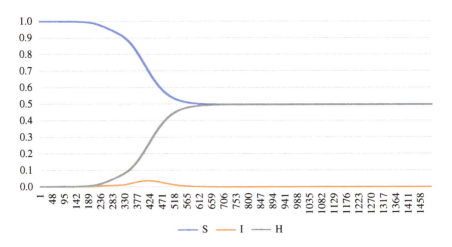

Figure 6.12 Trajectories of proportions S, I and H for scenario C₁ (without a vaccine). Source: the author's own study.

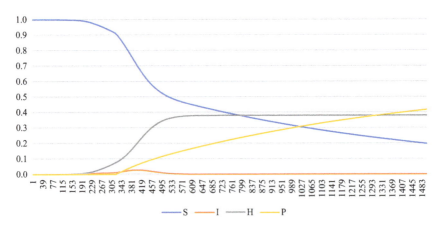

Figure 6.13 Trajectories of proportions S, I, H and P for scenario C₂ (50% of the population vaccinated). Source: the author's own study.

the population will include 28.1% vaccinated persons and 37.9% convalescents. Considering variant C₃ (75% of the population vaccinated) it can be seen that the peak of the epidemic would then fall on 1 April 2021 (day 394 of the epidemic).

The maximum proportion of people infected in this variant of scenario C would be lower as compared to both variant C₁ (reduction by 1.15 percentage points) and variant C₂ (reduction by 0.29 percentage points) and equal to 2.6%. The maximum proportion of deaths in variant C₃ would be 5.1‰, which, taking into account the population of Poland, translates into over 195,000 deaths. After 873 days (July 24, 2022) the epidemic would die out,

Pandemic simulations on Poland and Ukraine 131

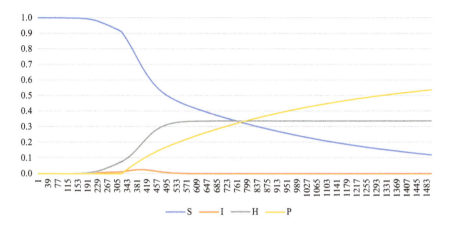

Figure 6.14 Trajectories of proportions S, I, H and P for scenario C₃ (75% of the population vaccinated). Source: the author's own work.

at which date there would be 37.2% vaccinated persons and 33.6% convalescents (see Figure 6.14).

In the final variant C₄ (25% of the population vaccinated) of this scenario, it is assumed that the proportion of the population declaring a willingness to be vaccinated is 25%. In this scenario, the maximum proportion of infected people would be 3.3% and it would fall on April 17, 2021 (the 410th day of the epidemic). Under option C₄, the maximum proportion of deaths would be 6.6‰, corresponding to more than 253,000 people dying from the epidemic. As compared with options C₁–C₃, the number of the deceased would be higher than under options C₂ and C₃ by about 31,000

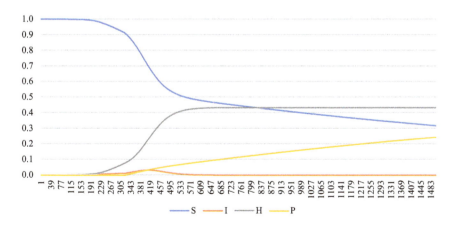

Figure 6.15 Trajectories of proportions S, I, H and P for Scenario C₄ (25% of the population vaccinated). Source: the author's own study.

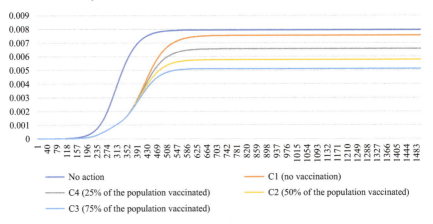

Figure 6.16 Trajectories of death rates for Scenario C. Source: the author's own study.

and 58,000 people, respectively, and lower by 38,000 people when compared with C$_1$ (see Table 6.3 and Figure 6.16). The epidemic following this variant would cease as of day 1,004 (cf. Figure 6.15). Moreover, on that day there would be 16.4% vaccinated persons and 43.2% convalescents.

6.3.2 Results of numerical simulations for Ukraine

The baseline scenario assumes that the government of Ukraine has not introduced any epidemic-related restrictions in March 2020. This scenario will serve as a baseline for the other scenarios. The peak of the epidemic would occur on day 283 after the outbreak (i.e. around 11 December 2020), and the maximum proportion of infections on that day would be 6.9%. The cumulative death rate would be 8.5‰, i.e. about 355,000 people would die. The epidemic would die out after about 2 years (day 774) with 43.2% uninfected persons and 55.9% convalescents at the end of the epidemic (cf. Figure 6.17).

In scenario A, it is assumed that the lockdown would be lifted when the proportion of infections falls below 50% of the empirical proportion on day 276. In the case analyzed, this proportion would be 4.21‰. In scenario A$_1$ (without a vaccine), the lockdown would end on 8 October 2021 (day 584 of the epidemic). The maximum proportion of infections is 1.46% on day 391 of the epidemic, which is 4.4 percentage points lower than in the baseline scenario. When the restrictions are lifted, the proportion of infected individuals would only rise to 5.9‰ on day 714 of the epidemic and then fall to 728 people on day 1,500 of the epidemic. In this scenario, the proportion of uninfected persons at the end of the epidemic was equal to 59.9%, while the proportion of convalescents was 40.2%. The cumulative death rate would be 6.1‰, i.e. about 256,000 people would die. This is about

Pandemic simulations on Poland and Ukraine 133

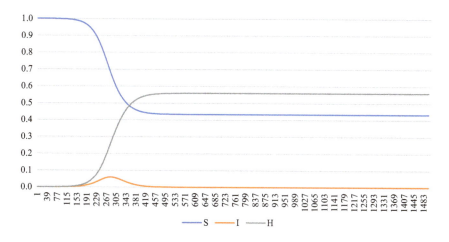

Figure 6.17 Trajectories of proportions *S*, *I* and *H* for the baseline scenario. Source: the author's own study.

99,000 fewer than in the baseline scenario. (See Figures 6.17 and 6.18, Table 6.4).

Scenario A, options A_2 (60% of the population vaccinated), A_3 (90% of the population vaccinated) and A_4 (30% of the population vaccinated), in addition to the lockdown abolition when the proportion of infections falls below 50% of the actual proportion on day 275, also took into account the spread of the epidemic when the vaccination process began. On 1 February 2021 (day 335 of the epidemic) the first people with immunity after vaccination will appear (thus reducing the proportion of the population at the risk of infection).

According to option A_2, 60% of the Ukrainian population will be vaccinated. In this situation, restrictions would be maintained until 11 July 2021 (day 495 of the epidemic).

The highest proportion of infections would be on day 364 of the epidemic and account for 1.36%. The cumulative proportion of deaths would be 3.4‰, i.e. approximately 142,000 people would die. This is 112,000 fewer than in option A_1 and 213,000 fewer than in the baseline scenario. The epidemic would die out around two and a half years (943 days) after its onset. The population would contain 14.9% uninfected persons, 20.6% convalescents and 39.4% vaccinated persons at the end of the epidemic (see Figures 6.19 and 6.22, Table 6.4).

According to option A_3, 90% of the Ukrainian population would be vaccinated. In this situation the lockdown would be maintained until 20 June 2021 (the 474th day of the epidemic). The epidemic peak would occur on 24 February (the 358th day of the epidemic) with the maximum rate of infections at 1.35%.

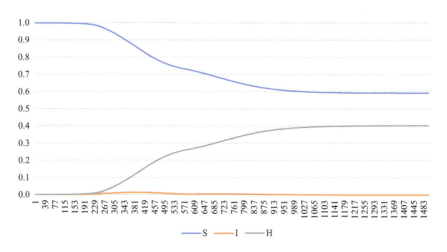

Figure 6.18 Trajectories of proportions S, I and H for scenario A₁ (without a vaccine). Source: the author's own study.

Table 6.4 Minimum proportion of uninfected persons (S_m), maximum proportion of infected persons (I_M), maximum proportion of vaccinated persons (P_M), maximum proportion of convalescents (H_M) and the deceased (D_M), day of the epidemic with the highest number of infections (T) for scenario A with different variants

variants	S_m	I_M	H_M	D_M	P_M	T
A₁	0.5923	0.0146	0.4016	0.0061	0	714
A₂	0.149425	0.013683	0.206078	0.003138	0.641359	364
A₃	0.065211	0.013493	0.186179	0.002835	0.745775	358
A₄	0.326729	0.014001	0.245820	0.003743	0.423707	373

Source: the author's own study.

The cumulative death rate would be 2.8‰, i.e. about 118,000 people would die. This is almost the same as under option A₂, 138,000 fewer than under option A₁ and 237,000 fewer than in the baseline scenario. The epidemic would die out 2 years (827 days) after its onset. There would be 6.5% uninfected individuals, 18.6% convalescents and 46.3% vaccinated persons at the end of the epidemic (cf. Figures 6.20 and 6.22, Table 6.4).

In scenario A₄, it was assumed that the willingness to become vaccinated would be low, thus 30% of the Ukrainian population would be vaccinated. In this situation, restrictions would be maintained until 12 August 2021 (the 527th day of the epidemic). The highest proportion of infected individuals would be on 24 February 2021 (day 373 of the epidemic) representing 1.4%. The cumulative proportion of deaths would be 3.7‰, or about 156,000 people would die. This is 200,000 fewer people than in the baseline

Pandemic simulations on Poland and Ukraine 135

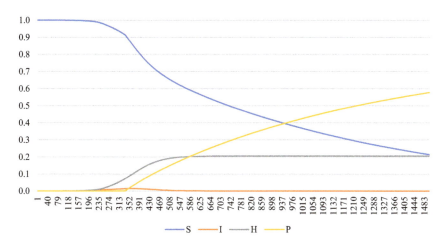

Figure 6.19 Trajectories of proportions S, I, H and P for scenario A_2 (60% of the population vaccinated). Source: the author's own study.

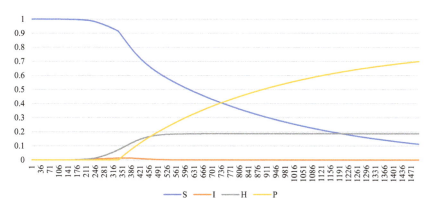

Figure 6.20 Trajectories of proportions S, I, H and P for scenario A_3 (90% of the population vaccinated). Source: the author's own study.

scenario. In contrast, this option predicts the highest number of deaths of all the variants that include a vaccine. The epidemic would die out three years (1,190 days) after its onset. There would be 32.7% uninfected individuals, 24.6% convalescents and 28.8% vaccinated persons at the end of the epidemic (cf. Figures 6.21 and 6.22, Table 6.4).

In scenario B, it is assumed that restrictions on socioeconomic life are to be gradually lifted starting from 30 January 2021 (the 333rd day of the epidemic). It is assumed that the rate of lockdown easing is 5% per week. In this scenario, restrictions will be entirely removed after four weeks, on day 362 of the epidemic. In variant B_1 (without a vaccine) the peak of the

136 *Paweł Dykas et al.*

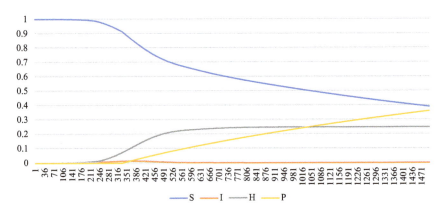

Figure 6.21 Trajectories of proportions *S*, *I*, *H* and *P* for scenario A_4 (30% of the population vaccinated). Source: the author's own study.

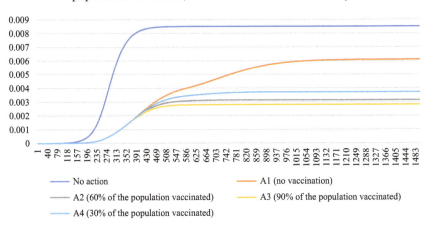

Figure 6.22 Trajectories of death rates for Scenario A. Source: the author's own study.

epidemic would be on 13 May (the 436th day of the epidemic) with the maximum proportion of infections at 4.37%, which is almost 2 million people. The cumulative death rate would be 8‰, i.e. about 334,000 people would die. This is 21,000 fewer than in the baseline scenario.

The epidemic would die out nearly three years (983 days) after its onset. There would be 46.2% uninfected individuals and 52.9% convalescents after the end of the epidemic (cf. Figure 6.23 and 6.27, Table 6.5).

The following variants of scenario B take into account the vaccination of the population. In variant B_2 it was assumed that 60% of the population would be vaccinated. In this situation the highest proportion of infected persons would fall on 27 April 2021 (the 364th day of the epidemic) at 3.12%. As a result of

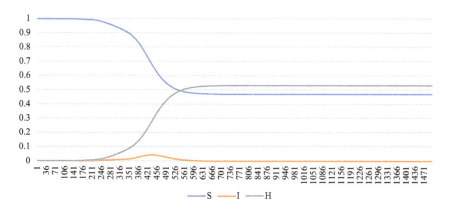

Figure 6.23 Trajectories of proportions S, I and H for scenario B_1 (without a vaccine). Source: the author's own study.

Table 6.5 Minimum proportion of uninfected persons (S_m), maximum proportion of infected persons (I_M), maximum proportion of vaccinated persons (P_M), maximum proportion of convalescents (H_M) and the deceased (D_M), day of the epidemic with the highest number of infections (T) for scenario B with different variants

variants	S_m	I_M	H_M	D_M	P_M	T
B_1	0.462102	0.043753	0.529830	0.008068	0	436
B_2	0.109040	0.031281	0.386877	0.005892	0.498192	420
B_3	0.050093	0.027247	0.334960	0.005101	0.609845	412
B_4	0.228571	0.036675	0.451814	0.006880	0.312734	428

Source: the author's own study.

the epidemic, 246,000 people would die. Thus, the cumulative proportion of deaths would be 5.9‰. This is 87,000 fewer than in variant B_1 and 109,000 fewer than in the baseline scenario. The epidemic would die out after two years (839 days). There would be 10.9% uninfected individuals and 38.7% convalescents after the end of the epidemic (cf. Figure 6.24 and 6.27, Table 6.5).

The following variants of scenario B take into account the vaccination of the population. In variant B_2 it was assumed that 60% of the population would be vaccinated. In this situation the highest proportion of infected persons would fall on 27 April 2021 (the 364th day of the epidemic) at 3.12%. As a result of the epidemic, 246,000 people would die. Thus, the cumulative proportion of deaths would be 5.9‰. This is 87,000 fewer than in variant B_1 and 109,000 fewer than in the baseline scenario. The epidemic would die out after two years (839 days). There would be 10.9% uninfected individuals and 38.7% convalescents after the end of the epidemic (cf. Figure 6.24 and 6.27, Table 6.5).

138 *Paweł Dykas et al.*

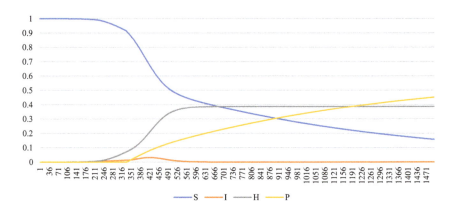

Figure 6.24 Trajectories of proportions S, I, H and P for scenario B_2 (60% of the population vaccinated). Source: the author's own study.

Variant B_3 assumed the most optimistic scenario in which 90% of the Ukrainian population would be vaccinated. The highest proportion of infections would fall on 19 May 2021 (day 412 of the epidemic) at 2.72%. The cumulative death rate would be 5.1‰. Approximately 213,000 people would die, which is 3.4‰ fewer than in the baseline scenario, 2.9‰ fewer than in option B_1 and 0.8‰ fewer than in option B_2. The epidemic would die out after two years (795 days). There would be 5% uninfected individuals, 33.4% convalescents and 37.8% vaccinated persons at the end of the epidemic (cf. Figures 6.25 and 6.27, Table 6.5).

On the other hand, variant B_4 is the most pessimistic scenario in which 30% of the Ukrainian population is vaccinated. In this variant the peak of the epidemic would fall on 5 May (the 428th day of the epidemic) with the maximum proportion of infections at 3.66%, i.e. 1.5 million persons. The cumulative proportion of deaths would be 6.88‰.

As a result, about 288,000 people would die. This is 75,000 more people than in option B_3, 42,000 more than in option B_2, 49,000 fewer than in the no-vaccine option and 67,000 fewer than in the baseline scenario. The epidemic would die out after two years (895 days). There would be 22.8% uninfected people, 46.4% convalescents and 16.1% vaccinated people at the end of the epidemic (see Figures 6.26 and 6.27, Table 6.5).

In the final scenario C, it is assumed that the lockdown restrictions are to be lifted on 30 January 2021 (the 333rd day of the epidemic). In scenario C_1 (without a vaccine), the epidemic peak would fall on 1 May (day 424 of the epidemic) with the maximum proportion of infections at 4.67%. The cumulative death rate would be 8.16‰, i.e. about 341,000 people would die. This is 14,000 fewer than in the baseline scenario. The epidemic would die out after almost three years (958 days). There would be 45.6%

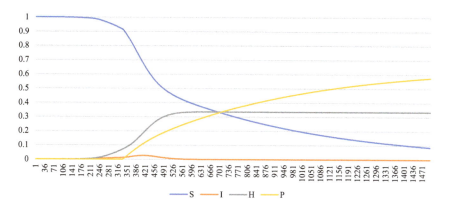

Figure 6.25 Trajectories of proportions S, I, H and P for scenario B_3 (90% of the population vaccinated). Source: the author's own study.

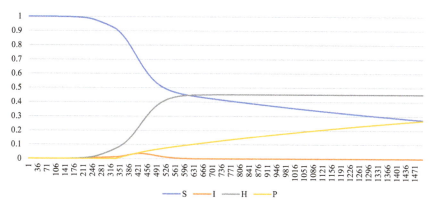

Figure 6.26 Trajectories of proportions S, I, H and P for scenario B_4 (30% of the population vaccinated). Source: the author's own study.

uninfected individuals and 53.6% convalescents at the end of the epidemic (see Figures 6.28 and 6.32, Table 6.6).

In the following variants of scenario C, the vaccination programme was taken into account. In variant C_2, it was assumed that 60% of the population would be vaccinated. On the basis of Figure 6.29 it can be deduced that the peak of the epidemic in this variant would fall on 18 April 2021 (day 411 of the epidemic) with the rate of infection at 3.56%. In this variant, 260,000 people would die. Thus, the cumulative proportion of deaths would be 6.2‰. This is 81,000 fewer than in option C_1 and 95,000 fewer than in the baseline scenario. The epidemic would die out after 2 years (821 days). There would be 31.8% uninfected individuals, 40.7% convalescents

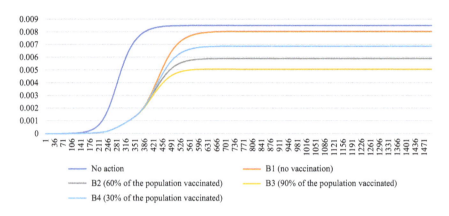

— No action
— B1 (no vaccination)
— B2 (60% of the population vaccinated)
— B3 (90% of the population vaccinated)
— B4 (30% of the population vaccinated)

Figure 6.27 Trajectories of death rates for Scenario B. Source: the author's own study.

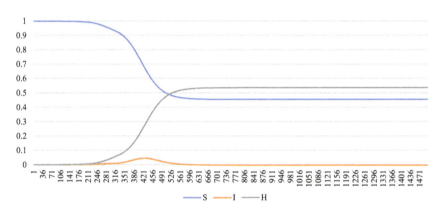

— S — I — H

Figure 6.28 Trajectories of proportions S, I and H for scenario C_1 (without a vaccine). Source: the author's own study.

Table 6.6 Minimum proportion of uninfected persons (S_m), maximum proportion of infected persons (I_M), maximum proportion of vaccinated persons (P_M), maximum proportion of convalescents (H_M) and the deceased (D_M), day of the epidemic with the highest number of infections (T) for scenario B with different variants

variants	S_m	I_M	H_M	D_M	P_M	T
C_1	0.455823	0.046713	0.536014	0.008163	0	424
C_2	0.105171	0.035679	0.407456	0.006205	0.481168	411
C_3	0.048006	0.031926	0.359403	0.005473	0.587119	404
C_4	0.222649	0.040525	0.466172	0.007099	0.304080	417

Source: the author's own study.

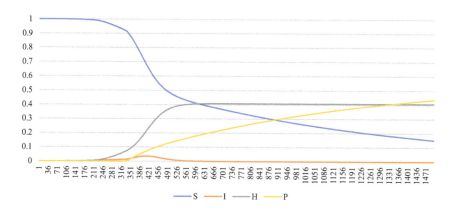

Figure 6.29 Trajectories of proportions S, I, H and P for scenario C_2 (60% of the population vaccinated). Source: the author's own study.

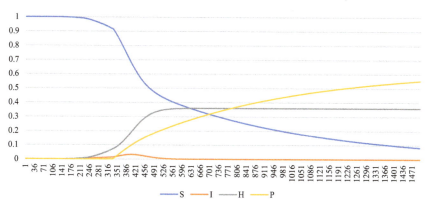

Figure 6.30 Trajectories of proportions S, I, H and P for scenario C_3 (90% of the population vaccinated). Source: the author's own study.

and 48.1% vaccinated persons at the end of the epidemic (cf. Figure 6.29 and 6.32, Table 6.6).

In scenario C_3, with 90% of the Ukrainian population vaccinated, the highest proportion of infections would fall on 11 April 2021 (day 404 of the epidemic) at 3.19%. The cumulative death rate would be 5.47‰. Approximately 229,000 people would die. This is 126,000 fewer people than in the baseline scenario, 112,000 fewer people than in option C_1 and 31,000 fewer people than in option C_2. The epidemic would die out after two years (782 days). There would be 27.6% uninfected individuals, 35.9% convalescents and 58.7% vaccinated persons at the end of the epidemic (see Figures 6.30 and 6.32, Table 6.6).

In the final variant C_4 of this scenario, 30% of the population is assumed to be vaccinated. In this, the most pessimistic variant, the peak of the

142 *Paweł Dykas et al.*

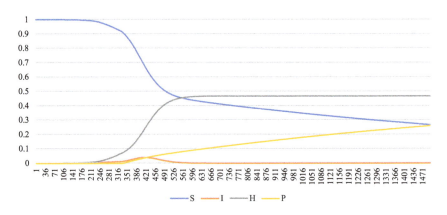

Figure 6.31 Trajectories of proportions S, I, H and P for scenario C_4 (30% of the population vaccinated). Source: the author's own study.

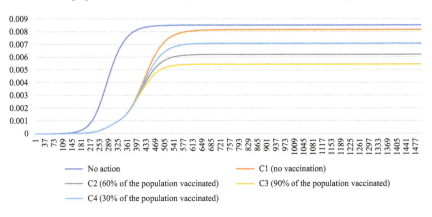

Figure 6.32 Trajectories of death rates for Scenario C. Source: the author's own study.

epidemic would fall on 24 April (day 417 of the epidemic). The maximum proportion of infections on that day would be 4.05%. The cumulative death rate would be 7.1‰, i.e. about 297,000 people would die. This is 58 000 fewer than in the baseline scenario. The epidemic would die out after 2 years (874 days). There would be 37.4% uninfected individuals, 46.7% convalescents and 30.4% vaccinated persons at the end of the epidemic (see Figures 6.31 and 6.32, Table 6.5).

6.4 Conclusions

This chapter analyzes three scenarios of the spread of the epidemic in two selected countries, Poland and Ukraine, depending on the actions taken by the government as regards the time and manner of the easing of socioeconomic restrictions. According to scenario A, the lockdown would be lifted when the proportion of infections fell below 50% of the actual proportion on day 275 of the epidemic. According to scenario B, restrictions would be lifted gradually over one month, beginning on 18 January 2021 in Poland and 30 January 2021 in Ukraine. According to the final scenario C, the lockdown restrictions would be lifted on a single date (18 January 2021 for Poland and 30 January 2021 for Ukraine). Additionally, each of the scenarios includes four variants, one without vaccination and three with the respective vaccination of 50% (60%), 75% (90%) and 25% (30%) of the Polish (Ukrainian) population.

An important parameter in the assessment of the course of the epidemic is the proportion of deaths. The best results for Poland are achieved with Scenario A in its variants with vaccination. Assuming that 75%, 50% and 25% of the population will express their willingness to be vaccinated, the proportion of deaths will be as follows: 3‰ (115,000 people), 3.4‰ (130,000 people) and 4.1‰ (157,000 people), respectively. For these variants the lockdown would have to be maintained until May 27, June 14 and July 12, 2021, respectively. The highest proportion of deaths can be observed for scenarios C and B without vaccination; they are respectively 7.6‰ (291,000 people) and 7.5‰ (288,000 people), differing relatively little from the base scenario as regards the free spread of the epidemic (7.9‰, 303,000 people).

Regardless of the variant adopted in Ukraine, the cumulative proportion of deaths would not exceed 8.16‰, which represents about 341,000 people. Therefore, the most pessimistic variant would be C_1 (lockdown restrictions are lifted on 30 January 2021, there is no vaccination). In the scenario without socioeconomic restrictions, the proportion would be 8.5‰ (355,000 people). The most optimistic variant of all discussed is the one where the lockdown would be lifted when the proportion of infections falls below 50% of the empirical proportion on day 275 and 90% of the A_3 population is vaccinated. In this situation about 118,000 people would die (2.8‰).

Another important parameter is the proportion of the population infected at the peak of the epidemic. This parameter indirectly affects the burden on the country's health care system – the more infected people there are, the more people are likely to require hospitalization. Also in this aspect the best results would be achieved by implementing scenario A. In different variants of this scenario, the value of this parameter for Poland oscillates between 1.20–1.24% (460–476 thousand people), and the pandemic peak would occur relatively early, i.e. on days 338–362 of the epidemic. In contrast, in scenarios C and B without vaccination and with the vaccination of 25% of the population, the proportion is between 3.01–3.79% (1,154,000–1,454,000 people) and the peak would occur on days 410–429 of the epidemic. With the free spread of the epidemic at the peak, i.e. day 311, the number of active cases would be 4.94% (approximately 1,895,000 people).

In each scenario, the peak of the epidemic in Ukraine would fall the soonest in variant 3 (90% of the population would be vaccinated). The most positive of these variants would be scenario A (socioeconomic restrictions are removed when the proportion of infections falls below 50% of the empirical proportion on day 275). In this case, the peak of the epidemic would occur on 24 February (day 358 of the epidemic). In addition, this variant has the lowest maximum proportion of infections at 1.35%. On the other hand, the highest maximum proportion of infections would be 4.67% in variant C_1 (the lockdown restrictions would be lifted on 30 January 2021). The peak of the epidemic would fall on 1 May (day 424 of the epidemic). The peak of the epidemic would occur the latest on 13 May 2021 (the 436th day of the epidemic) with the maximum proportion of infections at 4.37%, representing almost 2 million people. This would be scenario B in its variant without a vaccine (where the lockdown restrictions are gradually lifted starting on 30 January 2021). In the baseline scenario, the peak of the epidemic would fall on day 283 after its onset (i.e. around 11 December 2020) with the maximum proportion of infections on that day at 6.9%.

In Poland, high maximum recovery rates (42–50%) are observed in scenarios B and C without vaccination and with the vaccination of 25% of the population. Low recovery rates are observed in scenario A in its variants with vaccination, i.e. 20–27% of the population. Moreover, the fastest extinction of the epidemic can be observed in scenarios C and B with the vaccination of 75% of the population (July–August 2022). On the other hand, in the case of scenario A with the vaccination of 25% of the population, the epidemic would end in October 2023, and in scenario A without vaccination the epidemic would extend beyond the framework adopted in the simulations, i.e. 1,500 days (11 April 2024).

When analyzing the scenarios for the course of the epidemic in Ukraine, it is worth noting that the minimum timeframe for the epidemic to expire is two years. The epidemic would expire the soonest in the baseline scenario (day 774 of the epidemic). It would last the longest in scenario A – more than 1,500 days (variant 1 without a vaccine, the lockdown would be lifted when the proportion of infections falls below 50% of the empirical proportion on day 275). Out of all the variants, the epidemic would end the soonest in variant C_3 – on day 782 of the epidemic (90% of the population would be vaccinated and the lockdown restrictions would be lifted on 30 January 2021).

References

Atkeson, A. (2020). *What will be the economic impact of COVID-19 in the US? Rough estimates of disease scenarios*. NBER Working Paper, No. 26867. http://www.nber.org/papers/w26867 (accessed January 30, 2021).

Bärwolff, G. (2020). Mathematical modeling and simulation of the COVID-19 pandemic. *Systems*, 8(3), 1–12. https://doi.org/10.3390/systems8030024 (accessed January 30, 2021).

Glavcom. (2020, May 11). *V Ukrayini poslabyly karantyn: Shcho dozvoleno.* https://glavcom.ua/news/v-ukrajini-poslabili-karantin-shcho-dozvoleno-679172.html (accessed January 30, 2021).

Indexminfin. (2021, January 18). *Koronavirus v Ukrayini.* https://index.minfin.com.ua/ua/reference/coronavirus/ukraine (accessed January 30, 2021).

Kermack, W. O., McKendrick, A. G. (1927). A contribution to the mathematical theory of epidemics, *Proceedings of the Royal Society, Series A,* 115, 700–721 (accessed January 30, 2021). https://royalsocietypublishing.org/doi/10.1098/rspa.1927.0118

KMU. (2020a, March 11). *Postanova Kabinetu Ministriv Ukrayiny No.211 vid 11 bereznya 2020 roku "Pro zapobihannya poshyrennyu na terytoriyi Ukrayiny koronavirusu COVID-19".* https://www.kmu.gov.ua/npas/pro-zapobigannya-poshim110320rennyu-na-teritoriyi-ukrayini-koronavirusu-covid-19 (accessed January 30, 2021).

KMU. (2020b, May 20). *Uryad ukhvalyv rishennya pro poslablennya karantynu z 22 travnya.* https://www.kmu.gov.ua/news/uryad-uhvaliv-rishennya-pro-poslablennya-karantinu-z-22-travnya (accessed January 30, 2021).

KMU. (2020c, November 13). *Uryad zaprovadyv karantyn vykhidnoho dnya (onovleno).* https://www.kmu.gov.ua/news/uryad-zaprovadiv-karantin-vihidnogo-dnya-onovleno (accessed January 30, 2021).

Lotnisko Chopina w Warszawie. (2020, January 25). *Komunikat Lotniska Chopina.* https://lotnisko-chopina.pl/pl/aktualnosci-i-wydarzenia/0/976/szczegoly.html (accessed January 30, 2021).

Medonet. (2020, February 29). *NIZP-PZH przebadał 307 próbek pobranych od osób z podejrzeniem zakażenia koronawirusem.* https://www.medonet.pl/koronawirus/koronawirus-w-polsce,w-kierunku-koronawirusa-nizp-pzh-przebadal-307-osob,artykul,78353052.html (accessed January 30, 2021).

MZSU. (2020, September 30). *Uryad zminyv pravyla v'yizdu inozemtsiv v Ukrayinu na period diyi karantynu.* https://mfa.gov.ua/news/uryad-zminiv-pravila-vyizdu-inozemciv-v-ukrayinu-na-period-diyi-karantinu (accessed January 30, 2021).

Portal miasta Gdańsk. (2020, October 23). *Koronawirus - nowe obostrzenia. Nauka zdalna, zamknięte kawiarnie i restauracje. Co jeszcze?* (accessed January 30, 2021). https://www.gdansk.pl/wiadomosci/koronawirus-nowe-obostrzenia-nauka-zdalna-zamkniete-kawiarnie-i-restauracje-co-jeszcze,a,181595

Serwis Rzeczypospolitej Polskiej. (2020a, March 21). *Rozporządzenie Ministra Zdrowia z dnia 20 marca 2020 r. w sprawie ogłoszenia na obszarze Rzeczypospolitej Polskiej stanu epidemii.* https://www.gov.pl/web/rpa/rozporzadzenie-ministra-zdrowia-z-dnia-20-marca-2020-r-w-sprawie-ogloszenia-na-obszarze-rzeczypospolitej-polskiej-stanu-epidemii (accessed January 30, 2021).

Serwis Rzeczypospolitej Polskiej. (2020b, April 16). *Nowa normalność: Etapy znoszenia ograniczeń związanych z COVID-19.* https://www.gov.pl/web/koronawirus/nowa-normalnosc-etapy (accessed January 30, 2021).

Serwis Rzeczypospolitej Polskiej. (2021, January 20). *Raport zakażeń koronawirusem.* https://www.gov.pl/web/koronawirus/wykaz-zarazen-koronawirusem-sars-cov-255 (accessed January 30, 2021).

Ukrinform. (2020, February 25). *Sekretar RNBO proviv naradu shchodo sytuatsiyi z koronavirusom.* https://www.ukrinform.ua/rubric-polytics/2884185-sekretar-rnbo-proviv-naradu-sodo-situacii-z-koronavirusom.html (accessed January 30, 2021).

Unian. (2020, June 13). *Ukrayina hotuyet'sya do vidnovlennya aviaspoluchennya: Kudy ta za yakykh umov zmozhut' litaty ukrayintsi (video)*. https://www.unian.ua/tourism/news/kudi-mozhna-litati-ukrajincyam-vidnovlennya-aviaspoluchennya-novini-11035208.html (accessed January 30, 2021).

VRU. (2020, April 2). *Postanova Kabinetu Ministriv Ukrayiny vid 2 kvitnya 2020 r. No. 255 Kyyiv Pro vnesennya zmin do postanovy Kabinetu Ministriv Ukrayiny vid 11 bereznya 2020 r. No. 211*. https://zakon.rada.gov.ua/laws/show/255-2020-%D0%BF#Text (accessed January 30, 2021).

Key findings

Rafał Wisła and Paweł Dykas

The COVID-19 pandemic caused by the SARS CoV-2 virus, which struck in the years 2020-2021, was characterized by a global scale, an unprecedented pace of spread, fundamental uncertainty and interrelation of health, social and economic phenomena. The 2020+ pandemic entailed a worldwide exogenous demand and supply shock.

Restrictions imposed on social and economic activities in March 2020, aiming to contain the pandemic, involved dramatic changes in the economies of western and eastern regions of Europe. The economic collapse began at the turn of Q1 and Q2. Such dramatic and massive changes have not been observed in any business cycle after World War II. The sharpest fall in the value of GDP per capita between Q2 of 2019 and Q2 of 2020, in absolute figures, was experienced by the countries that in the years 2006–2019 were classified in the group characterized by mean, high and highest levels of wealth of an average citizen. All analyzed European countries experienced in Q2 of 2020 a dramatic fall in both exports and imports of goods and services compared to Q2 of 2019, due to restrictions imposed in H1 of 2020.

All countries except Sweden imposed a state of emergency with limited mobility of employees, closed border checkpoints, and a ban on certain business activities. The first lockdown lasted on average 20 to 94 days. Emergency programmes were launched and a record-breaking fund dubbed Next Generation EU was established at the European Union level. The methods employed to support the economies of Europe were convergent. All support packages imposed heavy financial burdens on the budgets of the states covered by the survey.

Russia faced an extremely high mortality rate caused by the COVID-19 pandemic in 2020. The Russian population decreased, in 2020, by almost 700,000 people. It was the deepest annual decrease in the last 15 years. Non-residents invested in the business enterprise sector in 2020 five times less capital than in 2019. The 2020+ pandemic was only one of the factors causing problems in the Russian economy.

The Ukrainian ministry of economy announced that inflation in 2020 reached 5%, principally due to a dynamic increase in revenues from retail sales and a rise in prices for energy sources on the global market that

DOI: 10.4324/9781003211891-7

affected local expenses on public utility services, finally reducing the consumer demand. The volume of passenger transport dropped in 2020 to 46% of its value in 2019.

The proposed multi-level pandemic narrative, a national and an international perspective, led us to a series of speculative scenarios.

In a theoretical analysis, falls in production in an economy without access to a vaccine reach, at peak incidence, 18.3% to 19.9% if severe restrictions are imposed in response to the epidemic, or 10.4% to 10.9% if a liberal approach is adopted. Slow progress in immunization coverage of the population combined with severe restrictions imposed in response to the epidemic reduces falls in production by 17.7% to 19.5%. If a liberal approach to the epidemic is adopted, estimated falls in production will reach (respectively) 10.2–10.6%. Additionally, rapid progress in immunization coverage has no material effect on falls in production at peak incidence.

Scenario analyses of the epidemic process in selected countries of Eastern Europe indicate that the minimum time required to curb the epidemic is two years in Ukraine and almost two and a half years in Poland.

The deep recession of 2020 and the great uncertainty as to the medium term (2021–2022) accelerated changes in the model of social and economic life, promoted by the technology revolution, towards a digital economy and remote education system. Those stimuli cannot be overestimated. Specific institutional consequences can be expected (established and commonly used telework and remote education models).

Secondary consequences of the 2020+ health disaster, including a fall in employment (in selected service industries), interrupted supply chains, a reduction in social capital level (repudiation and/or partial repudiation of contracts, limited social relations) and limited spatial mobility of workers and tourists, will be suffered for a longer period than drops in production, consumption spending, investment and trading turnover.

The post-pandemic economic recovery will be accompanied by an acceleration of the fourth industrial revolution. We can expect mass digitalization, common use of robotics in manufacturing processes and of artificial intelligence in services. Low labour costs will no longer represent an advantage. Advantages will include the quality of education, IT infrastructure, supportive business environment, transparency of law, the quality of the research and development (R&D) and science sector.

The COVID-19 pandemic caused by the SARS-CoV-2 virus will come to an end. But its economic and social consequences will be suffered for a long time. Digital tools and products will commonly and durably affect the ways we work, learn and relax. The popularity of countries still affected by the pandemic as tourist destinations will decline. Public debt will burden us for decades. Can we survive another exogenous global demand and supply shock without huge social costs?

Index

Note: Page numbers in *italics* indicate figures and **bold** indicate tables in the text.

agricultural sector 84
Alvarez, F. 90
Anti-Epidemic Protection Fund 61
Argente, D. 90
Argentina 4, 7
Asia Pacific COVID-19 (OCHA) 14
Asiatic pangolins 2
AstraZeneca 8, 9
Atkeson, A. 90, 120
Aum, S. 90
Australia 7
Austria 23, 24, 27, 28, 49; exports per capita 35, 37; gross fixed capital 31, 33; imports of goods and services 40; small and medium-sized enterprises (SMEs) in 48
Azerbaijan 5

balanced budget policy 47
Bank of Croatia 59
Bank of Denmark 60
Bank of Ireland 54
Bank of Slovakia 57
Bank of Slovenia 58
Bank of Spain 58
Bank of Sweden 63
Bärwolff, G. 89, 91, 120
bats *(chiroptera)* 2
Bazylyuk, Y. 68–69
Belarus 5
Belgium 22–24, 27, 28, 49–50; exports of goods and services 37, 38; gross fixed capital 31, 33; imports of goods and services 40, 42; small and medium-sized enterprises (SMEs) in 59
Berlin: protest in 6
BioNTech 8, 9
Bloom, D. 89

Bloomberg Covid Resilience Ranking 6–8
Bolsonaro, J. 5
Brazil 4, 5, 7, 11, 12
Breusch-Pagan test 81, 81n2, 83
Brock, W. 90
Bulgaria 23, 28, 59; central bank of 59; exports of goods and services 37, 40; gross fixed capital 31, 33; imports of goods and services 40, 42

Canada 12
capital accumulation 30, 90, 91, 95
"cavalier" leadership 5
Centers for Disease Control and Prevention (CDC) 14
China 7, 11
chi-squared distribution 81n2
climate change 12, 47, 48, 55, 90
Cobb-Douglas power production function 76, 94–95, 98
Colombia 4
communication activities 5–6
conspiracy theories about COVID-19 5–6
coronavirus disease 2019 (COVID-19) 1n2; caused by SARS-CoV-2 1–16; causing unprecedented human and economic costs 2; challenges 10–11; conspiracy theories 5–6; coping with pandemic 6–8; costs of 11–13; critical mental health services 13–14; databases 14; Delta Virus Pandemic 8; denial and miscalculations 5–6; effect on selected economies 68–87; first time identification 2; first worldwide wave of 4; fourth wave of 8; governmental

responses 4; hypotheses about 3; impact of 20–44; impact on the world 1–16; MERS-CoV and 3–4; mortality due to 6; number of cases of infection and death 4; origin and spread of 2–3; as a Public Health Emergency of International Concern 1; respiratory illness 1; SARS-CoV-2 and 3–4; second wave of 4; state governments action 2; survey 5; synthetic review of 69; third wave of 4; trade (especially online) and online games during 12; transport and tourism industries during 12; vaccination problems 8–10; vaccination process 4; Worldometer Data (WMD) 3; *see also* effect of the COVID-19 pandemic on economies; impact of COVID-19 pandemic on macroeconomic differentiation; lockdown; pandemic propagation simulations
Coronavirus in Asia and ASEAN–Live Updates by Country 14
Coronavirus Response Investment Initiative (CRII) 46, 48
Corporate Income Tax (CIT) 49
COVID-19 Research Response 14
critical mental health services 13–14
Croatia 22–24, 27, 28, 59–60; exports of goods and services 35, 37, 39; gross fixed capital 31, 33; imports of goods and services 40, 42
Croatian Bank for Reconstruction and Development 59
Cuddington, J. 90
Cuesta, J. 89
"Cura Italia" 54
Cyprus 22, 23, 28, 50; gross fixed capital 31, 33; imports of goods and services 40; small and medium-sized enterprises (SMEs) in 50
Czech Republic 23, 28, 29, 60; exports per capita 35, 37, 39; gross fixed capital 31, 33; imports of goods and services 40; quarantine in 60; small and medium-sized enterprises (SMEs) in 60

daily immunization coverage 97; *see also* immunization coverage
Delfino, D. 90
Delta Virus Pandemic 8
Demertzis, M. 46

Denmark 7, 22, 23, 28, 60; exports per capita 35, 37; gross fixed capital 31, 33; imports of goods and services 40
diphtheria 6
Drobot, Y. 68–69
Duda, A. 5

economic consequences 21
economic crises 12–13
economic module 94–97
Economic Stabilisation Funds 52
effect of the COVID-19 pandemic on economies 68–87, 89–113; calibrated model parameters 97–98; changes in GDP of Ukraine and Russia *vs.* the EU economy 70–75, *71, 72, 74, 75, 76*; economic indicators in consecutive scenarios 107, 108; epidemiological-economic model 91–97; epidemiological indicators in consecutive scenarios 100; fiscal interventions in Ukraine and Russia 83–86; overview 68–69, 89–91; scenarios and numerical simulation results 98–112, *100–105*; scenarios of epidemic development 99; social utility in scenarios *109–111* ; spatial interactions between European Union 76–83, *77, 78*; *see also* coronavirus disease 2019 (COVID-19); impact of COVID-19 pandemic on macroeconomic differentiation
Egypt 7
epidemiological module 92–94
epidemiological simulations 98n6
Estonia 23, 28, 50–51; exports per capita 35, 37; gross fixed capital 33; imports of goods and services 40
European Central Bank 47, 49
European Centre for Disease Prevention and Control (ECDC) 6, 14
European Commission 46, 47
European Investment Bank (EIB) 60, 62
European Stability Mechanism 49
Eurostat–COVID-19 14
eurozone states 47–59; Austria 49; Belgium 49–50; Cyprus 50; Estonia 50–51; Finland 51; France 52; Germany 52–53; Greece 53; Ireland 53–54; Italy 54; Latvia 54–55; Lithuania 55; Luxembourg 55–56; Malta 56; Netherlands 56; Portugal 57; Slovakia 57; Slovenia 57–58; Spain 58–59

EU Solidarity Fund 46
Eximbank state bank 61
exports of goods and services 34–40,
  36, 37, 38, 39

Federal Reserve (FED) 63
Finance Development Institution Altum 55
Finland 7, 8, 22, 23, 27, 28, 51; exports per capita 35, 37; gross fixed capital 31, 33; imports of goods and services 40; small and medium-sized enterprises (SMEs) in 51
fiscal interventions 46–65; comparative analysis of EU states' policies 46–65; eurozone states 47–59; fiscal measures 65; G20 countries 47; in Germany 46–47; overview 46–47; in Russia 85–86; series of fiscal measures 84; states with separate currencies 59–63; in Ukraine 83–85
fiscal interventions in non Eurozone states 59–63; Bulgaria 59; Croatia 59–60; Czech Republic 60; Denmark 60; Hungary 61; Poland 61–62; Romania 62; Sweden 62–63; United Kingdom 63
Flemish Region 50
France 4, 22, 23, 28, 52; exports per capita 35, 39; gross fixed capital 31, 33; small and medium-sized enterprises (SMEs) in 52
function of social utility 96

Gazeta Wyborcza 6
Germany 4, 22, 52–53; exports of goods and services 37; fiscal intervention 46–47; GDP per capita 22, 22–23; gross fixed capital 31, 33; imports of goods and services 40; protest in 6; small and medium-sized enterprises (SMEs) in 52–53; unemployment rate 12, 28, 30
Governmental Fund for Local Investments 61
Greece 7, 8, 22–24, 27, 28, 53; exports of goods and services 35, 37; gross fixed capital 31, 33; imports of goods and services 40, 42
gross domestic product (GDP) 7, 22, 22–24, 24, 25, 46; public health and 90; of Ukraine and Russia *vs.* the EU economy 70–75, 71, 72, 74, 75, 76

gross fixed capital formation per capita 30–33, 32, 33, 34, 35

H1N1 (swine flu pandemic) 1, 1nn3–4
Hancock, J. 90
High Indebted Euro Countries (HIDC) 47
HIV/AIDS 89, 90
Human Resources Development 59
Hungary 23, 24, 27, 28, 61; exports of goods and services 37; gross fixed capital 31, 33; imports of goods and services 40; small and medium-sized enterprises (SMEs) in 61

Iceland 28
immunization coverage 94, 97–98, 105
impact of COVID-19 pandemic on macroeconomic differentiation 20–44; exports of goods and services 34–40, 36, 37, 38, 39; gross domestic product (GDP) per capita 22, 22–24, 24, 25; gross fixed capital formation per capita 30–33, 32, 33, 34, 35; imports of goods and services 40–42, 41, 42, 43, 44; overview 20–22; unemployment 25–30, 26, 27, 29, 30; *see also* coronavirus disease 2019 (COVID-19); effect of the COVID-19 pandemic on economies
imports of goods and services 40–42, 41, 42, 43, 44
India 4, 7
Indonesia 4
Instituto de Crédito Oficial 59
International Monetary Fund (IMF) 12, 20, 47
InvestEU 48
Iran 4, 7, 11
Ireland 23, 24, 27, 28, 53–54; exports of goods and services 38; gross fixed capital 31, 33; imports of goods and services 40, 42; small and medium-sized enterprises (SMEs) in 54
Israel 8, 9
Italy 4, 7, 8, 11–13, 23, 28, 54; entrepreneurs in 47; exports per capita 35, 39; gross fixed capital 31; in High Indebted Euro Countries (HIDC) group 47; imports of goods and services 40; small and medium-sized enterprises (SMEs) in 54

Japan 7, 12
Johnson, B. 5

Johnson & Johnson 8, 9
Journal of Medical Virology 2, 2n5

Kermack, W.O. 89, 91, 119
Klose, J. 46
KMU Decree 116, 116n1
Kolomiyets,' O 68–69
Korea 7
Kovalivs'ka, S. 68–69
Kreditanstalt für Wiederaufbau (KfW) 52
Kulyts'kyy S. 68

labor supply growth rate 79n1, 80
Lancet–Regional Health 14
Latvia 22, 23, 28, 40, 54–55; imports of goods and services 40; small and medium-sized enterprises (SMEs) in 55
Lee, S. 90
Lik Ng, W. 90
Lippi, F. 90
Lithuania 22–24, 27, 28, 55; exports per capita 35; gross fixed capital 31; imports of goods and services 40; small and medium-sized enterprises (SMEs) in 55
lockdown 8, 11, 98; abolition 125; in Austria 49; in Belgium 49; in Bulgaria 59; businesses affected by 62; in China 11; in Croatia 59; in Czech Republic 60; in Denmark 60; duration of the 1st 65; economic and social costs of 4; economies suffering due to 15; efficiency and effectiveness of 73; end of 124; in Estonia 50; in Finland 51; in France 51; in Germany 52; in Greece 53; gross domestic product (GDP) in 46; during holiday season 119; in Hungary 61; in Ireland 53; in Italy 4, 54; in Lithuania 55; in Luxembourg 55; in Malta 56; measures 29, 43, 47, 63, 73, 83, 90–91, 100; mild 100, 102, 104, 105; in Netherlands 56; New Year 2021 10; in Poland 61, 117; in Portugal 57; on public holidays 73; in Romania 62; severe consequences of 90; severity 91; severity level of 90; in Slovakia 57; in Slovenia 57; socioeconomic restrictions 128; in Spain 58; strong rapid 29; in Ukraine 84, 116, 118; in United Kingdom 11, 63; value of social utility function 97; virus-related restrictions 7; *see also* coronavirus disease 2019 (COVID-19)
logarithm of capital–labor ratio 80
logarithm of labor productivity 77–78, 80
long-term bank refinancing mechanism 84
Lopez Obrador, A. M. 5
Lovasz, E. 90
Luxembourg 23, 27, 28, 55–56; exports of goods and services 35–36, 38, 39; gross fixed capital 31, 33; imports of goods and services 40, 42

macroeconomic variables 94
Mahal, A. 89
Makarov, I. 68–69
malnutrition 6
Malta 23, 24, 27, 28, 30, 56; exports of goods and services 35, 37–39; gross fixed capital 33; imports of goods and services 40
Malta Development Bank 56
Manasyan, S. 68–69
Mankiw, N. G. 90
McKendrick, A.G. 89, 91, 119
MERS-CoV 3–4
Mexico 4, 7
miscalculations of pandemic and virus 5–6
Moderna 8, 9
Multiannual Financial Framework 48, 48

National Bank of Ukraine 69
National Health Service 63
National Institute of Hygiene in Poland 116
natural logarithm of labor productivity 77
Nazarenko, V. 68–69
neoclassical model of economic growth 91
Netherlands 22–24, 28, 56; exports of goods and services 35, 37–39; gross fixed capital 31; imports of goods and services 40, 42; small and medium-sized enterprises (SMEs) in 56
"new normal" order 6
New Zealand 7–8
Nigeria 7
Norway 7, 8

Organisation for Economic
 Co-Operation and Development
 (OECD) 12
Our World in Data 14

Pakistan 7
Pandemic Emergency Longer-Term
 Refinancing Operations (PELTRO) 53
pandemic propagation simulations
 116–144; calibrations of 119–120;
 epidemiological model 119–120;
 overview 116–119; trajectories of
 death rates *125*, *131*, *136*, *140*, *142*;
 trajectories of proportions *122–142*
parameters of economic module 98
parameters of epidemiological module
 97–98
parameters of equation for the
 European Union, Russian Federation
 and Ukraine 81, 82
partial unemployment 84
percentage of dead 92, 92n1
Peru 7
Pfizer 8, 9
Poland 4–6, 22, 23, 61–62, 116–119;
 in *Bloomberg*'s ranking 7; Civil
 Status in 6; epidemiological situation
 in 119–120; exports of goods and
 services 35, 37, *40*; GDP per capita
 23, 24; gross fixed capital 31, 33;
 imports of goods and services 40,
 42; numerical simulations results
 for 121–132; quarantine in 61,
 117; small and medium-sized
 enterprises (SMEs) in 61; survey 8–9;
 unemployment rates in 27, *27*, 29,
 30; vaccination 6
Polish Development Fund 61
Polish Institute for Market and Social
 Research 8
Portugal 23, 24, 27–28, 57; exports of
 goods and services 35, 37, *39*; gross
 fixed capital 31, 33; imports of goods
 and services 40; small and medium-
 sized enterprises (SMEs) in 57
post-pandemic recovery 47
power generation sectors 47
protest 6
purchasing power parity (PPP) 70
Putin, V. 5

quarantine *see* lockdown
quasi-linear relation 77

REACT-EU 48
RescEU 48
Restart Fund 54
Riksbank 63
Romania 8, 23, 27, 28, 62; exports of
 goods and services 37, *40*; gross fixed
 capital 31, 33; imports of goods and
 services 40, 42; small and medium-
 sized enterprises (SMEs) in 62
Romer, D. 90
Russia 4, 5, 7, 70–87

SARS-CoV-2 *see* coronavirus disease
 2019 (COVID-19)
scaly anteaters *(manidae)* 2
Schipp, B. 90
seemingly unrelated regression (SUR)
 method 80, 81
severe acute respiratory syndrome
 coronavirus (SARS-CoV-2)
 see coronavirus disease 2019
 (COVID-19)
Shin, Y. 90
Simmons, P. 90
Singapore 7
Sinopharm 8, 9
Sinovac 8, 9
Slovakia 22, 27, 28, 57; quarantine
 in 57; small and medium-sized
 enterprises (SMEs) in 57
Slovenia 22, 23, 57–58; exports
 per capita 35, 37, 39; gross fixed
 capital 31, 33; imports of goods and
 services 40
small and medium-sized enterprises
 (SMEs) 68; in Austria 49; in Bulgaria
 59; in Cyprus 50; in Czech Republic
 60; European Investment Bank 49; in
 Finland 51; in France 52; in Germany
 52–53; in Hungary 61; in Ireland 54;
 in Italy 54; in Latvia 55; in Lithuania
 55; in Netherlands 56; in Poland 61;
 in Portugal 57; in Romania 62; in
 Slovakia 57; in Sweden 62; *see also*
 effect of the COVID-19 pandemic
 on economies; impact of COVID-
 19 pandemic on macroeconomic
 differentiation; lockdown
snakes *(serpentes)* 2
social capital stock 91
social distance 11, 90
Solow, R. M. 91, 94, 95
Solow growth model 90

154 *Index*

Solow long-run steady state 95–96, 98, 106
South Africa 4
South African Resource Portal 14
South Korea 8, 11
Spain 4, 11, 23, 27, 28, 30, 58–59; exports per capita 35, 39; gross fixed capital 31, 33; in High Indebted Euro Countries (HIDC) group 47; imports of goods and services 40, 42
spatial interactions between European Union 76–83, 77, 78
spread of epidemic, differential equations 92
Sputnik V 8
Support to Mitigate Unemployment Risks in an Emergency (SURE) 48, 82n2
Susceptible–Infected/Infectious–Recovered/Removed (SIR) 89–91
Sweden 4, 23, 24, 28, 62–63; exports 37; gross fixed capital 31, 33; imports of goods and services 40; small and medium-sized enterprises (SMEs) in 62

Taiwan 7
technical progress growth rate 80
Temporary Pandemic Emergency Purchase Programme (PEPP) 49
tetanus 6
Thailand 8
Tillmann, P. 46
Trump, D. 3n6, 5
tuberculosis 6
Turkey 4
Turkmenistan 5
typhus 6

Ukraine 70–87, 116, 119; epidemiological situation in 119–120; Health Ministry of 118; national quarantine 117; numerical simulations results for 132–142; quarantine in 84, 116, 118
unemployment rate 12, 25–30, 26, 27, 29, 30, 78–80, 95
United Kingdom 4, 5, 9, 11, 13, 21, 47, 63; quarantine in 11, 63; unemployment rate 12
United States 4, 5, 11; exogenous shock 71; protest in 6; quarantine in 63; unemployment rate 12; vaccination in 9
unplanned fiscal intervention 46
Uruguay 8
US National Institutes of Health 1n1

vaccination 4; differences in pace of 9; in Poland 6; problems 8–10; in United States 9
value of demand for labor 95
Vietnam 7
virus denial 5–6

Warsaw Chopin Airport 116
Weil, D. N. 90
WHO Coronavirus Disease (COVID-19) Dashboard 14
whooping cough 6
Wirtschaftsstabilisierungsfonds (WSF) 52
World Bank 11, 20, 68
World Health Organization (WHO) 1, 1n4, 6, 11, 21
Worldometer Data (WMD) 3
Worldometers 14
Wuhan 2–3

Xepapadeas, A. 90

yellow fever 6
YouGov-Cambridge Globalism Project 5, 9

Zellner, A. 80
Zhalilo, Y. 68–69

Lightning Source UK Ltd.
Milton Keynes UK
UKHW020102230722
406270UK00001B/26